No Girls in
the Clubhouse

D1246161

No Girls in the Clubhouse

The Exclusion of Women from Baseball

MARILYN COHEN

McFarland & Company, Inc., Publishers
Jefferson, North Carolina, and London

LIBRARY OF CONGRESS CATALOGUING-IN-PUBLICATION DATA

Cohen, Marilyn, 1952–
    No girls in the clubhouse : the exclusion of women
from baseball / Marily Cohen.
        p.   cm.
    Includes bibliographical references and index.

    ISBN 978-0-7864-4018-4
    softcover : 50# alkaline paper ∞

    1. Women baseball players — United States.   2. Women baseball
players — United States — Biography.   3. Baseball for women — United
States — History.   I. Title.
    GV880.7.C64   2009
    796.357082 — dc22   2008054774

British Library cataloguing data are available

On the cover: Lou Gehrig (left), Babe Ruth and Jackie Mitchell (National
Baseball Hall of Fame Library, Cooperstown, New York)

Manufactured in the United States of America

*McFarland & Company, Inc., Publishers
    Box 611, Jefferson, North Carolina 28640
    www.mcfarlandpub.com*

For my father, Harold Cohen

Acknowledgments

The successful completion of this book was made possible by the assistance of the following people and institutions. I am grateful to Saint Peter's College for a Kenny Summer Fellowship that funded my research. For their competent and cordial assistance, I thank James L. Gates Jr., library director, John Horn, the librarian, and staff of the A. Bartlett Giamatti Research Library at the Baseball Hall of Fame and the staff at the Little League Baseball Museum. I am grateful for the generosity extended to me by those whom I interviewed: Ernestine Petras, Maria Pepe, James Farina, and Vanessa Selbst. I thank Sean Aronson and Annie Huldekoper, public and community relations officers for the Saint Paul Saints, for generously providing a picture of Ila Borders, and Larry Lester, CEO of NoirTech Research, Inc., for his prompt attention to my requests for photographs. Finally I am grateful to those who read and commented on the manuscript in various stages of its completion: Alan Serrins, Lissadell Cohen-Serrins, David Surrey, Michelle Fine, Richard Blot, Dave Kaplan, Harold Liebovitz and Suzanne Chollet.

Table of Contents

PART II: THE EXCLUSION OF GIRLS AND
WOMEN FROM AMATEUR BASEBALL

Preface

Women have played and contributed to the sport of baseball for more than a century in the United States. Over the past fifteen years numerous books (Lois Browne, *Girls of Summer*; Sue Macy, *A Whole New Ball Game*; Barbara Gregorich, *Women at Play*; Gai Ingham Berlage, *Women in Baseball: The Forgotten History*; Marlene Targ Brill, *Winning Women in Baseball & Softball*; Michelle Y. Green, *A Strong Right Arm*; John M. Kovach, *Women's Baseball*; Jean Hastings Ardell, *Breaking into Baseball*; Merrie A. Fidler, *The Origins and History of the All-American Girls Professional Baseball League*; Leslie Heaphy and Mel Anthony May, *Encyclopedia of Women and Baseball*, many articles published in scholarly journals and in the popular press, the commercial success of the film *A League of Their Own*, and the subsequent exhibit devoted to women and baseball at the Baseball Hall of Fame have brought to light this long-erased topic in women's history. This initial "herstory" stage provides the essential documentation of women's varied contributions to baseball as amateur and professional players, umpires, sports commentators and writers, and enthusiastic fans. Several of these writers have also raised the key question relating to how male privileges in the sport of baseball have been maintained.

This book is intended to be a culturally informed history and theoretical analysis of girls' and women's exclusion from baseball. The book builds on the existing empirical foundation to extend analysis to a deeper theoretical level where gender is the central concept mediating social structures, forms of communication and social interactions among players and coaches, symbolic representations of female athletes, ideologies of inclusion and exclusion and subjective identities of players in the social settings of amateur and professional baseball in the United States.

1

The theoretical perspectives offered here to explain women's exclusion from baseball are informed by social science perspectives, principally critical feminist theory, anthropology, and sociology. Although gender is the central axis of analysis in feminist theory, I also include the intersections among gender, social class, race/ethnicity, age and sexuality since these social locations are significant in differentiating the experiences of women baseball players.

Sports are a core institution in our society's unequal sex/gender system. No single social institution, with the exception of the military, has influenced the cultural construction of masculinity more strongly or has justified in biological terms more directly the inferiority of the female body resulting in the acceptance of gender-based discrimination. Sport generally, with baseball as a case study, occupies a powerful position in our culture and is a reflection of it where symbolic notions of masculinity and femininity and the male and female body are constructed. These dichotomous constructions of gender are the result of a socialization process that generates real obstacles to participation by girls and women by scripting aggressive, rough, dirty, loud, sweaty and passionate athletic competition as masculine.

Culture is the socially generated system of symbolic knowledge shared by members of a society. As a historical anthropologist, I follow anthropologist Eric Wolf's historically specific conception of culture as permeated by symbolic representations of power beginning with naming or coding the environment with linguistic terms. Coding biological sex differences with symbolic meaning takes place within historically and culturally specific systems of power relations that have direct consequences for men's and women's lives.

For example, although in the past half-century women in the United States have made significant gains in access to resources, power and prestige, including access to amateur and professional sports, baseball lags behind other sports in the inclusion of girls and women. The ideological justification for exclusion based on cultural presumptions of female physical inferiority that emerged in the nineteenth century remains strong, justifying the bifurcation of the sport into softball for girls and baseball for boys. Baseball is a particularly interesting case study in this regard since it is a sport where, until recently, smaller male athletes have excelled. Following Henry Aaron, baseball does not depend on absolute strength but is a combination of strength, coordination, timing, strategy, control and knowledge. Although this combination should favor the inclusion of all prepubescent girls and some girls and women after puberty, it has systematically barred all from equitable participation, channeling potential female athletic talent into softball or into professional sports that offer more opportunities for women such as tennis, golf, ice skating, or basketball.

As a historical anthropologist I have long been interested in the application of anthropological concepts and theories to the explanation of events in the past. Anthropologists seek to retain a concrete focus on real people, in this case women athletes who experienced and coped with the structures of domination existing in baseball. Thus, the research methodology for this book involved combining archival evidence with extensive interviews and interpreting the accounts of baseball games and of women players written by sports journalists for cultural content. The key primary sources include articles by sports journalists, and visual images of women baseball players found in the A. Bartlett Giamatti Research Library at the Baseball Hall of Fame and at the Little League Museum, and legal cases involving sex discrimination suits brought by girls and women who were denied opportunities to play baseball. The evidence presented by expert witnesses on both sides and the decisions handed down by judges in the flurry of sex discrimination cases filed in the 1970s after the passage of Title IX are particularly enlightening since they demonstrate how "facts" relating to "real" biological differences cannot be separated from ideological constructions of gender and normative gender roles. Further these cases shed light on how the law can be retrogressive or progressive in addressing the social consequences of past and present sex discrimination.

In this book, I have limited the sources used and the analysis to girls and women who play(ed) baseball. Although umpiring and sports announcing are as exclusive of women as baseball teams, they have been covered by Jean Hastings Ardell. Also the theoretical perspectives offered here are equally relevant to these other settings. I hope that this book furthers the stimulating debates in feminist theory and women's studies involving men and women athletes and the political efforts that address the exclusion of women in sports. Since baseball is a sport that I have loved and followed since childhood, I also hope this feminist critique contributes to a reconsideration of the sport's enduring gender bifurcation.

1

Patriarchal Myths

This cultural analysis of gender dichotomies in the sport of baseball opens with two fabricated mythic accounts of the origins of pitching prowess. One originates in 1892 in Ragerstown, Ohio. It features a child who was always "naturally athletic and could hurl a corncob at the family cat with all the wrist-snap and follow-through of a major leaguer — at the tender age of two."[1] This gifted child, the father's favorite, was provided with every conceivable encouragement to develop its varied athletic talents which included baseball, rifle shooting, hunting, basketball and tennis. The father, an upper-middle-class pharmacist and doctor active in community affairs, spared no expense to further his child's athletic abilities. He established a two-year high school so that his child could pitch, founded a park so that his child might pitch for the town's second string team, built a heated gymnasium so that his child could weight train and practice skills during the off-season, and finally, purchased a semi-pro traveling baseball team so that his child could be featured as the star pitcher. This child's skills, as a strike-out pitcher who "seldom gives a base on balls," were publicized in the press and included a fast ball, curve, knuckler and sinker that were well known in Ohio and Kentucky. However, since a career in organized baseball was culturally impossible for this child, it followed the father into the medical profession, rarely thereafter talking about baseball.[2]

The second mythic story takes place today, 2006, in Orlando, Florida. It features a child who also "arrived on earth wanting to throw," beginning with toys and food from the high chair and graduating to throwing balls. Although many children throw such things, this child, according to its father, "had an especially determined arm." This child, like the first, is blessed with extremely supportive parents who are devoted

Pitcher Alta Weiss, "The Girl Wonder," pitched on men's semi-pro teams between 1907 and 1922. Weiss was a multi-talented athlete known for mastering a variety of pitches. She is pictured here in 1902, pitching in attire that reflected current standards of feminine respectability (National Baseball Hall of Fame Library, Cooperstown, New York).

to developing its talents. The father, a Division II baseball player in college, began practicing with his gifted child at age two, and both parents have structured their working lives around the elite travel team schedule spread out over a ten-month season and coaches who prepare the child for a bright future in the major leagues. Like the first child, the second is a "big-game pitcher — a precision right-hander whose fastball ... tends to cross the plate with uncanny and merciless accuracy." Since this second child is only thirteen, we do not know the myth's ending. What we do know is the child's dreams are built around succeeding in major league baseball, preferably as a pitcher for the Red Sox, and that there are no structural barriers to the realization of its ambition beyond the intense competition with other talented and privileged children.[3]

Eliminating the gender of the children highlights the structural similarities and the essential moral lesson of the key scenarios sketched above. Key scenarios symbolically communicate culturally valued outcomes and the correct means for achieving them. The moral lesson of the myths is that athletic talent regardless of sex should thrive when given encouragement and opportunity. However, to anyone who knows baseball, the gender of both is obvious, and is the essential structural factor determining the social contexts for and real outcomes of athletic capability, whatever they may be for the second boy child.

For Alta Weiss, the first child, the "Girl Wonder," her athletic talent, competitive drive, and the extraordinary dedication of her father, who rejected the prevailing view that baseball was not a game for women, could not overcome the discriminatory barriers blocking women's advancement in organized professional baseball at the turn of the twentieth century. After playing with the Weiss All Stars for seventeen years Alta Weiss earned enough money playing semi-professional baseball to pay for college where she intended to be a college physical education teacher. Her father, however, insisted she become a doctor. Alta Weiss then embarked on another pioneering direction in her "choice" of profession being the only woman in her medical school graduation class at Starling-Ohio Medical School in 1914.[4] Although women have made significant progress in the medical profession, gender barriers in organized baseball are still impermeable. Weiss did not have a brother. The second boy child has a sister, age eight, who plays fast-pitch softball. No matter how talented or motivated she may be, or how supportive her parents, she cannot share her brother's dream of pitching for the Red Sox.[5]

All human societies require predictability in social interactions and most people in a society at a given time accept the cultural and ideological constructs that justify established patterns of behavior. Social science perspectives "unpack" structured patterns of human interaction that are considered "normal" and, therefore, taken for granted by members of a society. For those social scientists committed to explaining and changing normative structures of inequality in a particular society, such as social class, gender, race/ethnicity, or sexual preference, "making the familiar strange" includes a critical political imperative to eliminate barriers to equal access to resources, power, prestige and opportunities. Structures of inequality conceptualize how power shapes human relationships at the social structural level where the social contexts for human interaction are generated, reproduced and negotiated over time. Structural power controls the contexts in which people exhibit their capabilities and interact with others. Individuals and groups operating within these specific settings have the power to direct or circumscribe the actions of others, including the actions of athletes.

The category of gender, the cultural meaning of sexual or biological differences, is an ongoing social creation involving myriad shifting biological and psychological assumptions concerning presumed essential differences between males and females. The recognition of gender as an ongoing social construction that varies over cultural space and historical time, rather than a fixed, essential, or natural category, has been instructive in analyzing how power relations shape the formation of cultural categories, social structures, settings and the social and political consequences of inclusion or exclusion. Gender is a cultural universal, and in all societies gender is a prestige structure, a mode of assigning people to statuses or positions in a society associated with command over material resources, political power, skills and connections to others with power. Prestige structures, like gender or race, are always supported by a legitimizing ideology, symbolic systems of meaning that make sense of and legitimize the existing order of human relationships in a society.

Kimberle Crenshaw points out that the social process of categorization is not unilateral but political with the naming of categories and the social consequences of naming interrelated yet analytically distinct political elements. There is power exercised by those engaged in the process of categorization — man/woman, Black/White, gay/straight — and there is power to cause that categorization to have social and material consequences for others.[6] Naming or coding the environment with linguistic terms, a uniquely human capacity, is not a politically neutral social process. Language is as much an instrument of power as it is an instrument of communication and knowledge. Constructions of gender as a cultural code take place within historically and culturally specific sex/gender systems or patterns of power relations that have direct consequences for women's and men's lives.

In patriarchal societies, where gender is a structure of inequality that limits women's access to resources, opportunities, power, and prestige, constructions of femininity and masculinity include dichotomous or oppositional understandings of difference. Although the rationales used to explain the physical inferiority of women's bodies have changed, the patriarchal assumption that women's bodies are essentially weaker (muscular strength, speed, height, reproduction) than men's persists as the principle justification for excluding girls and women from entering men's professional sports, including baseball, and relegating them to marginalized sports such as softball. Don Sabo argues that such ideologies, or "patriarchal myths," such as the myth of female frailty, function to legitimize structures of inequality in all sectors of society. In relation to sports, patriarchal myths "exaggerate and naturalize sex differences and, in effect, sustain men's power and privilege in relation to women. These same ideologies have also kept sport researchers from seeing women athletes as they really are as well as what they are capable of becoming."[7] Those struggling against gender-based inequality can challenge the "coherent" biological assumptions of weakness relating to women's bodies, they can challenge the construction of athleticism in culturally masculine terms and they can challenge the practice of discrimination based on those assumptions as injurious to those excluded, as intended by the passage of Civil Rights laws — Titles VII in 1964 and IX in 1972.

As the literature analyzing the gender anomalies and challenges faced by women athletes demonstrates, both participation in the full spectrum of sports and advancement into male professional ranks by women athletes in the United States is blocked by entrenched dichotomized cultural constructions of gender, and men's and women's bodies with sex discrimination legitimized in biological, psychological and normative terms.[8] Sport is a core institution in our society's unequal gender order and the legitimizing gender ideologies have constructed a predominant consensus or hegemony about the meaning of masculinity and femininity. Although constructions of gender have changed over time, no single social institution, with the exception of the military, has influenced the construction of hegemonic masculinity—the culturally idealized, persistent and widely accepted form of masculinity—more than sports, where masculine characteristics are learned and reinforced from childhood.[9] Aggression, physicality, competitive spirit, tolerance of pain and athletic skill have been scripted as masculine behavior.[10] Consequently, more girls than boys either do not participate in or drop out of sports. Women's sports, with the exception of tennis, are peripheralized, and few women attempt to play those sports labeled as masculine due to the social isolation and sanctions they will experience for transgressing normative gender boundaries.

A central task for social scientists analyzing sex/gender symbolism in any society is to assess the culturally specific contexts where notions of masculinity, femininity and the body are constructed and then function as ideologies to legitimize exclusion or inclusion. How are biological or sexual differences understood over time and space and used to legitimize segregation? How is gender difference made more or less significant in different social situations? How do social interactions and relationships strengthen or weaken gender boundaries? While all societies recognize as symbolically meaningful the biological differences between male and female bodies, in societies where the meanings of masculinity and femininity are framed in dichotomous terms, women are typically subordinate to men, and boys learn, through participation in gender segregated initiation rituals and social groups, essentialized gender distinctions.

Sports play a key role in the construction of gender symbolism in our society by generating culturally scripted ideologies about the male body and its biological superiority in strength, speed and endurance that legitimize discrimination against female athletes. It is essential to identify, differentiate and analyze biological sex difference to reduce the growing number of sports injuries to girls and women. However, it is equally essential to identify and analyze the masculine cultural dimension of sports injuries that link the tolerance of pain with a "warrior-girl (or boy) ethos" that encourages playing through injuries, returning to competition before full rehabilitation, and playing too long and too hard at one sport.[11]

When biological distinctions provide the rationale for exclusion and inclusion, a significant dimension of the justification is that the excluded group or category actually benefits from the exclusion. Since the excluded presumably cannot achieve at the same level as the included, the excluded will be intimidated by inclusion and therefore will perform better when grouped amongst themselves. Such dichotomous thinking is central to all ideologies of domination, since one element in the oppositional binary is objectified as "other" and viewed as an object to be manipulated, controlled, or excluded.[12] When the sexual female/male dichotomy is expressed symbolically in biological or psychological terms — i.e., pollution/purity, weakness/strength, emotional/rational — or in normative terms — i.e., male/public female/private spheres — women's access to social spaces, social groups and economic or political opportunities not associated with their private domestic roles as wives and mothers is often restricted. One result is that the relegation of excluded categories such as women or racial/ethnic groups to less skilled, less prestigious, underfinanced occupations and roles thus appears natural and rational.

Another patriarchal myth is that when women participate in and excel at sports their feminine gender identities become confused and they begin to act, think and feel like men. This myth, as Sabo points out, is rooted in the cultural assumptions that construct sports and athletes as masculine. Engagement in masculine activities by women will result in "abnormal personality traits" such as becoming too assertive, competitive or turning women into lesbians. Sabo suggests that sports "androgynize" rather than "masculinize" women's gender identities, resulting in a more balanced mixture of feminine and masculine traits. For boys, there is no cultural contradiction in gender socialization between the dominant construction of masculinity and the gender socialization that takes place during participation in sports. In fact, masculinization, one principle goal, is intensified and narrowed for boys in athletic social settings. However, for girls there is a contradiction between athletic culture and hegemonic constructions of femininity. Thus, gender socialization for girls participating in sports is expansive, widening what is possible physically, emotionally and socially. Research suggests that such gender broadening is psychologically beneficial. It also challenges hegemonic conceptions of femininity that reinforce and reflect male privilege in our society.[13]

However, women can also face sanctions when trespassing dichotomized cultural boundaries. Investigations of situations when men or women cross or transgress gender-dominated fields provide rich sources for analyses of the gender order. Women who attempt to gain access to male professional sports in the United States face structural and cultural barriers typical of societies where asymmetrical gender dichotomies restrict social relations between the sexes. Rituals reproduce though shared systems of symbolic meaning the social structure and cultural boundaries of a society, community or group, thus forging a shared identity. A ritual is patriarchal when it contains and reproduces elements of gender socialization that reflect institutionalized sexual separation and gender inequality. For example, in their analysis of football rituals, Sabo and Panepinto argue that masculinity rites in patriarchal societies share the following characteristics intended to reproduce prevailing gender dichotomies: man (officiate)/boy (initiate) relations, conformity and control, social isolation from the family and the feminine, deference to male authority and the infliction and tolerance of pain.[14] Timothy Beneke makes a similar argument linking manhood with tolerance of pain and psychological stress in baseball: "The whole domain of male sports constitutes an occasion for proving manhood. The ability to withstand physical pain and witness psychological pressure ... and remain competent, is a central part of this. Moments of physical danger, like facing a fast-moving baseball when at bat or on the field ... are similar occasions."[15] Anthropologist Alan Klein, who conducted ethnographic research in baseball academies in the Dominican Republic, draws parallels between Campo Las Palmas and the male initiation rites of age-graded sets of men in tribal societies involving ritualized gender bonding, isolation, instruction and anxiety.[16] Brett Stoudt's analysis of hazing rituals among athletes in an elite suburban boy's school reveals how hegemonic ideas about masculinity (inclusion) are constructed through misogynistic and homophobic dichotomies (exclusion). Conformity to the mandatory head shaving of freshmen crew team members was experienced as positive by those who participated since it established an oppositional foundation for and consensus about the criteria for inclusion "you're either in or you're out" and it "showed the guys that I'm not a pussy."[17]

While women in the United States have benefited from the erosion of gender dichotomies and sexual separation in many occupations and social spaces since the passage of the 1964 Civil Rights Act, Title IX in 1972, and Affirmative Action policies, they still face resistance to full integration into traditionally male occupations and activities, including professional sports. Women entering nontraditional occupations, including coal miners, construction workers, law enforcement, firefighters or the military, have frequently confronted occupational qualifications that are inherently discriminatory to women, hostile work environments where job performance and advancement were and are diminished by myriad forms of sex discrimination including sexual harassment, sexual objectification, glass ceilings, asymmetrical wages, pregnancy discrimination and legitimizing presumptions of physical and emotional inferiority.

Baseball is a sport where the cultural lag between the passage of civil rights and affirmative action legislation and the subsequent changes in symbolic culture necessary to eliminate prejudice and discrimination remains pronounced. The dearth of professional women baseball players is usually explained in biological terms: women's bodies lack the physical attributes (height, weight, upper body muscular strength) necessary to compete with men. While their exclusion thus appears legitimate, it is significant that baseball is a sport where smaller male athletes have long excelled because it is not a sport that depends on absolute strength such as weightlifting or offensive linemen in football. Baseball is a game involving a combination of skills including strength, coordination, timing, knowledge of the game, strategy and control. While strength is a factor in hitting and pitching, timing, bat control and coordination are also involved in bat speed and locating pitches. Despite average physical differences or sexual dimorphism between human males and females, there is no shortage of women athletes today who can compare favorably with small- to average-sized male athletes whose strength is not artificially enhanced by drugs. While male athletes are generally stronger and faster than female athletes because they are able to develop more muscle mass due to the hormone testosterone, women are more flexible due to estrogen. There are some women who are larger, faster and stronger than some men. Further, both men and women are getting larger, with bigger, stronger, faster women athletes becoming increasingly common. Physiological differences within the sexes are greater than the differences between the sexes. Some individual girls will be able to compete with and against boys, despite the physical advantages of most boys.[18] Baseball, in contrast to basketball or tennis, for example, offers talented women athletes no opportunities for inclusion.

The passage of Title IX in 1972 has dramatically increased participation rates by girls and women in sports at the high school and college levels. Still, inequalities exist. According to figures published by the Women's Sports Foundation for 2005–2006, male high school athletes receive 1.3 million more participation opportunities than their female counterparts. In collegiate athletics, male athletes outnumber female athletes 222,838 to 166,728, thus receiving 56,110 more opportunities to participate.[19] The gap is, of course much wider in professional sport that continues to be a male-identified social institution and cultural arena where men demonstrate their dominance.[20] This is partly due to the internal contradictions of Title IX itself, as Eileen McDonagh and Laura Pappano cogently argue. Title IX legislation both draws more females into sports and explicitly permits and encourages sex-segregated sports. The law allows for both the development and expression of female athleticism while it simultaneously reinforces assumptions of female athletic inferiority.[21]

Baseball, a core sport within the institution of organized sports in America, has been largely untouched by the passage of Title IX. Gender segregation, with baseball identified as a "He-sport" and softball as its "She-sport" alternative, emerged early in the twentieth century and continues today. This bifurcation reflects and reproduces gender as a structure of inequality because baseball, a core sport confined to men, dominates resources, opportunities and prestige in the sport at the amateur and professional levels. While softball is often regarded as the female equivalent of baseball, in fact, they are different sports. Baseball and softball are governed by separate national sport governing bodies in the United States and internationally. The rules, skills, competition fields and playing equipment are different for the two sports. A baseball field is significantly larger than a softball field, with 90-foot base paths compared to 60-foot paths in softball. Outfield fences for baseball are 100–200 feet longer than softball fields. Baseball has a grass infield with a raised pitcher's mound 60 feet from the batter, while softball uses a flat dirt infield with a pitcher's plate 40 feet from the batter. The pitcher in baseball throws overhand, while in softball the pitcher is required to throw underhand, two very different skills. A baseball is considerably smaller and denser than a softball and a baseball game lasts nine innings, while a softball game is seven innings.[22]

Men's sports culture in the United States includes dichotomous constructions of masculinity that both shuns and seeks women: shunning them as competitors challenging masculine privileges and seeking them as sexual partners. These constructions begin early. Gary Fine has demonstrated in his ethnography of Little League baseball teams that preadolescent boys spent considerable time discussing and constructing girls as feminine and their sexuality. These young boys have already established the link between masculinity and sexual prowess, and understood that masculinity was dominant. Boys avoided appearing too intimate with their girlfriends and "must never let girls replace other boys as the focus of their attention."[23]

These exclusive dualistic beliefs and practices structure social interactions extending to the homosocial or gender-segregated spaces associated with sports including athletic fields, locker rooms and, until recently, press coverage. The concept "homosocial" moves beyond gender demographics (i.e. single-sex teams) to focus analytic attention on social interaction. Messner and Sabo argue that locker rooms in particular are masculine spaces characterized by specific social interactions that intentionally exclude women.[24] Because locker rooms are socially isolated spaces, the social interactions taking place among the males that reproduce misogyny, homophobia, violence and homoeroticism are acceptable and rewarded elements of masculine athletic culture.[25]

Since hegemonic masculinity is also associated with compulsory heterosexuality, a parallel construction of maleness includes aggressively seeking sexual contact with women. Sexual access to women by male athletes is both expected and socially rewarded. Professional baseball provides a poignant example of men's sports culture with its contradictory mix of rigid sexual separation and heteronormativity. It is a sport where women have both participated as professional players on teams with men and in leagues of their own. Women have also made themselves available as sexual partners to professional male players — the notorious baseball Annies.[26] There is no shortage of media coverage of the multiple sexual partners linked with successful male sports figures.

In her critical assessment of "intersectionality," Kimberle Crenshaw argues that critical feminist theory focuses on gender as the central axis of inequality, but also includes the complex intersections of gender, race, class and sexuality in the construction of subjective identity and experiences.[27] The majority of women participating in baseball have been White. However, the participation of women of color has been erased by racist exclusion by the White male-dominated media who did not cover their games, by racist policies that excluded women of color from playing on all–White female teams, and by patriarchal exclusion of Black women from the Negro Leagues, with three notable exceptions. Further, since the evidence confirming the participation of lesbians in baseball as in all athletics has been shrouded in stigma, their subjective experiences and identities are only now being revealed.

Baseball, like other forms of entertainment performance, depends upon an audience or spectators. In sports the spectators include fans and the media, especially the sports media — writers, commentators, sportscasters. Both play powerful roles in creating or limiting cultural constructions of femininity and, therefore, the opportunities and success of women athletes. Fans witness, support and identify with athletes and sports teams that provide opportunities to reinforce, reflect upon and, at times, challenge prevailing gender ideologies. The sports media was and is central to the generation of cultural images of the bodies, capabilities and aspirations of women athletes that reinforce or challenge prevailing gender constructions and how these are mediated by race, class and sexuality. Media-driven images can be as powerful as athletic ability in determining the successful entry of women into male-dominated sports. Visual images in particular play a powerful role in constructing and circulating changing representations of femininity and masculinity in relation to broader social patterns of power structures and symbolic systems that govern sexuality, gender identities and roles. The visual images of women baseball players provide a rich source of evidence about the cultural contradictions presented by athletic women whose bodies signify strength and autonomy in a cultural context that justifies their subordination to men partly in terms of physical inferiority and the need for male protection.

Messner identifies four patterned ways that the media deal with women's sports: silence, humorous sexualization, backlash and selective incorporation of outstanding women athletes, all of which are useful to this analysis.[28] The representations of women athletes in the sports media have often reproduced prevailing gender binaries. However, at times, sports writers have helped to shape public knowledge about women athletes and push discourse and ideas in new directions. The balance between hegemonic constructions of gender and contested or counter-hegemonic ideas about gender is always in flux. Thus, attention will also be paid to the counter-hegemonic discourse relating to women's athletic bodies generated by the athletes themselves, by their family members, and by coaches (usually male) who encouraged their participation in baseball. Although the reality for women baseball athletes was defined and controlled by others, a persistent theme in this book is their attempts to transgress objectified constructions and define their own identities and experiences.

In the last decade, documentation of the long history of women's participation in professional baseball exists along with insights relating to how male privileges and social spaces in the sport have been preserved.[29] The structure of this book will, therefore, build upon the periodization and empirical research established by previous scholars. My purpose is to apply social science perspectives to analyze the connections between social constructions of gender at the societal level and the individual subjective identities and experiences of selected women athletes who chose to play baseball. In each chapter attention will be paid to the historically specific context for the construction of bodies and gender dichotomies, how these ideologies legitimized the exclusion or inclusion of women, and the language used by sports journalists to represent women baseball players' bodies and skills.[30] At the end of each chapter the principle theoretical arguments will be highlighted and linked with the empirical evidence.

2

"Contraband Pleasure": Victorian Era Baseball, 1866–1890

A significant cultural corollary of the physical separation of work and home characteristic of the capitalist mode of production was the emergence of a hegemonic femininity in the nineteenth century modeled on the experiences of middle- and upper-class White women that has proven resilient for more than two centuries. This cultural construction is part of a wider sex/gender system which divides social space into a masculine public domain and a private feminine domain closely associated with men's work roles outside the home and women's gender roles in the home. This gender binary was not unique to Western European or American societies. It existed in most state-level societies where elite males dominated settings of public power in the state, military, religious institutions and public family roles and where elite females led sheltered, protected lives.

With the rise of capitalism there were significant differences associated with the redefinition of "productive" work as an exchange of labor power for money. The home, rather than a site of production, structured by a complimentary gendered family economy and division of labor, was now a site of consumption and reproduction. Women, "angels of the hearth," who assumed control over reproductive work, were engaged in tasks that were unremunerated, resulting in their dependence on male breadwinners and their diminished power and prestige. Women's reproductive work was also redefined as love and nurturance, an extension of their "natural" capacity to care for others. Masculinity became associated with leaving the home to work for money to support one's family, thus increasing men's power in both the public and private spheres. However, as men left the home as breadwinners, women became the primary caregivers for both sons and daughters. Organized sports along with the Boy Scouts were homosocial institutions providing masculine social interactions to counter the feminized domain of the home.[1]

The construction of femininity as inferior to and dependent upon masculinity was woven into the cultural fabric of American life regardless of the hardworking accomplishments of many women in the eighteenth and nineteenth centuries. According to Rodger Streitmatter, women's limited domestic roles and expectations were promulgated in the publications of the eighteenth and nineteenth centuries such as *Ladies Magazine*, founded in 1792. The paternalism of late-eighteenth-century publications, rooted in the assumption of women's natural physical and mental inferiority, was replaced with hostility by the mid-nineteenth century in response to the Seneca Falls, New York, convention in 1848 that marked the emergence of the first-wave feminist movement in the United States. "American newspapers responded to the convention with a toxic mixture of outrage, contempt, and mockery—all forms of social control designed to slow the advancement of women." Not only was the new women's movement trivialized, feminists who participated in public political activities were attacked for abandoning their domestic roles and responsibilities and blurring the "natural" boundaries between men's public and women's private spheres. The male-dominated mainstream press continued to denigrate feminism throughout the nineteenth century, focusing in the later decades on the personal characteristics of feminists such as their single marital status or the perceived masculine behavior of the leaders such as Susan B. Anthony. "Miss Anthony is uncomely in person, has rather coarse rugged features and masculine manners." The connection between assertive behavior by women in the public domain and mannishness was easily extended to women's participation in athletics, particularly in "violent" public sports such as golf and cricket.[2]

Scholars who have documented the emergence of women's participation in baseball in Victorian nineteenth-century America have highlighted this patriarchal social context, including ideological assumptions about the female body as fragile. These assumptions were based on the experiences of privileged leisured White women since Black women and White working-class women were long engaged in strenuous work outside the home. Women's presumed frailty and the limitations on their physical exercise were associated with their reproductive capabilities, and women's presumed higher moral development was linked with their confinement to the private domain of the home and their roles as wives and mothers. Since the privacy of the home was women's "natural" sphere and the source of public morality, those women who crossed this cultural boundary to play a public sport—perceived from its inception as male, and as inviting male gaze and comment on their bodies—violated Victorian norms of feminine respectability.

Baseball, which began as a gentile homosocial sport played in White upper-class men's clubs, was introduced to common soldiers during the Civil War. It became a business by 1871 with the establishment of the first professional league, the National Association of Professional Baseball Players. In 1876, when athletic entrepreneurs formed the National League, pitchers threw underhand and the distance from the pitching mound to home plate was forty-five feet. Overhand pitching did not become the norm until 1884 and the distance from the pitcher's mound to home plate was not extended to sixty feet, six inches until 1893.[3] Home runs were a rarity in professional baseball until the "live ball" era of the twentieth century. In the early days of professional baseball, the balls were more suited to smaller parks often located in cities, and did not travel far when hit.

Observing baseball through a male lens, by the 1880s baseball was entering its golden era. It was anointed the national sport, with seventeen White and two Black professional leagues established, and deemed the great assimilator of urban immigrants into American values and communities.[4] Women's participation in baseball also emerged at this time beginning as spectators whose entrance into male homosocial space was justified by presumptions that their higher morality would uplift the rough side of the sport associated with gambling and drinking. The presence of women as spectators helped legitimize baseball and was an indicator of the sport's popularity.[5]

Soon women became interested in playing the game as well. Similar to men, their initial participation reflected the structure of class and race stratification in the United States. It also began at exclusive clubs and at the elite east coast White women's colleges. For example the Laurel Base Ball Club, with twelve members, and the Abenakis Base Ball Club with eleven members were founded at Vassar College in New York. The first nine-member college team was the Vassar Resolutes. Their uniform was a long skirt, long-sleeve blouse with a high neck, and a band around the waist bearing the team name, "Resolutes." The colleges known as the seven sisters provided one of the first opportunities for "respectable" participation by women in baseball, specifically at Vassar College in 1866 (eight players), 1876 (nine players); Smith College 1879; Mount Holyoke College 1891 and Wellesley College 1897.[6] At these elite White colleges, where elements of hegemonic femininity such as feminine propriety and sexual purity were reinforced by homosocial seclusion, the exclusive upper-class men's club provided the model for baseball rather than the popular but rough professional sport.

Elite college women benefited from the shifting discourse relating to the role of exercise in women's health in the late nineteenth century. Poor and working-class women were excluded from the construct of hegemonic femininity as they were engaged daily in physically demanding work in the public sphere, some indoors in factories and other working outdoors on the land. Prevailing medical opinion still discouraged vigorous exercise for women due to concern for their delicate reproductive and nervous systems. Some doctors were, however, beginning to extend the health benefits of exercise in the open air to women, whose physical fitness during their formative years had been neglected by parents and teachers. Many freshman arrived at college in poor physical condition with little or no previous experience with athletic exercise. The progressive views relating to the benefits of exercise for women were adopted by the founders of the new women's colleges who sought to reverse this trend. They believed that healthy minds and bodies were connected and required that all students be involved in physical activities as a necessary adjunct to the academic curriculum.

Administrators on elite women's college campuses still reflected the views of those who advocated a cautious approach to women's athletic activities, insisting on strict limits to reduce the possibility of reproductive dysfunction, competitive stimulation and sexual immorality.[7] Involvement in sports was limited to providing opportunities for exercise and social interaction, such as play days and interclass competition, among students on homosocial campuses so as not to appear competitive or to challenge the prevailing gender constructions. Intercollegiate sports were banned. Uniforms, consisting of long dresses with high necks and long sleeves, were modest to minimize male gaze. Unlike men's uniforms, these heavy dresses hindered baseball-related skills such as running and sliding, but the equipment used was standard, consisting of regulation hardballs, baseball gloves and face masks for catchers.[8]

The women players thoroughly enjoyed playing baseball, and sharing in this form of "contraband pleasure." As Debra Shattuck's research demonstrates, the players took the initiative to organize their own baseball teams, acquire their own equipment and proudly posed for team pictures emulating men's teams. However, evidence from their correspondence suggests that neither they nor college administrators took their play seriously, viewing baseball as a healthy form of social and recreational activity to be enjoyed only among themselves. Although players were proud of "attempting the unconventional," and proud of their physical abilities to pitch a ball or swing a bat, they remained committed to Victorian conceptions of femininity.

In all societies clothing is imbued with symbolic meaning signaling social status, power and appropriate roles for the categories of people. Among women involved in the first-wave feminist movement in the United States, bloomers were a symbol of freedom from restriction, a visual articulation of the broader political agenda for social inclusion that centered on the franchise. When elite White college women first began to play and enjoy the men's game of baseball, maintaining Victorian notions of respectability were paramount, to the detriment of players acquiring proficiency in baseball skills. They rejected wearing modern garments such as bloomers that allowed for greater athletic movement and openly displaying the competitive desire to win. The rejection of the more functional bloomer by women baseball players at elite colleges was linked with a rejection of feminist political goals. They did not adopt the bloomer due to its association with feminist activism and did not perceive a link between playing baseball and an extension of women's rights to include the franchise or work opportunities. Rather they sought to assure themselves and others that participation in baseball did not conflict with prevailing ideas of femininity that excluded appearing competitive. "It was unladylike for us to be playing baseball just like men."[9] Many students playing baseball were concerned with how the sport was perceived by outsiders and their peers, "its reputation for dignity among the undergraduates may be regarded as a minus quality."[10] In fact, baseball was not especially popular at Vassar with only 25 of 338 students in 1877 choosing the sport.[11]

Although there were women sportswriters by the late nineteenth century, such as Ella Black and Sally Van Pelt, as we would expect, the sports media gave little coverage to women's collegiate play. The few accounts were usually trivializing or demeaning. "It must be admitted that few are good at the game." Nevertheless, among the upper class, baseball continued to be a respectable pastime for women, played as it was in private clubs where proper dress and decorum were maintained.[12]

In contrast to such baseball "madonnas" there were "other" women players, those who invited male gaze and sexual desire in public social spaces. These players' alternative marginalized femininities and heightened sexuality were defined in class and racial terms. Promoters of baseball realized as early as the 1860s that attractive women willing to play baseball against men would draw paying crowds. These were working-class women who had already transgressed hegemonic femininity by working outside the home and were presented as sexually attractive. Although the recruited women were presumed to be and advertised as morally respectable, they were watched by and commented upon by men and received their share of public censure regarding their respectability.

For example, in 1890, the *Washington Post* reported on a baseball game at Capitol Park between the Young Ladies Baseball Club, "nine sprightly and uncommonly well-built young women, two of whom had long hair," and a team of men who were "of sufficient good taste to play under assumed names." Although the women's athletic skills at running and hitting were mentioned, these were assumed to be inferior to the opposing men's talents who allowed the women to score purposely to gain the support of the crowd. Far more attention was paid to their bodies and "costume" consisting of "a black bodice and black stockings, which really seemed to have no ends. They also wore brief yellow and black striped skirts that neither impeded the girls' movements, nor the crowd's full appreciation of the girls' physiques."[13]

Another example was the theatrical Dolly Vardens in 1867, an African American women's professional team from Philadelphia who based their image on a "busty working class flirt" from a Charles Dickens novel. Their sexualized image was fashioned by their made-up faces and uniforms: red calico dresses "shorter than propriety allowed for."[14] The Dolly Vardens are perhaps the first organized women's baseball club whose players used baseballs made from tightly wound yarn.

A third example was the Blondes and Brunettes of Springfield, Illinois, and later Philadelphia, who were teams of nine White women who barnstormed and gained widespread publicity. In 1875 the Blondes and Brunettes played the first game of baseball for money between two women's teams. Although these White women were described in the press as "reputable," their skills as "baseballers" were described as inept and their appearance, "the attraction is the novelty of seeing eighteen girls prettily attired in gymnastic dress," emphasized. An exhibition game between the Blondes and Brunettes in New York attended by 1,500 people at the Manhattan Athletic Club in September 1883 was covered by a reporter for the *New York Times*. Calling the game "a base-ball burlesque" he described the skills of the girls: "They played base-ball in a very sad and sorrowful sort of way, as if the vagaries of the ball had been too great for their struggling intellects. At the bat most of them preferred to strike at the ball after it passed them ... the girls displayed an alarming fondness for making home runs on three strikes ... often when the fielders could not stop the ball in any other way they sat down on it. This was at once effective and picturesque, and never missed gaining a great howl of applause." The reputation of the Blondes and Brunettes for "ridiculous exhibition" to attract male attention spread to major cities in the United States and extended across the Atlantic to England.[15]

At the turn of the twentieth century, there were a few women such as Lizzie Stride (Arlington), Lizzie Murphy, Mabel Schloen, and Josie Caruso with exceptional athletic skills who played on men's teams. Such women were working class and recruited primarily as novelties to draw paying spectators.[16] Lizzie Arlington was the youngest of six children and introduced to baseball and pitching by her father and brothers. She was the first woman to receive a minor league contract and to play a regulation game on July 5, 1898. After pitching four innings, collecting two hits and playing second base for the Philadelphia Reserves in their victory over Richmond, a baseball representative at the game, Edward Grant Burrow, signed Arlington to an official minor league contract with Reading. Arlington again played second base and pitched the ninth inning. The game was won by Reading 5–0, and among the 1,000 paying spectators were 200 women. A sports writer for the *Reading Eagle* covering the game reflected the prevailing ideology that women players were attractive novelties, but inferior athletes. "The spectators beheld a plump young woman with attractive face and rosy cheeks ... her hair was not cropped short, but was done up in the latest fashion.... Miss Arlington might do as a pitcher among amateurs, but the sluggers of the Atlantic

League would soon put her out of the business. She, of course, hasn't the strength to get much speed on and has poor control. But, for a woman, she is a success." Arlington was paid a relatively high salary to draw large crowds of paying spectators, but when the number of spectators dwindled her contract was terminated.[17]

In the nineteenth century, the emergence of a distinctly feminine athleticism that included some women playing baseball was part of a broad social revolution in the United States associated with modernity. With the transition to industrial capitalism as the dominant way of life, new ways of working arose with people leaving their homes to work for wages in a variety of worksites. The new manufacturing worksites employing both men and women were public spheres where monetary wages were earned to support the private sphere of the home. These changing economic relations of production generated new contexts for the construction of gender in the home, the workplace, the new colleges for women and in other public political events associated with the first-wave feminist movement. Although many working-class women worked for wages at this time, the public domain of productive or waged work was masculinized and associated with autonomy, competition and bread-winning. The home was gendered feminine and associated with dependence, consumption, nurturance and morality. Women who transgressed these cultural boundaries as workers, political activists or athletes faced sanctions and questions in the press concerning their moral respectability. Further, since the women and children who organized domestic life were often dependent on men's waged work and public representation for sustenance, women's bodies and minds were constructed as weak, fragile, inferior, hence "naturally" requiring the leadership and protection of men. Those women who challenged these hegemonic oppositional constructions of femininity—first-wave feminists, former women slaves such as Sojourner Truth, or women athletes—were classified as mannish, another deviant gender transgression.

Working-class women, whose femininity was marginalized due to the necessity for them to earn wages outside of the home, had greater freedom to play baseball competitively in public spaces. Those like Lizzie Arlington, who played baseball for the entertainment of paying male crowds, had to contend with prevailing ideologies of femininity and respectability that emphasized private domestic roles. Dichotomized gender ideologies rooted in the presumed biological inferiority of the female body diminished women players' athletic skills and relegating them to novelties whose principle function was to boost ticket sales. Their struggle to be taken seriously as skilled ball players was undermined by women who played "baseball burlesque" such as the Blondes and Brunettes.

Upper-class women, who had the privilege to lead leisured lives, did not work outside the home for wages. They too had the freedom to experiment with playing baseball at elite college campuses, at home or in exclusive clubs. These homosocial settings ensured that the women players did not violate Victorian norms of feminine behavior. While many elite college women accepted the new notion that exercise in the open air was a healthy activity for women, they distanced themselves from the first-wave feminist movement and its political goals symbolized by less constraining garments such as the bloomer.

3

"Playing to the Surprise and Delight of the Crowd": Bloomer Girls and Barnstorming Exhibition Players, 1890–1935

By the 1890s the novelty of watching women's teams composed of attractive women with inept skills had worn off and the public wanted to see skilled women players competing against men's teams. Some newly formed teams were composed of both men and women who played locally, such as the one in Lenox, Massachusetts, described in 1893: "One of the most amusing entertainments of the week was a baseball game gotten up by the young men and women, a mixed team. The girls could play quite as well as the boys. Some of them were really expert with the bat, in fact, they could bat better than they could throw. The game was won by a woman who hit a double, stole third and scored."[1] Better known were the new barnstorming or traveling teams of skilled women and men who played against local men's amateur or semi-professional teams known as Bloomer Girls. Although these teams were advertised as women's teams, they included men who played key positions such as catcher, pitcher or shortstop.

Bisocial or gender-integrated teams provide a useful focus for the assessment of culturally specific contexts where gender is constructed and negotiated, especially as both women and men on these teams crossed gender-dominated fields. During the Progressive Era, 1890–1920, Victorian sexual codes were being challenged by a "boldly sexually assertive working class youth culture" and a "playfully erotic" pleasure-oriented consumer economy.[2] Also, more women were engaged in the public arena: at work, in various political movements, in the new women's colleges and as social workers. The golden years of baseball were a time when the boundaries for women's participation in the periphery of the sport were somewhat permeable. Although women's bodies were still constructed as inferior and the Victorian cultural ethos of separate gendered spheres was still pervasive, contradictions between emergent egalitarian ideals and the rigidity of prevailing gender and racial binaries in the United States were being voiced.

The professional mixed gender barnstorming teams that appeared in the 1890s and lasted until the 1930s were called Bloomer Girls, after Amelia Jenks Bloomer, a pioneer suffragette and advocate for less restrictive women's clothing. Bloomer responded to the desire by some women for greater range of movement to engage in physical activities. Playing baseball in long heavy skirts with restrictive stays was difficult and those women determined to excel, such as Alta Weiss and players on Bloomer Girls teams, discarded their skirts in favor of bloomers or loose fitting pantaloons. Bloomer Girls teams were predominantly working class and composed of six or seven women and two or three men who initially dressed as women.

Although early promoters were primarily interested in the profit-earning potential of Bloomer Girls teams by marketing the heterosexual appeal of the women players, men known as "toppers" were also hired. These men wore curly wigs and dressed in skirts.[3] Promoters had no trouble finding sufficient numbers of men to fill these positions, despite prevailing notions of hegemonic masculinity that excluded cross-dressing. The pay was sufficient, and according to Gae Berlage, some men were able to use the experience on women's teams as a stepping stone to successful careers in the major leagues. Bloomer Girl teams, despite their popularity, were peripheral in baseball. For the male players, this brief period of transgressing gender boundaries by cross-dressing was justified by their ambition to eventually play on the core men's major league baseball teams. Those men who did advance included such stars as Smokey Joe Wood and Rogers Hornsby. By the early 1900s, women discarded their skirts and bloomers and wore traditional baseball pants. It was also accepted that some members of the teams would be men, so they were no longer disguised as women.[4] Still, some "ballpark announcers and sports reporters thought it humorous to call a male player by a female name," chiding them for gender bending.[5]

For women at this time, advancement into the center of organized baseball was structurally blocked. Even the famous Bloomer Girl pitcher Maud Nelson, "champion lady baseball pitcher of the world," an "expert at twisting the pigskin" who regularly struck out men batters, was not considered eligible for promotion to the minor or major leagues.[6] Nelson played for decades pitching for the Boston and Chicago Bloomer Girls and the Star Bloomer Girls Baseball Club of Indianapolis. Nelson's baseball skills included pitching, hitting and fielding at third base. In 1903 the *Boston Herald* reported on a game in Maine attended by one thousand spectators. Nelson was the only player mentioned in the article by the reporter. "The feature of the game was the pitching, batting, and fielding of Miss Neislon [sic]. She made three base hits, and had four put outs and four assists and made no errors. In the five innings she pitched she struck out seven men."[7] In 1911 Nelson eventually became a manager, scout of both male and female talent and owner of the highly successful Western Bloomer Girls, a team consisting of eight women and three men. They barnstormed widely in the United States and in 1926 visited Cuba where they played against men's amateur teams.

Pitcher Lizzie Arlington, who was coached by Baltimore Oriole pitcher Jack Stivetts, also "had a really good windup and delivery," and was considered by him to be "quite a hurler." She was also sufficiently talented to pitch in regulation minor league games around the minor league circuit. However, after failing to attract crowds she was released from her expensive contract and joined a Bloomer Girls team.[8]

Given the concrete ceiling barring women from advancement in professional baseball, accounts of women's athletic skills by sportswriters were expectantly contradictory. Some writers deplored the Bloomer Girls as "a traveling female aggregation of alleged ball players," while others praised their skills. Most assumed that women's athletic skills were inferior and if the men's team lost, it was due to "laxness" or "chivalry." In a game featuring the New York Bloomer Girls team and the Judson Class A Red Coats, a team in the men's King Cotton League: "Male pitcher chivalry didn't put as much stuff on the ball as he otherwise could have done. The visiting girls (two men as catcher and short stop) didn't have trouble hitting him. The Judson infielders, imbued with the same sense of chivalry or something, were also a bit lax in their fielding accounting for a number of visitor runs."[9]

A reporter for the *New York Tribune* perceived the Bloomer Girls teams as "disgraceful," emphasizing women's inferior athletic abilities. "Probably the most disgraceful feature in baseball is the female baseball crowd now traveling over the country giving a burlesque of the sport. The women cannot play baseball and never will be able to learn how to play the game. It is safe to say that nine boys in Knickerbockers picked up at random could defeat this women's team without any difficulty. The exhibitions are disgraceful and ought to be stopped by the police. The manager of this team tried to get the Polo grounds for the women's team, but the grounds like all reputable baseball enclosures in this neighborhood were refused to them."[10]

Another sports writer for *The Nashua Reporter* in Iowa in 1907 lamented that, "The Ball game last Friday between Nashua and the Bloomer Girls was a disappointment to those who attended expecting to see a close game. The girls were no match for our boys who could have shut them out entirely if they had been on their mettle, but in the 9th inning they got indifferent and the girls ran in one lone score. Three of the girls were boys but we could not see that they played any better than the real article."[11]

In contrast, coverage in the *Cincinnati Enquirer* of a game where a Bloomer Girls team defeated the Cincinnati Stars 12 to 7, praised the determination of the players and skills of the pitcher Maud Nelson and first basemen Miss Day. "The girls played as if their lives depended on winning the game and though they were up against one of the strongest amateur teams in the city, they never showed the white feather, but kept working hard for victory. Pitcher Maud Nelson gave up 4 runs (3 unearned) in 4 innings. The work of Miss Day at first base was a revelation to the large crowd in attendance. No matter where the ball was thrown she would get it. Some of her pick ups of low thrown balls were remarkable. She also led her side in batting."[12]

Existing documents relating to the women players suggest that they played baseball with competitive spirit and took their skills as athletes seriously. Their accounts also suggest that they developed a love for baseball and an appreciation of their athletic skills as children who played baseball wherever and whenever they could usually with their brothers. Although prevailing gender dichotomies linked athleticism with masculinity, ideologies can be mediated by the needs of real people, particularly children, in real situations. As research on "doing gender" among children has revealed, gender separation can be fluid and situated. Baseball could be an occasion when local girls, due to their emersion in local social networks, could cross gender boundaries without suffering stigma.[13] If a neighborhood baseball team were short of players, a sister who could play would be recruited or taught to play. While institutionalized sexism discriminated against women as athletes, on the local baseball diamond, individual males (brothers, fathers, uncles, and friends) often encouraged androgynous tomboys who resisted feminine games, pursuits and dress to join a game. For these girls playing baseball provided an alternative means for self-definition and gender identity, empowering them to experience their own physical competence.

Such was the case with Sister Miriam Cecil, a former New York Bloomer Girl interviewed at age 96 in 2003. "I started at home with my two brothers. There was a baseball field the next block ... and my oldest brother was a big fan and he put me on. I could play if I wanted and I sure wanted because it was fun then. Anytime I saw people playing baseball I was always there." Sister Miriam played first base and pitched for the New York Bloomer Girls team that traveled throughout the United States, Mexico and Canada for twenty weeks. It was her mother who gave the initial go-ahead to play in a charity baseball game in 1923 in Brooklyn. Two New York Bloomer Girls watched her play and gave her the invitation to join. She earned $15.00 a week plus expenses. In 1929 Sister Miriam joined the Kitty Kelly All Stars, a men's team featuring a few of the best women players of the day where she earned $25.00 a week plus expenses. Mindful of her respectability when traveling with men, she owned a car and her sister traveled around the country with her as companion and chaperon. Sister Miriam's career batting average was .323 and ended in 1941 when she joined a convent. There she continued to enjoy physical work including painting, carpentry, and lawn mowing. She stated that traditional feminine roles never held much importance for her. "Girls should play sports. It proves that they are just as good as men. Anyone who loves baseball and wants to strive to play the game right, as it should be played, should be allowed to play. Men shouldn't have, and don't have, anything over women in the area of sports. We are just as capable." After 50 years of not playing, Sister Miriam still felt "spring fever." "We didn't care if we lost 30 to 1 ... baseball to us was baseball."[14]

Alma Korneski, interviewed in 1994 at age 83, joined the New York Bloomer Girls in 1933. She first encountered the team as an opponent on the Lehigh men's city team which included women players. She played second base and although Lehigh won, Korneski wanted to join the Bloomer Girls team. "My family never minded me playing baseball. They knew I was a tomboy." She was the only girl in a family of six brothers and learned to play baseball by being the odd man out. "My brothers always called me outside to come and even up the sides in the neighborhood games. So I've been playing baseball since I was old enough to run around the diamond." Although her team lost most of its games against men's teams, crowds came to see women play baseball. After the Bloomer Girls Team disbanded she formed a softball team in Perth Amboy to continue playing the sport.[15]

Bloomer Girls teams barnstormed in Canada beginning in the 1890s. Another former New York Bloomer Girl, Edna (Lockhart) Duncanson was Canada's only player between 1910 and 1935. Duncanson, a five-sport star from Avonport, Nova Scotia, pitched and played third base for the New York Bloomer Girls. She also developed her athletic skills on the local school playground with her thirteen siblings. While visiting one of her siblings on Staten Island at age seventeen, she was spotted by the manager of the team. "I could throw, I could bat and I could run. I had great coordination." Duncanson played 100 games per year, all against men's teams and everywhere they drew large crowds. However, as members of Margaret Nabel's team they "had to be ladies after the game. We had to change into skirts after the game. We couldn't smoke, couldn't drink beer. If you were caught in a pub in those days you would get a pink slip. The manager would never stand for it. All we had to do was keep our health and stay in shape. And toe the line." Duncanson stated that the fans treated them with respect as professionals. After the New York Bloomer Girls team folded, she returned to Canada and continued to play basketball, softball and bowling.[16]

The New York Bloomer Girls team was founded in 1910 in Staten Island by Dan Whalen, Joe Manning and Eddie Manning and continued for twenty years with their booking and promotion handled by Syd Pollock, a promoter of barnstorming Negro League teams. Staten Island was supplying ballplayers to the majors by the 1880s and by 1928 there were 250 baseball teams, many sponsored by local companies. These companies would hire ballplayers as workers. On Staten Island, baseball was a passion and played by working-class men, women and children.

Margaret Nabel joined the team in 1914 after graduating high

Billed as the "undefeated female champs," the New York Bloomer Girls, managed by Margaret Nabel (pictured here with her team that included Edna Lockhart), continued to play until 1935. The women players wore uniforms similar to men's. Front row (left to right): Julie Gressek, Dotty Ruh, Helen Demarest, Ginger Robinson. Back row (left to right): Hattie Michaels, Margaret Nabel, Alma Pucci, Shank Nelson, Edna Lockhart, Mary Ontek, Mel Pearsell (National Baseball Hall of Fame Library, Cooperstown, New York).

school. She played as a pitcher and outfielder and assumed management of the team by age twenty. Nabel built a superlative team, recruiting skilled local talent and managing them according to her own rigorous standards. At first her team consisted of seven women and two men who comprised the battery. In her view, "we feel no female player can do justice to the pitcher's burden and you will agree that the catching job belongs to a man, too." Women pitchers, including Helen Demarest and Ethel Condon, were used when the New York Bloomers played against other women's teams.[17] Her eastern team was as highly regarded as the Western Bloomer Girls, managed by Maud Nelson, barnstorming from Nova Scotia to Florida, challenging men's company sponsored teams. Nabel promoted her team as the "the undisputed female champions of the world."[18]

In male homosocial sports the relationship forged between managers or coaches and players is central to the engendering process where boys are socialized to be masculine. Team managers, coaches and their assistants teach required skills, lore, language, and behavioral norms in ways that help prepare boys for participation in larger gendered spheres of life.[19]

On bisocial Bloomer Girls teams the socialization process between manager and players was complicated by several factors: the feminine gender of successful managers such as Nabel and Nelson, the feminine gender of the majority of players, the masculine gender of a few key players, the prevalence of Victorian cultural constructions of respectable femininity in terms of passive domesticity, female frailty and the cultural links among athleticism, baseball and masculinity. Women who transgressed gender boundaries as baseball players were perceived by many as "unnatural."

It is reasonable to assume that women managers of the caliber of Nelson and Nable profoundly influenced the young women players on their teams who were usually teenagers traveling on their own for the first time. The socialization process involved traversing the murky gender contradictions posed by young single women leaving home and *temporarily* transgressing gender boundaries by playing a masculine sport with men as teammates in public arenas where men were the majority of spectators. It was important that they retain their respectability so as not to limit their future prospects either as dependent wives or independent employees. Similar to boys on homosocial teams, these young women learned many attributes scripted as masculine: independence, hard work, discipline, commitment to one's team, and athletic competence while conforming to the authority and discipline of the manager. However, they were learning these attributes at a time when most women received contradictory messages based on the assumption that their future would be as wives and mothers supported by husbands. Evidence suggests that the women players experienced this androgynous socialization as positive with some continuing to pursue sports and alternative occupations. Most of what is known about Bloomer Girls teams relates to White women, and although evidence relating to sexual preference is also lacking, these teams offered a space for participation by lesbians and other single women who rejected the normative dependence on men inherent in marriage practices at the turn of the twentieth century.

Interviewed in 1931, Margaret Nabel commented on the myriad difficulties involved in building a solidly committed team of women players at a time when autonomy was not a feminine trait. "It is comparatively difficult to locate, develop and retain capable and reliable girl players, as you can well imagine. Sometimes the parents object and sometimes it's a steady boyfriend; oftimes the girls are too young, they wish to remain strictly amateur, or they tire of steady play."[20] Nevertheless, Nabel was a skillful manager with an eye for young talent. The team boasted a twenty-year winning streak against women's teams and in the east they were considered the team to beat. They also played against Black men's semi-pro teams such as the Jersey City Colored Athletics on September 16, 1932.[21] Nabel successfully recruited young Philadelphia Bobbies star player Edith Houghton in 1925. Houghton later became the first woman to be hired as a scout for a major league team by the Philadelphia Phillies. In April 1931, after Jackie Mitchell's minor league contract was voided by Commissioner Kenesaw Mountain Landis, Nabel immediately offered her a contract. Mitchell turned it down and decided to play on another men's team, the Lookouts in Tennessee. Nabel, known to never miss an opportunity to promote her team, traveled to Tennessee and challenged the Lookouts to a big game. Mitchell and the Lookouts won 7 to 4, but the New York Bloomer Girls pitched and fielded well. Although Nabel was adept at promotion, her team became well known primarily because her players gave "the best teams a close game." Town teams and semi-professional teams looking for a competitive game sought them out as rivals.

Although professional promoters advertised the Bloomer Girls teams and made sure that paying crowds knew that the women were skilled ball players, not actresses or prostitutes, sometimes the teams faced irate ministers, misogynist fans and a skeptical press. In an interview with Nabel in 1961, she was asked if people ridiculed the girls. Her answer reflects that the link between female athleticism and mannishness had not yet fully crystallized. "No, we were accepted. Women were starting to move into sports and business then. People seemed to like to mix with us. Fellows used to like to come over and feel our arms. They were always surprised at how hard, how in shape we were."[22] Nabel herself was described by a former player as a solidly built woman. While prevailing constructions of female bodies based on elite, leisured, White women emphasized delicacy and softness, these Bloomer Girls reconstructed their bodies in masculine athletic terms — hard, strong and fast — and displayed them with pride.

Margaret Nabel and Maud Nelson were successful team managers, scouts and promoters, positions of authority usually reserved for men. "Many adventurous female ball players relied on one or another of Nelson's teams to earn a living." Although Nelson is described by her players as quiet and modest, she was very capable at balancing multiple responsibilities: training the players, consulting the booking agents, handling the myriad needs of her players, including injuries, homesickness or replacement. Although quiet, Nelson was competitive and strove to recruit talented players for her teams. "No fake attractions." For example she wrote to Toney and Margaret Gisolo, whose talent as a player on a successful American Legion team had been widely publicized. Margaret Gisolo, despite her talent, was banned in 1929 at age fourteen from further participation on American Legion teams on the basis of her sex. Nelson recruited her as a player for the All Star Ranger Girls. Nelson retired when the Great Depression made it difficult to finance a baseball team and when women began to play softball rather than baseball.[23]

Nabel's management style was masculine, employing a stern paternalistic style rather than nurturing surrogate mother to mold her players into a disciplined unit. Prior to her assuming management of the team, the New York Bloomer Girls "were a rowdy bunch gaining notoriety in 1913 when they trashed a hotel in Raleigh, North Carolina — breaking windows, mirrors, and chairs and beating back the police with bats and balls."[24] Nabel "ran the Bloomer Girls with an iron fist" with no tolerance for rowdy, rough behavior that would tarnish the respectability of her players. "Players are strictly disciplined, as we cannot tolerate looseness of any kind. We allow absolutely no drinking, no carousing, and we all observe a regular curfew at 11:00. In addition, players must write home at least once a week."[25]

Barnstorming teams received a share of the gate which was divided between the park, the team, and the promoter/booker. Reputed to be a tough but fair businesswoman, Nabel immediately divided the team's share among the players. If the teams were not paid their agreed upon share before the game started, she pulled the players off the field. According to former player Ella Birmingham, "she was a business woman, very much so. Nobody could put anything over on her. When we got money it was all split up and that was it. We had traveling expenses and other expenses that were paid for us. She was a congenial person, but a business woman. She knew what she was doing. She was a good manager, very good to the girls who played for her."[26] Nabel was also an intelligent enough business woman to know when to disband the team in 1933 when the Depression years made it difficult to meet expenses.

Although Nabel's team played against African American men's semi-professional teams, there were no integrated Bloomer Girls teams. There were however, African American Bloomer Girls teams such as the Black Broncho Baseball Club of St. Louis managed by Mr. Conrad Knebler. These teams were ignored in the White mainstream media during the Jim Crow years. In 1910, the *Indianapolis Freeman* billed the team as "the only Colored Female Baseball Club in the world today." The Black Bronchos toured the central states "taking on all comers." A picture of the team shows six women and four men who were "getting into shape for a good season of ball." In a game between the St. Louis Black Broncho Baseball Club and the East St. Louis Imperials, "the base running of Lilly and Bess was wonderful. Nellie who played first is a star. She can throw to third like a man and also pick them up off the ground in great style."[27] Referring to women players by their first name only or preceded by the honorific "miss" could signify familiarity and affection or reflect prevailing deference rituals and subordinate status depending on the race/ethnicity of the sports writer. Another early African American women's team located in Kansas City, Missouri, was covered in 1907 by *South Bend News Times*. The article focuses on the surprise felt by a man strolling by a park and encountering a "practice of aggregation of colored female athletes." This "full team of negro girls, ranging in age from 18 to 22 years, clad in short blue skirts, white shirtwaists, black stockings, and regulation baseball shoes" were "equipped with every modern device for capturing the frisky baseball."[28] A Maryland-based team, the Baltimore Black Sox Colored Girls, was being followed by the *AfroAmerican* in 1921. The team was reported to have "played well to the surprise and delight of the crowd."[29]

The Bloomer Girls and other women who played on professional bisocial exhibition teams were agents at a historical moment, the Progressive Era, when women were beginning to negotiate the rigidity of Victorian gender separation. Playing on teams with men and against men is an experience that only a handful of women have duplicated since. Their bloomer uniforms (later replaced by pants), unlike those uniforms which preceded (long skirts to the ankle) or followed (short skirts worn by the All-American Girls' Professional Baseball League), provided them with the freedom of movement to play baseball efficiently, safely and modestly. Their skills were often recognized in the sports media, and although concern with moral respectability, social class and race segregation remained, owners like Margaret Nabel sought to insulate their players with rigid codes of feminine conduct.

Not every adventurous female baseball player at this time joined barnstorming Bloomer Girls teams. Jackie Mitchell posed the first real challenge to professional baseball as a male preserve. The daughter of a doctor, and therefore middle class, Jackie Mitchell "was out at the sandlots with my father from as long as I can remember" and was the star pitcher at her prep school — the Signal School. She was also coached by Hall of Fame pitcher Dizzy Vance. In 1929 at the age of seventeen, the

In 1931, seventeen-year-old Jackie Mitchell (right), a southpaw pitcher, signed a minor league contract with the Class AA Chattanooga Lookouts. Team owner Joe Engel announced that Mitchell would pitch an exhibition game against the New York Yankees, creating a media sensation. Although Mitchell struck out Babe Ruth (center) and Lou Gehrig (left), Commissioner Kenesaw Mountain Landis voided her contract (National Baseball Hall of Fame Library, Cooperstown, New York).

southpaw attracted the attention of scouts when playing on the Engelettes, a girls' team managed by Joe Engel. She joined Kid Elberfeld's baseball school in Atlanta in 1931 and later in that year signed a contract with the Chattanooga Lookouts, a Double A minor league team in the Southern Association also owned by Engel. This was the second minor league contract signed by a woman. Engel announced that he would use her in a game against the Yankees. At an exhibition game on April 2, 1931, between the Lookouts and the New York Yankees, Mitchell struck out Babe Ruth and Lou Gehrig, causing a media sensation.[30]

Engel intended to retain Mitchell as a pitcher with the Lookouts. However, her contract was voided by Commissioner Kenesaw Mountain Landis who claimed that baseball was too strenuous for women.[31] During his tenure as commissioner, Landis was responsible for decisions based on fabricated biological distinctions that were detrimental to the integration of both women and African American men into the core of organized baseball. Although Landis intended his action to set a precedent for all women aspiring to play professional baseball, he did not object to women playing amateur baseball. In a 1933 forward to the Spalding Guide, Landis stressed the benefits of amateur baseball for women as long as they played exclusively among themselves. "It is indeed a wonderful thing that these benefits may now be enjoyed by our girls and young women under the supervision of properly constituted authorities on women's athletics." These authorities regulated play on homosocial teams and competitions on "playgrounds, schools and colleges."[32]

As Messner argues, women athletes often appear in the media as sexual objects, a representation that silences them as athletic agents.[33] While sportswriters acknowledged Jackie Mitchell's skill as a left-handed pitcher, with a career record of 60 wins to 40 losses, they also constructed her as "other," an essentially feminine object who was merely a sexualized publicity stunt. In the media account of the exhibition game against the Yankees, Mitchell is described in humorous sexualized terms intended to detract attention from her athleticism. "The bobbed hair pitcher pulled out her mirror and powder puff and dusted the shine off her nose. She then went into an intricate windup and the ball whizzed toward the Babe." Again, "The curves won't be all on the ball when pretty Jackie Mitchell of the Chattanooga Lookouts in the Southern League takes the mound against the New York Yankees in an exhibition game."[34]

An article in 1933 emphasized her respectable femininity, informing the public that her mother always traveled with her as chaperon, and her domestic skills. "It might be supposed that having adopted the exciting and strenuous profession of baseball that Miss Mitchell has abandoned the usual feminine arts, but the contrary is true. She can sew and make a dress, she cooks with skill and success and even plays the piano ... she is charming and has the unassuming title: the little blonde southpaw from sunny Tennessee."[35]

Jackie Mitchell put the Lookouts in the national spotlight and after Landis' decision she continued to play baseball, touring with men's semipro teams who were beyond his jurisdiction. Although such teams were peripheral in baseball, they allowed her to continue to play baseball and to transgress gender boundaries. She died in 1981 at age 73. In 1975, at age 67, she was interviewed again in the *Chattanooga News* where her own subjective androgynous gender identity differed dramatically from the earlier feminized images constructed by the media. "Of course we never heard of women's lib' back then, but I guess you could say I was a pioneer at it. Back in my younger days, I wasn't a person who wanted to settle down. I didn't get married until my 50s and then it was someone I had known for a long time. I'm interested in keeping up with what's happening in female athletics and efforts of the girls to play with the boys. I think they ought to be allowed to, if they are good enough."[36]

Commissioner Landis's decision also immediately affected another talented woman athlete, Mildred "Babe" Didrikson. Mildred's nickname Babe was given to her by the boys in her neighborhood since she could hit a baseball hard like Babe Ruth. Didrickson was perhaps the greatest woman athlete, proficient at running, basketball, baseball, tennis, billiards and golf, all with her parents' encouragement. She pitched about 200 games for the House of David barnstorming team in 1934 and as a promotional gimmick in exhibition games in the "grapefruit circuit" during spring training. There she pitched against minor and major league teams including the Philadelphia Athletics, the Brooklyn Dodgers and the St. Louis Cardinals, performing well against minor league hitters. Despite her talents as a pitcher, hitter and runner, Landis's decision eliminated any possible career for Didrickson in organized baseball. She therefore turned to women's golf, dominating that sport until her death in1956.[37]

Barnstorming exhibition players like the Bloomer Girls teams, Jackie Mitchell, Babe Didrickson and managers like Maud Nelson and Margaret Nabel emerged during the Progressive Era and lasted until the Depression and World War II. Although the cultural assumptions relating to the inferiority of women's minds and bodies underpinning Victorian gender constructions still dominated, the ideologies that justified their exclusion were challenged by greater numbers of women moving into the public domain as workers, political leaders and participants, college students and athletes. Women's participation in competitive athletics, including bisocial baseball teams that played games viewed by paying spectators, was one outgrowth of these larger forces of social change. If we shift our perspective on this period to marginalized African Americans, it also coincided with the passage of Jim Crow laws that legally sanctioned and institutionalized race-based discrimination. Although some African American women also assumed positions of leadership in the struggle to extend the franchise to women and equal opportunities to African American men and women, attended college, and played sports, there were no racially integrated Bloomer Girls' teams or in men's organized baseball.

The 1920s and '30s were also periods of anti-feminist backlash in response to women's newly won franchise and included the medicalization of homosexuality as a congenital or psychological pathology. The typology of the "mannish lesbian" appeared with "depraved sexual appetites and preference for masculine dress and activity were identified as symptoms of psychological disturbance." The result was an emerging taboo on lesbianism and a fear of female homosocial environments including women's colleges and sports teams "where mannish lesbians lurked."[38] To counter the mannishness image, the eroticized heterosexual sports competitor also emerged as female athletes began to face a new image problem—a contradiction between their athleticism and femininity—reflected in press accounts stressing their appearance, (i.e. "feminine charms") heterosexuality and traditional domestic gender roles.[39] Significantly, by the end of the "the bold years," this backlash also included formally codifying discriminatory barriers for women's participation in professional baseball at the minor league level.

Although Bloomer Girls teams were bisocial teams, the principle attraction for spectators was the women players who challenged local men's teams. These teams played baseball competitively with a high level of skill and the most successful Bloomer Girls teams were managed by women: Maud Nelson and Margaret Nabel. These teams challenged the assumption that athletic competition between or among both sexes is harmful since men would presumably lose self-esteem and women would presumably be vulnerable to physical injury and emotional stress due to contradictions in their feminine self-image. Evidence from the women players does not suggest any physical or emotional harm from participation on these integrated teams.

The men players, who usually filled the battery positions of pitcher and catcher, are interesting cases of negotiated gender identity. Only men at this time were eligible to advance into organized baseball, and some male Bloomer Girls players were spotted by baseball scouts. However, in the early years men players had to cross-dress and cope with the derision of male sports announcers and writers. It is reasonable to assume that cross-dressing and the accompanying negative comments might have injured the self-esteem of some of the men. However, these men players also experienced the athletic prowess, competitive success and competitive drive of their women teammates. Those men playing for Nelson or Nabel had to accept the authority and competency of a woman manager. It is also reasonable to assume that these experiences could translate into enhanced respect for their female teammates and the ability to work with and for women.

The situational complexity of gender symbols and relations on Bloomer Girls teams is evident in the press coverage of games where some journalists held the teams in utter distain, some continued to feminize the men players after they ceased to dress as women, and others recognized the skills and contributions of exceptional women players in the competitive effort. While the journalistic technique of selective incorporation of outstanding women athletes expands the public perception of women's athletic capabilites, it also reproduces ideologies that justify the exclusion of women from organized baseball since the majority are assumed to be incapable of competing successfully with or against men.

While the majority of Bloomer Girls players were working class and, therefore, accustomed to women working for wages outside the home, most accepted middle-class Victorian codes for respectable feminine behavior and morality. Women managers thus negotiated a morally ambiguous social context where very young single women, many of whom had never left home before, were traveling around the country with young men playing a man's game of baseball for a largely male-paying public. Protecting the respectability of these young single women players by setting strict curfews, limiting alcohol consumption, wearing feminine clothing off the playing field, writing regularly to parents was a significant concern of manager Margaret Nabel.

Although homophobia in sport had not fully emerged, Nabel was careful to promote an acceptable feminine image for her players both in terms of dress and conduct. These young women baseball players were already challenging prevailing gender constructions identifying as androgynous "tomboys" who enjoyed playing baseball with brothers or local neighborhood boys more than accepted feminine pursuits. They took their skills as athletes seriously and their gender-neutral uniforms provided them with both freedom of movement and feminine modesty. Young female players also learned, as did young boy athletes, such "masculine" values as hard physical training, commitment to a team, earning and managing their own money and thus enjoyed considerable autonomy within the boundaries of feminine respectability. Nevertheless, since women players could not enter the ranks of organized baseball, even at the minor league level, most were only expected to play for a short time before leaving the sport to assume traditional feminine lives as wives, mothers or in the occupations currently open to women. While it is reasonable to assume that many former Bloomer Girls players did assume such roles, evidence also suggests that many continued to play competitive sports, some never married, and others pursued occupations and careers that were pioneering for women.

4

"More Than the Usual Variety of Curves": The All-American Girls Professional Baseball League, 1943–1954

World War II was another historical moment when constructions of feminine gender identity were negotiated. After the United States joined the Allies in the war effort, many occupations that were previously limited to men were now open to women, including baseball. In 1943, Philip K. Wrigley, owner of the Chicago Cubs and president of Wrigley's Chewing Gum, decided to form a woman's league since he feared that major league baseball would have to be suspended due to the number of men enlisting in the military. By 1943 only eleven of forty-one minor league teams were operating and the manpower shortage also threatened major league baseball teams. However, by this time women's softball was established and well attended. Originally named the All-American Girls Softball League, the League was originally a hybrid of fast pitch softball and baseball.[1] Wrigley provided the start-up money, between $200,000 to $250,000, as a patriotic endeavor, a non-profit organization to boost the morale of factory workers during World War II. Wrigley recruited the support of major league general managers Ken Sells of the Chicago Cubs and Branch Rickey of the Brooklyn Dodgers to become League Trustees.

The era of the All-American Girls Professional Baseball League (AAGPBL) between 1943 and 1954, is replete with cultural contradictions. The Progressive Era, with its concern for social equality and justice for women and workers, was over and the world was at war. However, during this short period, a woman's golden age of baseball unfolded, when men were overseas and women were needed as "patriotic pinch hitters" to fill various required occupations including baseball players. During the war years, women baseball players who lined up before each game in a "V" formation, were to "exert a Betty Grable quality reminding America what it was fighting for."[2]

The War was also the heyday of the Negro Leagues. White and Black workers flooded into the Northern industrial cities, there was near full employment and attendance at available forms of popular entertainment, including Negro League baseball games, soared. The participation of African American men in the War effort provided a powerful justification for their integration into the major leagues in 1947. Although this justification did not result in women's integration, this was a historical moment when women's professional baseball also moved briefly to the semi-periphery, a position closer to the core of organized baseball than ever before or since. However, it is significant that this golden age of women's baseball was limited to White women, as racism and Jim Crow segregation excluded African American women from participation on AAGPBL teams.

Gae Berlage argues that, "A certain irony is obvious when one looks back on this era — an era of unprecedented opportunity for women to participate in baseball. After all, women today are barred from playing baseball, which remains a male preserve. Yet the women who played baseball during World War II were treated as children and depicted as the weaker sex. There was still strict sex-role segregation. Women could be 'feminine' players and chaperons, but they were not allowed to be managers or coaches. The teams were forbidden to play even exhibition games against male teams. Yet the League was billed by Arthur E. Meyerhoff Associates, Wrigley's principle advertising agents, as the third major league and the women players were expected to possess all the skills of professional baseball players."[3] The organizational structure and culture of the League — its bureaucratic hierarchy, rules for play on the field, rules for conduct off the field, rules regulating the social interactions among players, managers and chaperons and the dominant symbols used to represent and promote the teams and players — reproduced rather than challenged the male-dominated gender regime of baseball. The creation of a women's "league of their own" was an outgrowth of legitimized exclusion from men's organized baseball and did not challenge or eliminate either the exclusive ideologies or discriminatory barriers.

This golden age for women's baseball did not challenge prevailing dichotomous gender constructions of male and female bodies. The League's ideology constructed a "socially acceptable athletic femininity" in terms explicitly oppositional to male athleticism premised on the assumption of women's physical inferiority.[4] Although the women players were recognized as talented athletes with enough skills to play highly competitive baseball games, it was assumed that they could never and should never compete with men. To do so would subject women to injury and humiliation. It was in women's best interest to play on exclusively homosocial teams in a homosocial league of their own. "It is an iron rule of the league that the girls shall never play against teams of boys or men. Every single member of our board agrees ... this is a girl's game, and our girls are not imitating men. It wouldn't prove a thing; it would simply be carnival stuff if we played one of our teams against men. We think we are doing a little something to give girls confidence in themselves, the players and the women who come to watch the players. We are not interested in a meaningless competition with men."[5] Even when the Class B Florida International League, a men's minor league team, tried to buy the contract of talented All-American first basemen Dorothy Kamensek of the Rockford Peaches (the first such attempt since Jackie Mitchell), Fred Leo's refusal illustrated how women's athleticism was to be understood and controlled. "Rockford couldn't afford to lose her. I also told them that we felt women should play baseball among themselves and that they could not help but appear inferior in athletic competition with men."[6]

The media — newspapers, magazines, radio — played a vital role during the War in reconstructing hegemonic femininity, which rested on assumptions of female fragility and dependence. It was essential to reconcile the need for middle-class women's labor power with their domestic reproductive work for which they were "naturally" suited. Rosie the Riveter was "young and beautiful, but also strong and confident with a powerful rivet gun resting across her muscular thighs and a copy of *Mein Kampf* under her feet." The media provided a "flood of positive images" of working women to alter the consciousness of the White middle-class public toward married women working outside the home. To eliminate the "stigma of economic necessity" working women were glamorized in images and words. Assembly-line workers were described as "alluring Grable-like damsels, clad in slacks and bandannas, and oozing glamour from every pore." Women's talents, work habits and productivity were praised as equal to those of men. Since one-third of working women were mothers, the public was assured that they were adept at balancing their domestic and workplace responsibilities.[7]

Further, in the interwar years and those following World War II, "the stereotype of the lesbian athlete emerged full blown. The extreme homophobia and the gender conservatism of the postwar era created a context in which longstanding linkages among mannishness, female homosexuality and athletics cohered around the figure of the mannish lesbian athlete."[8] Although the athletic skills of League players were recognized by everyone involved with them, their athletic prowess should be displayed in ways that were not "mannish." The construction of feminine athleticism by the leadership of the League, the players and media included an "apologetic stance" toward women's athleticism.[9] Women were expected to play baseball with high levels of competence, competitive motivation and a stoic disregard for the inevitable injuries inflicted by the game and exacerbated by their short-skirted uniforms that exposed their legs to unnecessary injuries, all the while conforming to myriad rules governing their femininity on and off the playing field. The emphasized femininity of League players was an attempt to demonstrate that their players were not being masculinized by playing baseball. The League focused public attention on White heterosexual standards of beauty among their players.[10] Also, since feminine athleticism was presumed to be inferior to masculine athleticism, future careers in organized minor or major league baseball were inconceivable. After a stint at playing professional baseball, the women players should assume heterosexual lives in supportive dependent reproductive roles for which they were "naturally" suited.

The AAGPBL followed quickly on the heals of the Bloomer Girls teams which disbanded in the 1930s, and League ideology actively sought to sharply distinguish the image of their players from both the rough, "carnival," Amazon, sexually permissive Bloomer Girls and the enormously popular "masculine, physical freaks" who played softball in modified men's uniforms in approximately 600,000 teams across the country.[11] In 1943, women's softball players in Kenosha, Wisconsin, were depicted in the press as having a "tendency to lean toward emulating their male brethren in the game of baseball. Their mode of dress, carriage, and actions ... have been annually moving toward the male side."[12] A 1948 piece published about the Bloomer Girls also reflected a backlash against the rugged image of these bisocial teams vigorously shunned by the League. "When ... Ty Cobb was burning up every diamond the Bloomer Girls were the red-hot mammas of the national pastime. That was nearly forty years ago and the Girls' first women's professional ball teams of record played only exhibition games against male nines. Those rugged Amazons usually abetted by a male pitcher and catcher, played a man's game against men, with regulation bats and balls on regulation fields. What's more they won games."[13] Questions about the sexual morality of Bloomer Girls players also continued, as Merrie Fidler's brief account based on evidence from New Orleans-based teams suggests.[14] In contrast, the feminine All American "girl baseball players" were not "giant huskies ... they are feminine American girls of better than average beauty ... the AAGBL refuses to hire the masculine rough neck type of player...."[15] Thus the League constructed a dichotomous athletic femininity understood as not masculine, not lesbian and conforming to prevailing White standards of beauty.[16]

This hyper-emphasis on feminine image-making highlights the differences between the Bloomer Girls teams and the AAGPBL: homosocial teams managed and coached exclusively by men, feminine uniforms featuring tailored tunics, short skirts and knee socks rather than pants, institutionalized markers of feminine respectability including charm schools, the first of which was run by Helena Rubinstein, published codes of conduct, dress and appearance including make-up, uniformed chaperons, curfews and the strong link between the teams, individual players and the communities supporting them.

Several examples from the AAGPBL rules of conduct will illustrate:

1. ALWAYS appear in feminine attire when not actively engaged in practice or playing ball. This regulation continues through the playoffs for all even though your team is not participating. AT NO TIME MAY A PLAYER APPEAR IN THE STANDS IN HER UNIFORM, OR WEAR SLACKS OR SHORTS IN PUBLIC.

2. Boyish bobs are not permissible and in general your hair should be well groomed at all times with longer hair preferable to short hair cuts. Lipstick should always be on.

3. Smoking or drinking is not permissible in public places. Liquor

drinking will not be permissible under any circumstances. Other intoxicating drinks in limited portions with after-game meals only, will be allowed. Obscene language will not be allowed at any time.

4. All social engagements must be approved by the chaperone. Legitimate requests for dates can be allowed by chaperones.[17]

League players, unlike the barnstorming, gender-transgressing Bloomer Girls, were constructed as America's daughters who were "quartered" in private homes when playing in their home cities. "The townspeople love them dearly and care for them as though the girls were their own daughters."[18] Two or three players would live with families, paying their expenses and tending to their own domestic needs. The kinship term "daughter" signified in this historical and cultural context respectable, young, White, single women who required protection and care by parents or their surrogates until marriage when they would be protected by their husbands. Players responded to the loyalty and affection of local fans and most adhered to the League rules governing their respectable behavior. In addition to dress codes prohibiting slacks, players would not be seen drinking alcohol in local establishments, preferring to drink in bars located outside of the team's home town.[19]

Although the differences between the Bloomer Girls teams and the AAGPBL were substantial, there were significant continuities that are more easily overlooked given the emphasis on constructing a hyper-feminine athleticism. As the New York Bloomer Girls under Margaret Nabel's management illustrate, concern for the respectability and sexual propriety of female players, strict codes of conduct governing appearance, dress, behavior and interactions with the opposite sex had already existed. These codes regulating feminine conduct were formalized and institutionalized by the AAGPBL as were chaperons.

League chaperons, who were paid seventy to eighty dollars per week, served numerous crucial functions, including arranging for hotels and restaurants while on the road, arranging doctors' appointments, providing first aid, choosing roommates, checking rooms, dispensing paychecks and filling in as surrogate mothers to players who could be as young as fifteen.[20] While Bloomer Girl teams did not have uniformed chaperons to monitor players' behavior on the road, it was not uncommon for individual female players on bisocial teams to travel with members of their family—usually a sister—who acted as chaperon. Even Alta Weiss, whose protective father owned the team of men for whom she pitched, traveled with her sister Irma.

The social origin of League players was, however, the same as the Bloomer Girls: tomboys who played baseball as children in local games on diamonds and sandlots with their brothers or neighbors. As children they were recognized and accepted as androgynous tomboys who crossed gender boundaries, preferring baseball to girl's games, who excelled at the game and enjoyed the support of family members, particularly fathers and teammates.[21] For example AAGPBL player Ernestine "Teeny" Petras, who played shortstop, began playing softball with local children on mixed gender teams. Since there were shortages of boy players, girls were needed to fill the gaps, with Petras playing pitcher and shortstop. They played every day from morning until dark, bringing their lunches to the playground. Petras learned many skills from the boys since they respected the girls as players and taught them essential skills. Some of the boys played baseball for their local high school teams. Although this opportunity was not open to the girls, Petras thoroughly enjoyed her athleticism, feeling like she "was on cloud nine."[22] Despite this androgynous socialization by mixed-gender peers, in the League's revision of the athletes' origin myths, the label "tomboy" suggested mannishness, and was rejected. The androgynous tomboy label originally implied a similarity of athleticism in children regardless of sex and a relative absence of stigma for the girl who crossed, while the League's ideology intended to sharply distinguish an inferior feminine from masculine athleticism.

Ironically, while the League's ideology emphasized heteronormativity (examples of players who were wives, pregnant, and mothers were widely publicized) lesbianism was a silenced reality in the AAGPBL — recognized by the players and management, but never openly discussed by the team managers or in the press.[23] Pat Griffen argues that "silence is the most consistent and enduring manifestation of homophobia in women's sport." Lesbians "are expected to maintain deep cover at all times."[24] As an AAGPBL player interviewed by Susan Cahn explained, "tomboyish girls who wanted to go with other girls" signaled their preference by the mannish shoes they wore and how they dressed.[25]

Players who were outside of this narrow heteronomative mold could be subjected to condescension in the press where they were depicted as the inevitable asexual spinster. "The game has been a godsend for some other girls, the ones who are plain and not the marrying type, but still have lives to live. They have gained poise and assurance from performing before crowds and the knowledge that they can make use of a talent has done something for their egos. In the towns where they play they are looked up to as civic assets."[26]

Some players married out of the game while others remained as players after marriage or motherhood. A married catcher for the Kenosha Comets featured in the local press exemplifies the heteronormative image of players. "Mary Bonnie Baker is really Mrs. Baker having been married nearly 10 years ago. Last season after 3 years of stellar play she almost retired from baseball to devote herself to homemaking upon the return of her husband from over seas with the Canadian forces. After passing up spring training she reported late to the Sox camp when the lure of the game and the clamor of the fans proved too much for her to resist."[27]

The rejection of the label "tomboy" is also evident in an interview of Chicago Colleen's pitcher Gloria June Schweigerdt in 1950 by reporter Jennie Vimmerstedt where her feminine appearance and manners are stressed: "If we had any idea that professional baseball gals are rough necks or tomboys, we lost it after that visit. Gloria is so sweetly feminine you can easily picture her in laces and ruffles across a candle lit room. She was neatly dressed in a plaid cotton blouse of beige, tan and green with green skirt and black and white saddle shoes. Natural and unassuming she left us with the impression of a good wholesome All American sports-loving girl whose ambition is to be a physical education teacher when she finishes high school and college.... We learned from her that teams had intensive courses in make-up and grooming from beauty experts."[28]

Players attended charm school when they first joined the League. In charm school, players, many of whom were very young, learned how to speak with the public and how to act in public within respectable feminine norms. "Teeny" Petras, for example, considered this socialization to be valuable. However, she questioned the relevance of walking with books on her head after six hours of practice with her legs aching from exhaustion.[29]

Given the contradictions and apology inherent in negotiating the hyper-emphasis placed on feminine appearance and roles and the expected high levels of athletic skill, it is not surprising to find both elements of the League player emphasized by sportswriters, including the few women journalists. Both men and women journalists recognized the skills of the players. "The girls are capable batwielders fast on the base paths and play a high caliber of baseball generally. They are an interesting group to work with because the youngsters keep a fast moving pace with plenty of baseball sense. Many men leave the ball parks amazed at the ability of the girl stars."[30]

At times, when a player was considered outstanding, such as Dorothy Kamensek, she was not sexually objectified, but rather described in gender neutral terms. Wally Pipp, former Yankee first basemen, considered Kamensek to be the "fanciest fielding first baseman I've ever seen, man or woman." "You should see that girl. She's a slugging 135 pounder who wows 'em in the East. Manager Bill Allington of the Peaches has a piece of property that might bring some big dough, if the majors were game enough to try using girl performers."[31] Pipp's assessment of Kamensek's athletic ability was shared by League players who considered her to be one of the few women talented enough to play at a man's level.[32]

Too often, however, sportswriters were more concerned with the players' appearance than their abilities. Players were described in humorous sexualized terms stepping out of the shower in full makeup. "The girls and their 'skoits' are not expected to cause too much of a furor ... maybe the frocks won't attract much attention but it's an accepted fact that the pigtails, sultry eyes and pitchers with more than the usual variety of curves will bring out plenty of males and several members of the opposite sex who are always interested in watching their colleagues show off their athletic abilities."[33] Another example from the *Little Rock Gazette* in 1946: "This is my first injection of bobby-pin baseball and it's water on my wheel. The girls' uniforms are something on the order of a majorette's regalia and I saw better curves than I have seen since Dizzy Dean was in his shining prime. These quails all looked healthier than water buffalo and had the complexion of peanut butter. When I commented on their husky arms and well developed legs, it was explained to me that these were built up by throwing the ball and running so much."[34]

Unlike the major leagues, where individual teams "owned" the contracts of individual players, the League players' contracts were "owned" by the League and players were allocated where needed. If a new team needed a shortstop, one would be relocated from an existing team, even if she enjoyed a close connection with teammates and the city's residents.

Ernestine "Teeny" Petras played shortstop for several All-American Girls Professional Baseball League teams between 1944 and 1952. Here she is pictured in her Grand Rapids Chicks uniform, a team and town with whom she was closely bonded (Courtesy of Ernestine Petras).

League teams were located in Midwest war production cities (Kenosha, Racine, Springfield, Rockford, Battle Creek, Grand Rapids, South Bend) to serve as family entertainment for war workers. Gas was rationed, games were inexpensive — fifty cents — and whole families attended after working hours at 8:00 P.M. In larger cities such as Milwaukee and Chicago, where men's major league teams were firmly established, there was less interest in women's teams. The Milwaukee Chicks only played half a season in 1944 because too few fans paid to see them. When the Chicks gladly transferred to the smaller city of Grand Rapids, they enjoyed a close bond with the community and the stands were always filled with fans. Local families would invite players to their homes for dinner, sometimes did their laundry, and often requested that they pose for pictures with family members. Popular shortstop Ernestine "Teeny" Petras received fan mail and a proposal of marriage and made many close friends while playing in Grand Rapids. Unfortunately for Petras, shortstops were frequently in demand when new teams were formed and she was transferred several times. When she was transferred from the Grand Rapids Chicks to the new Chicago Colleens team, a public plea was written by the Club President Nate Harkness to accept her departure. An enormous crowd attended her last game as a Chick and Petras felt "heartbroken" to leave her loyal fans and the inter-reliant playing relationship formed with second basemen Alma Ziegler.[35]

The support from local fans, especially from enthusiastic children, was extremely important to the players who clearly recognized and appreciated their fan's loyalty. That the League players were eagerly watched and supported by many female fans is a significant phenomenon. Women had been regular enthusiastic spectators of baseball since the 1880s. Although the League kept yearly attendance figures, demonstrating the consistent popularity of the teams located in small cities, these figures were not broken down by gender. The athletic skills displayed by women players confirmed not only their own possibilities as professional athletes but expanded the horizons of those women watching them as fans. Women fans, through their enthusiastic support for the women players, were essential to the players' successful transgression into male athletic space. Although players were objectified by the League's publicity, often by male fans and in the media, they were also viewed as subjects who controlled their own experiences. As sportswriter Morris Markey noted:

In 1948, the Grand Rapids Chicks won the League pennant. They also won championships in 1947 and 1953. Front row (left to right): Unidentified, unidentified, Alma Ziegler, Marilyn "Corky" Olinger, unidentified. Middle row (left to right): Jaynne Bittner, Ruth "Tex" Lessing, Lavonne "Pepper" Paire, Alice Haylett, unidentified, Inez Voyce. Back row (left to right): Johnny Rawlings (manager), Millie Earp, unidentified, Earlene "Beans" Risinger, Connie Wisniewski, Doris Satterfield, Dorothy "Dottie" Hunter (chaperone). Other team members possibly pictured here but not identified include Merle Keagle, Joan Fisher, Helen Smith, Ruth Barney, Betty Jamieson, and Betty Petryna (National Baseball Hall of Fame Library, Cooperstown, New York).

Just abut a million spectators bought tickets last year to watch the All American Girls ... and it seems significant that more than half the customers were women. Men are ardent and vociferous fans to be sure. The first time they go to the park they are likely to be thinking of bare knees (a masculine failing which is not to be condemned too readily) but after the first inning they have forgotten the knees and are gawking with wonderment at the skill of the infielders, the lusty swings of the batters, the assortment of "stuff" the pitchers display. But women make the game possible. Housewives and cooks, clerks and secretaries, and salesgirls find a delight which they make no effort to conceal in watching members of their own sex play a game just about as well as their brothers can play it. The spectacle feeds their pride and goes a long way toward dispelling the myth of inferiority, the myth of the weaker sex. Coaches and managers discovered that the old notions about a girl's structural inability to throw a ball — that she must push or toss it — were a lot of tosh. The modern girl if properly taught can heave a ball that will put a blister in the palm of most men trying to catch it.[36]

In addition to admiring the players as women athletes who transgressed normative gender boundaries competing in the male public domain, women spectators could also relate to them as women whose existential concerns and experiences paralleled their own in terms of gender-specific roles as daughters and wives with gender-specific sexual scripts, patterns of speech, forms of team camaraderie and means of enforcing conformity to team-established norms. Sports writers emphasized the similarities between players and fans as women rather than their differences. "Are these girls different from other girls? No. They are just as feminine, just as attractive, have the same problems and aspirations in life as any girl working in a Kenosha office, in a bank or in an industrial plant."[37] Women sportswriters wrote about the players' lives off the field, helping to construct their respectable public personas as the community's daughters. For example, Betty Brennan fed the interest of women fans in the gendered lives of players off the field, portraying them as America's daughters whose responsibilities included doing their own washing, ironing, and mending.[38] These written accounts were read by many, facilitating a broad public acceptance of these transgressing women athletes partly on the basis of athletic merit, but also because they were scripted as "normal" (attractive, heterosexual, respectable) feminine daughters who were only temporarily independent agents (albeit under strict supervision) before assuming their permanent roles as wives, as mothers or in traditional female occupations.

Brennan also emphasized the close bonds formed amongst the players who worked, traveled and lived together kindling "remarkable" team spirit. Chaperons, such as Dorothy Hunter of the Milwaukee and Grand Rapids Chicks, who understood how to manage the different unique dispositions of twenty-five young women, were catalysts in establishing bonds between players. Many chaperons including Hunter were themselves players and understood the difficulties involved when traveling on hot, rundown busses for many hours and then playing single games that began at 8:00 P.M. or double headers. Hunter would choose hotel roommates when on the road, insisting that these rotate to facilitate the players' forming friendships with one another.[39]

At this time, respectable sexual scripts for women emphasized virginity before marriage and marital fidelity. These ideals were often mentioned in the press, justifying the close supervision of the players by chaperons who were stereotypically depicted as strict, unattractive women. "The AAGBL goes all out to protect its players from guys they meet on the road. They can't go out on dates without the approval of the chaperone, who looked at me like she had just finished eating a green grapefruit."[40] Chaperons were also depicted as knowing "how to discourage bleacher wolves and dugout-door Johnnies." If a man wished to date one of the players he had to receive the approval of the vigilant chaperon. "Most of the girls in the league are unmarried and during the regular season they don't get much opportunity to toy with Cupid. Parents or husbands know that the girls are well chaperoned. Girls are kept busy with practice, playing and domestic chores. So if any handsome young gentlemen in the grandstand tomorrow night wait for potential dates outside the dressing quarters it behooves them to write a formal note to that effect addressed of course to one of the chaperons. Perhaps they will be able to walk downtown with some of the pretty players — but there'll be that two-hour curfew to observe. We can picture a cutie walking in the moonlight with her escort's arm around her waist, ruminating, 'Oh why didn't I pull that drive a little more in the sixth inning tonight. It looked like a sure double.'"[41]

League rules that regulated players' decorum after games included a limit of two beers and a two-hour curfew. However, girls just want to have fun and they discovered ways to break these rules. Some chaperones were easier to trick than others, and some managers were stricter than others. The players from California had a reputation for both being very good, since the weather permitted year-round play, and for knowing how to party. Chicks shortstop "Teeny" Petras recalled that players would tie sheets together and stack milk crates to escape from their hotel rooms to go out. One evening a player fell. When discovered by manager John Rawlings, one of the stricter managers who stayed in the hotel to make sure his players did not violate the curfew, she was benched for a week. Petras also served as a player chaperon for the Kenosha Comets. Since the team was in last place, she employed a flexible approach letting the players do as they pleased.[42]

Close bonds enabled players to sanction deviant "trouble makers" by exposing them to the "League's gossipy grapevine" and to ostracism "until they come to terms."[43] Both gossip and ostracism are common sanctions among social groups with no formal or codified sanctions for deviant behavior and are often gendered as feminine. Many male writers also commented on the "constant stream of shrill chatter" or feminine speech patterns characteristic of the women players while in the dugout. "One of the gals on the bench commented on the beauty of the moon as it rose over center field. All hands then stopped making noise and commented ecstatically on how romantic it looked."[44]

However, League players were competitive and would break feminine behavioral norms in the heat of competition. For example, players would informally sanction the few players who broke norms governing sportsmanship such as trying to spike an opposing player when sliding into a base. These deviant players would face the same spikes or a pitch thrown at them. Players also did not hesitate to voice forcefully their displeasure when an umpire made a call they considered "bad" or incorrect. Although players usually did not curse at umpires, they often felt strongly enough to do so. "Teeny" Petras recalled a game where she was ejected in the second inning after calling an umpire an S.O.B. She was also fined $5.00.[45]

One persistent problem for the League was the high rate of turnover among the male managers partly due to the pressure placed on them to win. "The All-American League is the Little Big Horn of the managerial profession. You've got to see those girls play to believe it. They slide, steal bases, throw overhand and pitch curves — and the fans love it. That's why so many of us get fired — every city wants a winner or else!" During the League years there were forty-plus managers with twenty-eight quitting.[46] Contemporary media often depicted these managers as harried or henpecked: "You've got troubles? Listen, have you ever tried to manage a girl's baseball team?" The troubles plaguing manager Dick Bass of the Fort Wayne Daisies, for example, included two of his married players becoming "acutely pregnant" and his "personal relationship" or engagement to his second baseman, resulting in his dismissal just before the playoffs. Bass "did the best he could" under the circumstances, placing the expectant mothers on the voluntary retired list. The years Chet Grant spent as manager of teams in South Bend and Kenosha were described as a "sentence." He was terminated after Kenosha sunk into sixth place.[47]

The goal of Philip Wrigley and Arthur Meyerhoff was to recruit retired major league stars as managers to boost fan attendance. Most of the managers had no previous experience with girl or women athletes. Only one of these stars, Hall of Fame centerfielder Max Carey, had a major impact on the League, serving as manager of the Milwaukee Chicks in 1944, as president of the League between 1945 and 1950 and as manager of the Fort Wayne Daisies in 1950. Carey, who studied for the ministry, was a scholarly man who maintained a paternalistic mentor relationship with the women on his team, some of whom called him "Pops." According to "Teeny" Petras, who played on Carey's 1944 Milwaukee team, he was highly respected by his players both for his style of managing and for his baseball skills. She and the other players thoroughly enjoyed playing for him. He encouraged his players to bring their issues to him directly and he would not tolerate troublesome players. If a player made an error on the field, broke one of the rules, or if the team lost a game, Carey would never embarrass them in front of their teammates, but rather called players into his office for a private discussion.[48] As a manager, Carey was respected for his ability to teach baseball skills, particularly the running game (sliding into bases and stealing bases) and run-generating "small-ball" strategies to his players, most of whom were former softball players. Carey's own skills at base stealing were renowned and he held seminars with his students on how to read a pitcher's moves to enhance base-stealing success and how to hold base runners. Petras, a shortstop with over 100 stolen bases in her career, learned much from Carey.

Involved from the onset, Carey was instrumental in changing the League from softball to baseball and was committed to the continuity of a women's baseball league after the end of the War. His vision was that women's teams would fill in while men's teams played away games. "Big-league ball parks are in use only 75 days or nights during the season. As we develop more and better girl players, we'll be able to move in while the home team is traveling and fill those vacant dates — the owners will operate their parks at a profit all summer long."[49]

Over the twelve-year existence of the League, the game evolved steadily toward regulation baseball. Carey respected the athletic abilities of the women players, but felt adjustments had to be made to accommodate the physical differences between men and women. To create the optical illusion that women were as fast or threw as hard as men, he spaced the bases 72 feet apart as opposed to 90 feet, the pitcher's mound

Ernestine "Teeny" Petras was known as a slick fielding shortstop and proficient base stealer during her long career in the AAGPBL. She considered hitting to be the weaker side of her game. She is pictured here with Hall of Fame slugger Jimmy Fox, who was imparting tips on hitting (Courtesy of Ernestine Petras).

was 50 feet from home plate, and players used a ball "that was not quite as lively as that big-league jack rabbit."[50] When the season closed in September, Carey organized all-star teams for barnstorming trips through Mexico, Central America, Puerto Rico and Cuba.

As League president, Carey was also involved in overseeing League development and scouting for new talent. Carey considered the women's game to be "much superior to the game I was mixed up in for 25 years as a player and coach." "Baseball men themselves — executives, players old-timers — who have seen it are amazed. Not only the speed and color of it, but the skill of these girls. I'm telling you that a lot of them perform as gracefully and with as much talent as good men players."[51] In his retirement letter to the players, Carey stated how the "AAGBL has pioneered the way for a grand new sport" with a framework to ensure its continuity.[52]

Another highly successful and competitive manager who was not a major league star was Bill Allington, manager of the Rockford Peaches for eight years and the Fort Wayne Daises for two. In a League where the pressure to be successful was considerable, Allington's teams were on top five of eight years and the Peaches were the closest approximation to a dynasty. His success was partly attributed to his patience and techniques in teaching rookies. Allington also had years of experience coaching women's softball in California before managing the Peaches and was proficient at teaching baseball skills to softball players, many of whom were recruited by him to play on League teams. He also was a professional minor league baseball player for twenty years with the Pacific Coast League.

Known as a tough taskmaster, Allington drilled his team on baseball basics at his mandatory daily practices covering hit-and-run, bunting, fielding and rules of the game. Allington also strictly supervised his players' after-hour activities and maintained a strict curfew. Although Allington's manner was abrasive and at times sarcastic, he respected the athleticism of his players and was committed to the continuity of women's baseball. His players, in turn, respected his knowledge of the game and teaching skills.[53] According to "Teeny" Petras, who did not play for Allington, some of his players did not like playing for him, but they respected him. She considered Allington to be a great manager because "baseball was his life."[54] Carey's style was paternalistic, respecting his players but never losing sight that they were women with less athletic capabilities than men. Allington, however, approached his women play-

The combined talents of competitive manager Bill Allington and the players resulted in the Rockford Peaches winning more League pennants and championships than any other team. Here they are pictured as 1949 champions. They won the pennant in 1945 and 1950. The Peaches were League champions in 1945, 1948, 1949, and 1950. First row (left to right): Dorothy Ferguson Key, Melba Alspaugh, Manager Bill Allington, Lois Florreich, Dorothy Green, chaperon; Charlene Barnett, Irene Applegren. Second row (left to right): Ruth Richard, Alice Pollitt, Jean Lovell, Jacqueline Kelley, Louise Erickson, Betty Werfel, Helen Fox. Top row (left to right): Dorothy Kamenshek, Dorothy Harrell Doyle, Eleanor Callow, Rose Gacioch, Doris Neal (National Baseball Hall of Fame Library, Cooperstown, New York).

ers in somewhat more gender-neutral terms, expecting the former softball players whom he recruited to work hard to develop baseball skills and to display masculine levels of competitive drive and commitment.

The relationship and socialization process between managers and players on League teams was also replete with cultural contradictions. Managers and coaches were mostly men whose masculinity was largely formed in the homosocial context of male organized sports with all its patriarchal rituals and oppositional gender dichotomies. Managers had the task of developing the women players as athletes and as leaders in a cultural context where athleticism, independence, leadership and authority were masculine attributes. While some managers like Carey and Allington were committed to the continuity of women's league baseball, the League was established as a temporary substitute for men's baseball until the end of the War. As "pinch hitters" none of the women players were expected to aspire to play organized baseball as a career. The players were young women, tomboys who loved baseball, many of whom were leaving home for the first time. These women learned the essential knowledge and skills of baseball and conformity and deference to authority from their older male coaches while their respectable femininity was presided over by the chaperons. While the players had gender-expanding androgynous experiences, including independence and competitive drive that separated them from other women, they were represented by the media and League ideology as normative daughters, signifying their dependence on surrogate fathers (managers), mothers (chaperons) and neighbors (the families that temporarily sheltered them). After their stint as baseball players, these daughters were fully expected to marry and assume the dependent roles of wives and mothers, as were other employed women after the men returned from the war.

Although the manager's job was made easier by the cultural expectation that men should have authority over women, managers were assisted by women chaperons and team captains who were socialized to act feminine. All teams had captains chosen by the managers who would earn slightly higher wages. If players did not like a particular captain, they could discuss this with the manager, who usually would choose another. A team captain's responsibilities included meeting with players and managers to plan strategies during a game.

Only four women served as managers, all of whom were hired as short-term midseason substitutes for convenience and economy. Bonnie Baker was the only woman who signed a contract to manage the Kalamazoo Lassies in the 1950 season. The other three were appointed as interim managers but did not sign a contract to manage. Ernestine "Teeny" Petras served briefly as manager of the Kenosha Comets for the last six weeks of the season in 1951. She was chosen by manager Johnny Gottselig and was assisted by the first and third base coaches, who were also women. As team manager Petras's responsibilities included making up the batting order, coaching third base, giving signs and holding team practices. She was respected by the players, who could come to her or the chaperon with problems, and she received a pay raise.[55] In 1950 the

League Board of Directors voted to prohibit women managers. The Directors justified women's exclusion by stating that players disrespected them, would not follow their directives on the field, and that fans objected to women assuming the masculine role of managers.[56]

When the League was first organized there was no shortage of interested players. The locations for initial tryouts were publicized in newspapers and many young hopefuls responded. For example Petras learned about the tryouts from the *Star Ledger* at age seventeen. Since she lived in Irvington, New Jersey, she attended the one-day tryout in Newark that was organized by Max Carey. She estimated that 150 girls competed for two openings, ultimately offered to herself and Kay Blumetta. The larger centralized tryout to determine who would make the initial four teams was held about six months later in Chicago. There hundreds of girls again competed for positions on the newly forming teams. Men with baseball and softball experience were there to evaluate their potential. Successful names were posted on lists and assigned to teams. Petras was assigned to the Milwaukee Chicks.[57] The players selected were then sent money for plane fare to spring training in Florida.

However, in later years, the recruitment of new talent to replace players who left when they married, after they bore children, when their once supportive husbands grew tired of double duty, were injured, or when they aged beyond twenty-six or -seven ("That's when we begin to put on weight") became a persistent problem. The recruitment problem intensified as the women's game evolved away from softball and toward regulation baseball. Since high schools and colleges discouraged intercollegiate women's sports, in 1946 cities with League teams began offering Junior League Girls Baseball through parks and recreation departments. These Junior Leagues were actively encouraged by the AAGPBL as a source of new talent. Also in Chicago, a minor league, the Chicago Girls Baseball League, emerged which signed girls to contracts and trained them to play the unique AAGPBL game. By 1948 there were four teams in the Chicago Girls Baseball League which functioned as a farm system.[58] Canada was another source of players for the League. While most Canadian women played softball, women's baseball developed rapidly in Toronto and Western Canada during and after World War I. Between 1943 and 1954 about ten percent of the AAGPBL players were Canadian, the majority of who were from Manitoba and Saskatchewan.[59]

In 1948 a new rival, National Girls Baseball League, presided over

by Lou Hanelis and Eddie Ainsmith, was formed. The four-team franchises of this new League initially caused lawsuits to be filed against them
by Max Carey and AAGPBL for "raids" on their players. The National
Girls League offered the same salary and no extensive traveling; some
star players, such as Audrey Wagner, who played eight years as a
centerfielder with the Kenosha Comets, and some players who spent
most of their time on the bench made the switch.[60] The agreement
reached between Carey and Hanelis banned "raids" and respected the ter-
ritories and contracts between the Leagues and their respective players.
A future plan, which never materialized, was for a World Series between
the two Leagues.

Most of the new recruits for the AAGPBL and the NGBL were
softball players and the development of baseball skills required time.
"Scouts would watch the games to determine by evaluation of timing,
throwing arm, swinging bat, coverage of sliding which girls might be
able to play the totally different game of hard baseball. They are then
interviewed to see if they are our type of girl." Some girls were still in
high school and would leave early to begin training.[61] The NGBL proposed that an educational campaign be launched to interest high schools
and colleges in adding girls baseball to their sports curriculum, a proposal that still has not been adopted in 2008.[62]

Spring training was a time when all the League teams came together,
usually in Florida or Mississippi, which provided an opportunity for
publicity. The most widely publicized spring training took place in "baseball mad" Havana, Cuba, in 1947 where the public lavished the players
with attention and attendance at their four exhibition games. Players
stayed at an American hotel and toured extensively. All eight teams held
two weeks of spring training in Havana, drawing larger crowds at their
exhibition games than the Dodgers then visiting with Jackie Robinson.[63]
The women's tour inspired the Latin American Feminine Baseball
League, and League scouts noticed that some Latina players were talented. Eleven of these players eventually played for the AAGPBL, nine
of whom were Cuban.[64]

As Cuban men entered the major leagues in the 1940s, a wealthy
distillery owner named Rafael de Leon formed a women's baseball league
named *Estrellas Cubanas* (Cuban Stars), modeled on the AAGPBL, late
in 1946 or 1947 in preparation for the spring training arrival of the
League. The women players, who represented the most talented on the

island, wore similar uniforms and became a minor league farm system for training talented players. Rafael de Leon built a baseball park and house for the players to train and hosted the young women players on his estate where he taught them the AAGPBL game. "Working in close cooperation with Max Carey and other AA League Officials, the Latin American loop was patterned after Carey's Organization. The All-American game, known as Girls Baseball, was adopted along with all of the AA rules and regulations." As a result of the 1947 link between the AAGPBL and Cuba that included well attended (by men) exhibition games, the Latin American Feminine Basebol League was developed as a source of players and post season tours in 1947–1949.[65]

The Latina players on League teams are an interesting case study for the social construction of race and intersectionality. Unlike major league baseball, the AAGPBL teams remained all White. Since the Latinas who played for the League were all fair-skinned, the League did not perceive them as breaking racial barriers, or necessitate an expanded definition of an All-American girl to include women of color. However, from the perspective of the Latina players, their acceptance and assimilation on League teams was understood as opening a new opportunity for women of color. Their construction of difference emphasized ethnic markers such as language and food and class markers since many who emigrated from Cuba were poor. All of the Latina players were young — twenty years old or less — and confronted the emotional challenges posed by leaving their native country and assimilating to a new culture compounded by language barriers. "Compared to the American girls in the League, the Latina players faced prejudice or discrimination on two fronts — since they were both women and Latina. Perhaps the biggest challenge was in the name."[66]

The first Latina player to join a League team, the Racine Belles, was nineteen-year-old Eulalia Gonzales, who played on junior girls teams in Havana and in exhibition games with and against men's teams. Although special permission was granted to admit her to the United States without a birth certificate, Gonzales returned shortly to Cuba due to loneliness and homesickness.[67]

Isobel "Lefty" Alvarez, who was encouraged to play baseball by her baseball-loving mother, arrived in the United States in 1949 to pitch for the traveling Chicago Colleens. These road trips included other Spanish-speaking Cuban players who were pictured together, suggesting a support system while they learned English and adjusted to the cultural differences. When Alvarez joined the Fort Wayne Daisies she was alone with no roommate, shy by nature and felt the language barrier acutely. "I was alone in Fort Wayne. Sometimes when you can't communicate, you feel maybe [others] don't want you around. Everyone has a clique, they run around in groups." Alvarez also felt that the language barrier affected her ability to improve as a player since players benefited from talking to one another about the games. Alvarez would return home to Cuba during the off-season, but her mother insisted that she remain in the United States where "she wouldn't have to worry about me. I had a job to do. I wasn't allowed to say, 'Ma, I'm homesick.' I had to do my job and forget about Cuba." A few of her teammates and coach Bill Allington helped Alvarez to gradually assimilate and improve her skills as a player.[68] For example, "Teeny" Petras and Jane Moffet often roomed with Alvarez over the years until she was paired with another Spanish-speaking player. Jane Moffet, a catcher and first baseman, was particularly helpful to the Cuban players who came to her with any problems they were having with their

rooms or in restaurants due to the language barrier.[69] Alvarez remained in Fort Wayne and in 1959 became a U.S. citizen.

Class was an important factor shaping the experiences of these young Cuban players, given their impoverished lives in Cuba. As the example of Isobel Alvarez illustrates,

Ysora Castillo, first baseman for the Muskegon Lassies, was one of several Cuban players who came to the United States in 1949 after the All-American Girls Professional Baseball League held spring training there in 1947 and an exhibition game in 1948 (National Baseball Hall of Fame Library, Cooperstown, New York).

these Latinas were encouraged by their family members to leave Cuba to pursue a better life through baseball. Ysora del Castillo also joined the Colleens in 1949 at age seventeen hoping baseball would be her ticket out of poverty. "From the perspective of Latina ballplayers, the league must be viewed as a tremendous success. They brought national attention to Cuban baseball, made their places in this country and transcended race and gender by being widely accepted into a domain previously dominated by white males."[70]

By 1954 the era of the AAGPBL ended. The League had reached its peak in 1948 and by 1950, in spite of the close connections between the League teams and their local communities, several teams had folded as men and women were expected to resume their traditional roles after the War. Television also diminished attendance at baseball games. All of the historians of this Golden Age point out that despite the showcasing of White women's athleticism by the League during the War and after, access for any woman into organized baseball remained unattainable.

This women's golden age was erased from baseball's history until recently. Given the publicity that the AAGBPL has enjoyed since the 1992 film *A League of Their Own*, numerous interviews, oral histories of the players, and books are now available. These interviews demonstrate that the players were intent on playing baseball at the highest level possible. The players all understood the League's marketing plan to initially attract people by insisting on impractical uniforms that focused attention on women's exposed legs or sexual attractiveness and to keep them coming back by displaying athletic skills. They were also aware that they were role models for children and that their conduct was to be closely monitored. These women were both subjects and objects, attempting to negotiate the confines of an externally controlled construction of femininity and their subjective experiences as competent women athletes. It was forty years until another financial backer financed an all-women's professional baseball team.

A year after the League disbanded, Bill Allington organized a team called Allington's World Champion All Americans that barnstormed throughout the United States and Canada between 1954 and 1957. Like the former Bloomer Girls teams the All Americans challenged the best of men's White semi-pro teams. Although the team was advertised as available to play any men's team, their only game scheduled against a Black team, in Jasper, Texas, was cancelled due to racial tensions. Always reputed to possess an expert eye for spotting talent, Allington's team, billed as "the battle of the sexes," caught on quickly.[71]

The All Americans had much in common with the barnstorming Bloomer Girls teams and Negro League teams who combined exhibition baseball games with pre-game attractions of various types. Although this team of twelve was composed of all women, when they played men's teams they exchanged batteries, pitcher and catcher, reminiscent again of the Bloomer Girls teams. In Allington's view, to compensate for differences in strength, men pitched against men and women against women. If a male player was sliding home he would encounter another man and the same for women, thus decreasing the chance for injury.[72] This strategy proved successful and showcased the skills of women pitchers to the coaches of men's teams. The team wore the same uniforms as the AAGPBL. They traveled together, slept together in motels, changed together either at the ball park or in the basements of private homes, and were well supported, particularly in former League towns like Fort Wayne. This kept their costs down. Similar to the New York Bloomer Girls, the women were paid by the game, equally splitting a percentage of the game's receipts. However, the players earned less than they did with the AAGPBL and most continued for love of the game until the end of 1957.[73]

It is significant that despite the public exposure of women's athletic abilities during the League years, and the convic-

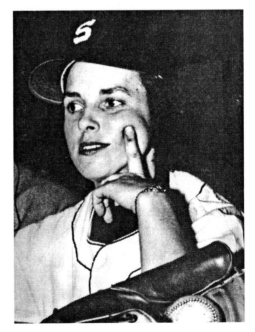

In 1952, Eleanor Engle was signed by the Harrisburg Pennsylvania Senators, a Class B Minor League Team. The response was vitriolic. Her contract was quickly voided by Minor League President George Trautman and confirmed by Major League Baseball Commissioner Ford Frick. Their decision banned women from minor and major league baseball (National Baseball Hall of Fame Library, Cooperstown, New York).

tion by some men that women could play baseball well, opportunities for women to play organized minor league baseball were definitively eliminated during this golden age. On June 23, 1952, George M. Traut-man, head of the minor leagues, voided the minor league contract of twenty-four-year-old shortstop Eleanor Engle with the Class AA Harrisburg Senators of Pennsylvania, a dying team in a dying league.

As soon as the signing was announced on June 21, 1952, controversy ensued. General Manager Howard Gordon insisted Engle was signed because of her ability. "She can hit the ball better a lot better than some of the fellows on the club." Engle was given a uniform, told to field some grounders and allowed to hit balls during batting practice. However, team manager Buck Erickson was not consulted by team officials before the team signed Engle and he was determined to resist this transgression. "I won't have a girl playing for me. This is a nowoman's land and believe me I mean it. She'll play when hell freezes over." The manager of the Allentown club, Whitey Kurowski, threatened to protest the game if she was in the lineup and Umpire Angstadt flatly declared, "If she ever comes up to bat I quit."[74] Although Engle practiced with the team, she was not permitted to sit in the dugout, was not included on the June 22nd roster and spent her first game in the press box.

Troutman's official statement clarified beyond any doubt the unwritten law barring women from the minor leagues established when Jackie Mitchell's contract was voided. He stated, "so as to remove any possible doubt as to the attitude of the National Association office toward any such contract, I am notifying all Minor League Clubs that no such contract will be approved and that any club which undertakes to enter into such a contract, or to go through the motions of entering into such a contract, will be subject to severe disciplinary action ... it is not in the best interest of baseball that such travesties be tolerated."[75] Although Engle had the support of her husband, she was dismayed and hurt by Troutman's decision stating, "I'll never try to get into baseball again." "I think baseball is making a big mistake. I love the game. More women should be playing. I'm sure that I would have been able to remain as a player with the Senators."[76]

These sentiments linking the presence of women to the devaluation of baseball were reminiscent of the view taken by a steering committee of major league executives on the "race question" in 1946 that integration would lessen the value of baseball franchises. These executives included Phil Wrigley of the Cubs, Larry MacPhail of the Yankees, Tom Yawkey of the Red Sox and Sam Breedon of the Cardinals who stated that the facts proved that no Black player was capable of playing major league ball and that increased Black patronage would discourage White patrons from attending.[77]

Engle and her contract were the "talk of the nation," unleashing a media frenzy that affected Engle so deeply that in a 2002 interview, at age seventy-six, she avoided the topic.[78] The frenzy included Hollywood stars, women baseball players and sportswriters. The Hollywood stars included Marilyn Monroe, Larraine Day and Doris Day, all of whom were of the opinion that women should be allowed to play with Monroe in character, declaring, "I can think of no better way to meet outfielders." Brad Crawford, Bob Hope and Bing Crosby gave opinions conveying the absurdity of the prospect. Hope's ugly sexist comment will serve to illustrate. "I bought into the Cleveland Indians because I thought they had squaws on the team."[79]

Women baseball players interviewed included Jackie Mitchell, whose voided minor league contract set a precedent for Trautman's decision, and AAGPBL pitching star Jean Faut. Mitchell, who played with and against men during her entire career, had the hindsight of twenty years. She stated, "Frankly baseball is a hard game for a woman to play. It's exhausting and rough. I think if a girl wants to play, she should play on a woman's team only. In particular, it's hard to be the only girl on a man's team." Faut spoke as a contemporary of Engle. "I don't see why girls couldn't play although I realize competition would be very tough. But then again with travel and all that I don't really think there's a chance that women will break into men's baseball."[80]

Sportswriters' views were generally negative, some vitriolic, and focused on Engle's appearance as "a 24 year old curvaceous brunette."[81] Engle's audience consisted of the media and male spectators who erased her athleticism, her potential contributions to the Senators and sexually objectified her, thus contributing to this aborted short transgression into male baseball. "A 24-year-old stenographer, Eleanor Engle, signed to play with the Harrisburg (Inter-State) club, worked out in practice, then was told to go home and forget the whole thing."[82] Engle fit the ideal "All American Girl" image of a woman baseball player: she was married (read heterosexual), "comely" and wore shorts, exposing her legs and heightening her sexual attractiveness like the other League players, separating her from her male teammates. Men in the stands were hostile, subjecting her to sexual harassment or "wolf calls" during batting practice, resulting in the decision to move the batting cage to deep center field.

Engle downplayed her feelings of isolation from her teammates, "it felt kind of funny sitting in the dugout, but the fellows didn't seem to mind." However, editorial comments on a picture showing a smiling Engle wearing a short skirt sitting apart from her teammates in the dugout, focused on her social isolation as the inevitable outcome of a preposterous violation of gendered space.[83] "It is not easy to embarrass a ball player, but as the above picture shows members of the Harrisburg Interstate League Team obviously were made ill at ease by the presence of a young woman on the bench, June 22, garbed in what club officials apparently believed was the proper costume for a female diamond performer. The reasons should be readily apparent. Opposing players would be reluctant to slide into a base guarded by a girl infielder, pitchers would hesitate to throw close to a feminine batter, tagging would be a problem, baseball could not afford to take a chance of injury to a woman in a game played for keeps by men. Dugout language is too sulphuric for the ears of lady-like performers, special dressing rooms would have to be provided and there would always be the risk of insulting remarks hurled by smart-alek fans. The *Sporting News* hopes this is the last time it will ever find it necessary ... to print the picture of a woman ballplayer on a man's team. Woman's place may not be altogether in the home, feminine athletes have their own distinction in many sports where they can compete with others of their own sex. But as far as Organized Baseball is concerned, a woman's place is in the grandstand."[84] As Baseball Commissioner Ford Frick fully concurred with Trautman's decision, this ruling barring women from minor league contracts, stubbornly premised on nineteenth-century assumptions of women's biological inferiority and moral superiority, remained in place for forty years.

Contradiction, as Berlage argues, is the key concept in analyzing the brief golden age for women's baseball represented by the AAGPBL. Comparison between the earlier Bloomer Girls and the League teams is a useful starting point in highlighting these contradictions. In several significant respects the League was a step backward for women's baseball. Gone were bisocial teams, women in managerial roles, and functional gender-neutral uniforms. The link between female athleticism and mannishness became strongly established. Although the women who comprised the League's players were talented athletes whose skills at playing baseball were recognized, their athleticism and athletic potential were presumed to be inferior to men's. Consequently, it was the League's policy to segregate the teams by gender in terms of player composition, opportunities for athletic competition, and positions of power and prestige, including team managers and coaches. Such exclusion was justified as a natural consequence of feminine mental and physical inferiority.

Since the dichotomous construction of femininity and feminine athleticism hardened during the League years and in the years following the War, a transgression into the privileged male space of organized baseball by Eleanor Engle was met with fierce hostility and resistance by men players, coaches, spectators and sports writers, the intensity of which surpassed previous attempts by women players to join men's teams in the Progressive Era. Although women at this time were playing professional baseball in a league of their own, AAGBPL players were guided by the strictly gender exclusive regulations formulated by the League. During the League years, when gender segregation in baseball became normative, Engle sought to play on a men's minor league team, a violation of male privileged space that necessitated a permanent legal solution.

Engle's case is comparable to other patriarchal societies where rigid cultural codes separate women's lives from men's in physical space. In many such societies, contact with women in particular social settings is taboo, and severe sanctions exist to control women's behavior and limit their access to resources, statuses or power. These include displays of sexual aggression and intimidation by men or social isolation, as Engle experienced, to remind women of their rightful place. Engle was deeply shocked and hurt by the hostility that she encountered and by Trautman's ruling barring women from minor league teams. Thirty years later, an evaluation of Engle's rejection by a man sports journalist reveals a changed perspective on gender exclusion generated by the second-wave feminist movement. "She was cut short by some chauvinistic overlord, before she cracked the line-up."[85]

Thus the contradictory women's golden age during the League years were a moment in baseball history when the formation of dichotomous or oppositional constructions of gender was clearly intentional. The gender identity of the female "pinch hitters" who replaced male baseball players during the War years had to be carefully constructed so that feminine athleticism would not challenge masculine dominance and privilege. Since the link between athleticism and mannishness was firmly established, the femininity of players was hyper-emphasized in terms of their appearance (i.e., attractive), behavior (i.e., charm school, curfews, chaperons) and, by their inappropriate uniforms that drew attention to their legs and away from athletic skill and the need to protect their legs from injury. League players were not to be viewed as androgynous tomboys or mannish, but as thoroughly feminine young women whose only difference from other ordinary daughters was that their athletic talents allowed them to temporarily transgress accepted gender boundaries by leaving home to play a traditionally male sport that they loved. The sports media played a vital role in orchestrating and spreading these saturated feminine images of League players by focusing on their attractive physical appearance, emphasizing their "curves," their heterosexuality, their ability to balance playing baseball with feminine behavior and roles characteristic of their future domestic lives as wives and mothers.

One significant advance made by AAGPBL teams for women's baseball, the close relationship established between the small industrial cities of the Midwest and their teams, exposes another cultural contradiction: feminine autonomy. The young women players, most of whom were single and working-class, were characterized as America's daughters. The kinship term "daughter" and its associated symbolic meanings provided a comfortable normative framework for White working-class families of European origin whose single daughters wanted to leave their protection to play on League teams that were located in distant cities and managed by men. Although working-class daughters were expected to work outside the home for wages, in these patriarchal families daughters were to remain home under the protection of fathers and male siblings until marriage when their protection passed to their husbands. Since young League players led relatively autonomous lives, surrogate "parents" temporarily assumed this role. Team chaperons who were women protected their players' respectability. For example, manager Max Carey, called "Pops" by his players, took a paternal interest in his players. Finally, families in the community housed and cared for players when they played at home. Domestic environments provided security and care and allowed for the continuity of socialization by performing feminine domestic tasks such as washing and mending clothes.

The close ties between the League teams and their sponsor-cities generated an enthusiastic fan base whose loyalty was deeply meaningful for the players. In addition to the close ties with teammates, players became members of families and objects of desire and were adored by young girls and women who attended their games in significant numbers and who admired their athletic skills and independence. Players opened new possibilities for women by stretching old gender conceptions within the confines of respectability.

Unfortunately these new possibilities were open only to White women. Although light-skinned Cuban women were recruited as players and fit the image of the All-American Girl, African American women were excluded from these constructions of respectable femininity and from participation on League teams. League teams remained racially segregated even after African American men began to integrate organized baseball, thus wasting a needed pool of talented new recruits. A precious few of these talented African American women athletes nevertheless found alternative avenues to pursue their dreams of playing baseball.

5

"A Woman Has Her Dreams Too": Three Women Players in the Professional Negro American League, 1952–1954

The race barrier in baseball was removed for African American men after the death of Commissioner Landis, integration's "implacable foe," in 1944.[1] As a result of integration in 1947, the barnstorming Negro Leagues withered, with only six teams remaining in 1951. Although in baseball, as in our society generally, the experience of racism by males "determined the parameters of anti-racist strategies," the disintegration of the Negro Leagues briefly opened the door to the participation of three African American women as novelties to bolster declining attendance.[2]

In 1892 African American scholar, sociologist, and feminist Anna Julia Cooper argued that the marginalized, doubly oppressed social location of Black women generated a unique angle of vision on the social world and the analysis of forms of domination.[3] "The colored woman, then, should not be ignored because her bark is resting in the silent waters of the sheltered cove. She is watching the movements of the contestants nonetheless and is all the better qualified, perhaps, to weigh and judge and advise because not herself in the excitement of the race. Her voice too, has always been heard in clear, unfaltering tones, ringing the changes on those deeper interests which make for the permanent good."[4] A century later, feminist bell hooks locates this angle of vision in Black women being denied an "institutionalized other" whom they could oppress. While White women and Black men are both oppressed and oppressors, the totally marginalized worldview of Black women, who dominate no category of people, possesses a uniquely counter-hegemonic potential.[5] Critical race theorist and feminist Kimberle Crenshaw's concept of "intersectionality" focuses on how patterned structures of inequality—racism, sexism, class, age, heterosexism—intersect in the situated lives of real people. "Women of color are situated within at least two subordinated groups that frequently pursue conflicting political agendas. The need to split one's political energies between two sometimes opposing groups is a dimension of intersectional disempowerment that men of color and white women seldom confront."[6]

In the early twentieth century some clandestine efforts were made by organized baseball to hire light-skinned male Cuban ballplayers and in 1947 Major League Baseball slowly began integrating Black players by signing Jackie Robinson. However, "the closest the League [AAGPBL] came to integration was the signing of a few light-skinned Cuban ballplayers. Darker-skinned, homegrown talents like Stone, Johnson and Morgan were ignored."[7] The erasure of the presence and contributions of Toni Stone, Mamie Johnson and Connie Morgan, the three African American women athletes who played professional baseball with men in the Negro American League in 1952–1954, had been complete until quite recently. Toni Stone was the first woman professional baseball player in an organized major league playing second base for the Indianapolis Clowns. She was the second woman to play in the Negro Leagues (preceded only by Isabel Baxter in 1933 who played three innings of one game at second base for the Cleveland Colored Giants).[8] Mamie "Peanut" Johnson was the first woman to pitch on a men's major league baseball team as a member of the Indianapolis Clowns. They were both ignored in the 1989 "Women in Baseball" exhibit at the National Baseball Hall of Fame at Cooperstown which revived the public memory of the AAGPBL. The Hall of Fame subsequently did honor Toni Stone along with seventy-three Negro League players in 1991. They were also ignored by Mike Wallace of *60 Minutes* in 1998 who incorrectly identified Ila Borders as the first woman to pitch for a men's professional team, and by such authoritative encyclopedias as *Total Baseball* where even Effa Manley, influential owner of the Newark Eagles with her husband Abe, merits only a few sentences in a chapter devoted to the Negro League.[9] Finally, Stone, Johnson and Morgan were virtually ignored by contemporary sportswriters in the mainstream press.[10] Only in the last decade, several published accounts of Stone's, Morgan's and Johnson's athletic careers have appeared.

These three women were given the opportunity to play when Negro professional ball teams were declining after 1947. Although women were barred from minor league play in 1952, the Negro League, a semi-peripheral institution in organized baseball, did not have as powerful a commissioner as the core White minor and major leagues. By the early 1950s the Negro American League had declined from twenty to four teams and the Negro National League had folded in 1948 as the departure of talented black players for the major league reduced attendance and diminished media coverage of Negro League teams by the Black press.

In 1952, thirty-two-year-old Toni Stone was hired by Indianapolis Clowns' owner Syd Pollack to increase attendance as a novelty female ballplayer. She played second base in fifty of the 175 games the Clowns played that season, batting .243. In 1954 her contract was sold to the Kansas City Monarchs and Pollack hired Connie Morgan, as an infielder to replace her, and Mamie Johnson, a pitcher.[11]

Marcenia Lyle (Toni Stone) like the other women baseball players described above, began playing baseball as a child on the sandlots of St. Paul, Minnesota. She also played softball with the Girls Highlex Softball Club at second base. At Humbert High School Stone's athletic talents were displayed in a variety of sports including tennis, high jump and baseball, where she was the first girl to play for the baseball team. Given Stone's intersecting identity as an African American woman athlete, she "endured the typical sexist slurs, along with some racial epithets."[12]

Stone's parents often took her to see Black baseball teams playing at St. Paul Stadium. After one game in 1943 or 1944 at age thirteen or fourteen, Stone approached Bunny Downs, the business manager for the Indianapolis Clowns to promote herself as a potential player. Downs encouraged her to finish high school and contact him after graduating.[13] Although Stone's father encouraged her athleticism, her parents did not want her to play professional baseball, emphasizing the value of an education. "They would have stopped me if they could, but there was nothing they could do about it."[14] For Toni, "whose athletic ability overshadowed her work in the classrooms," education would come later.[15] Rejecting traditional feminine roles, she was anxious to define her own experience through travel and playing baseball. Stone was fortunate to

attend Gabby Street's local baseball school where she learned sound baseball fundamentals. Street had been a catcher in the major leagues and a
manager of minor and major league teams. Recognizing Stone's talent
and persistent motivation, he bought her a pair of cleats and allowed her
to attend the all-boy's baseball clinic.

Stone rejected softball as too slow, and at fifteen she began to play
on baseball teams with boys or men, a choice that continued for her
entire athletic career. In 1943 Stone wrote a letter to the Chicago
Colleens, an AAGPBL team, asking for a tryout. She received no response
since the League was racially segregated.[16] Thereafter, Stone played for
the Wall Post #435 American Legion boys' team from 1943 to 1945,
joined the House of David barnstorming team, pitched for the semi-pro
Twin-City Giants, joined the integrated San Francisco Sea Lions, and
Negro Minor League teams—the New Orleans Black Pelicans and the
New Orleans Creoles from 1948 to 1950. With the Creoles, Stone earned
about $300 a month playing various positions and honing her infield
skills. She left the Creoles batting .265.[17]

Stone also honed her emotional skills as the only woman player for
the Creoles learning to negotiate gender transgression—conforming to
male speech norms ("They didn't spare me because of my sex") and
adjusting to sexual harassment while confined with fifteen men on the
bus rides. "The self-described tomboy walked with the bow-legged strut
of a bronco rider, and talked trash that would make a sailor proud. Her
rhubarbs with umpires turned the air blue and ears red."[18]

In 1950 when the Indianapolis Clowns faced the Creoles, Stone
once again approached Bunny Downs about signing her to play. Downs
eventually mentioned her to owner Syd Pollock.[19] After the 1952 season
Pollock hired Stone to boost attendance as the first and only woman
player on an all-male professional Negro League team. Pollock was principally motivated by her publicity value. "Toni will be our regular second baseman. This girl is no freak and although I wouldn't deny that
her publicity value is very great for our team and its games, we expect
her playing to help us a lot."[20] Although Pollock reduced her age to
twenty-two and exaggerated her salary for publicity as $12,000 a season,
she was actually paid $300 a month, then $350, then $400. She was the
highest paid Clowns player at a salary twice that of a major league
rookie.[21] When she arrived at spring training in Norfolk, Virginia, Stone
attracted the level of public attention from agents and the media that

Pollack had hoped for. She, however, felt like a "goldfish."[22] Stone played the first three innings at second base, replacing second baseman Ray Neil, the batting star of the team, who moved to left field.[23]

There are two very different accounts of when and how Marcenia Lyle assumed the "playing" name Toni Stone. Barbara Gregorich states that Lyle assumed the name in San Francisco, choosing Toni because it sounded like "tomboy," a subjective identity she always embraced. Larry Lester, who interviewed Stone in 1991, also attributes the choice to Stone. "Toni was short for tom boy. I wanted my name to reflect what I was all about." Alan Pollock maintains that his father Syd chose the name. "We can't sign a player named Marcenia Lyle Alberga or Mrs. Aurelious Alberga. Her names need to be short and easy for fans to say and remember." Syd Pollock chose Toni from the popular Toni Home Permanents for the hair.[24] While in San Francisco Stone had married Aurelious Alberga, who also would have stopped her playing baseball if he could, but since he could not, he consented to both Toni's new career and name.[25]

Stone's transgression into male privileged space was qualitatively beyond that of any previous woman baseball player, threatening many male players, managers and owners in the Negro League. That baseball is and should remain masculine was made clear to Stone beginning as a young teenager. Nevertheless, she rejected the sexual segregation of the sport along with the ideologies justifying gender exclusion and aspired to succeed in the male leagues. "There was nothing else I was interested in. I figured that then was the time for me to try out and make the grade as the first woman player with an all-male team. I dreamed about it every night. I imagined myself on the way to something real big and with a big payoff. I found it wasn't too hard for me to hit curve ball pitching and the faster the pitching the better I liked it."[26]

Once she achieved her dream as a member of the Clowns, her aspirations grew to join the major leagues. "I've got my own ideas. Who knows? Maybe I'll be the first woman to play major league baseball. At least I may be the one who opens the doors for others. A lot of things can happen, you know. There's got to be a first in everything. Before 1946 nobody thought Negroes would be in the big leagues. But we've got 'em there today. A woman player might have a chance, also. Maybe it will be me."[27]

Stone also rejected the dichotomized feminized athleticism constructed by the AAGPBL. She identified herself as an androgynous tomboy who grew up to be an athletically built "big sassy girl" of 5'7" and 148 pounds. "I wasn't real popular with the girls because I loved to play with the boys."[28] When Pollack wanted Stone to wear a skirt or shorts like the League players, she refused, stating she wanted to dress like the rest of the men players on the team. "I went to Indianapolis to learn the fundamentals of the game. But they hired me as a drawing card and wanted me to wear shorts. I cussed [Pollock] out and told him: 'No ... I came to play ball.'" Determined to look androgynous while on the playing field, she wore a man's uniform with "an oversize 42" shirt to accommodate her 36" bust."[29]

Stone also rejected the hyper-feminine image of players off the field constructed by the AAGPBL, presenting a gender conundrum for the media. "Stone walked with the strut of a man, had unmanicured fingernails and had a rough appearance."[30] She was an athletic and competitive woman who "belts home runs as easily as most girls catch stitches in their knitting." Yet sports writers sought to construct her as feminine—"a cute second baseman" or a "lithe limbed lassie."[31] In 1953 Syd Pollock had publicity shots taken of Stone portraying her as feminine and alluring, leaning on a Cadillac in an attractive dress and high-healed shoes. "Toni Stone is an attractive young lady who could be someone's secretary, but once in uniform she is all ball player."[32] Stone responded to Pollock "that the car reminded her she needed a raise."[33]

Stone "played with the vigor and spirit of a man." Her consistent desire was to play baseball like a man and be held accountable like any other man on the team. She "traveled and practiced and played eighteen hour days, immersed in the game."[34] "I know what I'm doing and what I am in for. I don't want anyone playing me 'easy' because I'm a woman and I don't play 'easy' against them. I'm out here to play the game and I'm sure I can take the knocks as well as anyone else. Don't worry I can take care of myself." Stone remained proud of the scars on her left wrist inflicted by a runner trying to intimidate her when sliding into second base.[35]

Tracy Everbach, who has compared media coverage of Stone in *The Call*, a Kansas City–based African American newspaper, and in two mainstream papers, *The Kansas City Star and the Kansas City Times*, demonstrates that Stone was given considerably more coverage in *The Call*. Sportswriters were unsure how to treat Stone's and the other two women players' gender: at times they focused on their uniforms and at other times on their athletic abilities. Although the three women were referred to as girls or gals in *The Call*, they were recognized as possessing "amazing ability in playing the men's game. They handle their chances in the field speedily and they take their cuts at the ball at the plate." Stone was described as a "rough and tumble player" and a "tough sister" who was "murder minded in her effort to aid her team."[36] Her dedication earned the respect of some of her teammates. According to Gentry Johnson, shortstop and friend of Stone's, "when she was on the field, the ball was hit to her as sharp as it was hit to me, and she would pick it up and throw it. She was a pretty good ballplayer; she wasn't just a lady in a uniform."[37] Frank Ensley stated, "Toni was great for a female. She had a lot of desire. Gave 100 percent. She was flashy, and that was her strength for the Clowns."[38] In the mainstream press such as *The*

In 1953, second baseman Toni Stone was the first woman to play on a major league baseball team, the Indianapolis Clowns, a team in the American Negro League. Here she is pictured with manager Bunny Downs and teammates Ray Neil and Buster Haywood (Courtesy of NoirTech Research, Inc.).

Sporting News, coverage of Negro League games appeared only in the back pages along with minor league games. Stone's brief mention was positive focusing on her skills as a second baseman playing five innings of errorless ball or her batting average. "One of the most surprising batting sprees has been put on by Toni Stone, the Indianapolis Clown's girl second baseman. In three weeks, she hiked her average to .368, fourth highest in the league, and has stolen one base."[39]

Still, in ways similar to the experience of the Black men players who first integrated major league teams, whose physical capabilities and "steadiness" were questioned, Stone confronted and negotiated frequent hostile reminders of her trespass of gender boundaries and her subordinate status as an inferior woman player from managers and many of her teammates who ignored her. "There are people who try to make it hard. There are people who call you names. But you have to keep trying."[40] Although the Clowns had a 175-game schedule and Pollack counted on her to increase attendance, Stone was only a part-time player who played fifty games. Buster Haywood, manager of the Clowns, considered her to be "mostly a show.... She did pretty good, but she couldn't compete with the men to save her life. Now in a women's league she would be a top player."[41] Haywood, known for his competitive zeal, deeply resented having to play Stone for three innings in 1953 when Ray Neil was considered a superior second baseman and hitter, batting .397 in 1953. "She wasn't a ballplayer and I'm playing to win. It was the worst season of my life; made me sick."[42]

Stone also did not play second base for more than two or three innings per game with the Monarchs. Although coach Oscar Charleston of the Clowns treated her well, when she was traded a year later to the Kansas City Monarchs, coach Buck O'Neal repeatedly told her he did not want her on the team. With the Monarchs Stone earned $400 a month and a $200 signing bonus. She was resented by many of her male teammates and opponents who believed she was on the roster only as a gate attraction, not as a worthy second basemen.[43]

Interviewed in the 1990s by Alan Pollock, Buster Haywood still recalled with anger Stone's playing time with the Clowns. "I disliked Toni Stone as a player. She couldn't play. She couldn't catch a damn pop-up, and that's why Syd got rid of her. It upset me no end to play with her. She drew well for us one year, and that was it.... He [Richard King/King Tut] told Toni, 'Shit woman. You can't play no ball. You ought to be home washing dishes.' ... She'd swear right back at Tut, but he'd walk off and do his act. She couldn't field grounders to her right. She'd make an error, come in and slam her glove down in the dugout. It gave me headaches. I had about a heart attack."[44]

Stone also had to adjust to the all-male speech community who exposed her to language "most ladies wouldn't want to hear.... I had to keep my composure, never using profanity to respond to critics. I knew that men could drink hard and use lots of profanity, but that if I did I would be criticized."[45] Pollock, however, maintained that if profanity was directed at her, she "hurled it back" and she was notorious for creating a spectacle after a called third strike. "Immediately after the call, her visitation with the plate umpire was like no one else's. Her bat already thrown to the ground ... her face inches from the umpire's or pressed against his mask, her head bobbing with anger and agony; she screamed her thoughts on his call, his ancestry, his body parts and the amazing things she strongly suggested he do with his body parts. Crowds roared."[46]

Similar to the experience of the first Black players on all-White teams, being the only woman on an all-men's team was socially isolating. Like Jackie Robinson, who in 1946–1947 faced hostility from fans, opposing players, pitchers and some Dodgers teammates, Stone was often ignored or shunned by her teammates who called her "so many bad names." She was told to "to home and fix your husband some biscuits, or any damn thing. Just get the hell away from here."[47] Locker rooms are settings for social interactions among teammates. Since separate changing facilities for women did not exist, Stone was excluded from this form of bonding with teammates. Stone would arrive at the ballpark early and dress in the umpires' room. She would play three or four innings and leave the game in the seventh or eighth inning to shower before the others finished.

Negro League teams played for nine months a year, seven days a week and sometimes played two games a day. Players usually slept on the bus. On the buses traveling with twenty-one to twenty-five men, Stone, a married woman, encountered sexual harassment but established clear boundaries. "At first, the fellows made passes at me, but ... once you let the guys know that there isn't going to be any monkey business, they soon give you their respect."[48] During the Jim Crow years, despite the long distances traveled, toilet facilities for Black men players were few, but there were no accommodations for a Black woman. Alan Pollock ruminated, "I've often wondered about the loneliness of Toni Stone in the woods in the night by herself while her teammates lined up at the bus during a Clowns rest stop."[49]

For African American women who were involved in rejecting externally defined controlling images as sexually promiscuous, special emphasis was given to possessing self-respect and demanding respect from others, especially from African American men.[50] *The Call's* articles on Stone sometimes referred to Stone by her first name, but also referred to her as "Miss Toni Stone," with the honorific "miss" signifying respect.[51] When asked why she put up with these hardships to play baseball, Stone responded, "A woman has her dreams too. When you finish high school, they tell a boy to go out and see the world. What do they tell a girl? They tell her to go next door and marry the boy that their family's picked for her. It wasn't right. A woman can do many things."[52]

The women Clowns fans who responded to Stone with "joyous laughter or tears of pride ... screaming with arms extended over their heads in adoration" clearly agreed.[53] Unfortunately, the Monarchs did not, and after unsuccessfully attempting to gain more playing time, Stone quit baseball in 1954. Her statistics with the Negro American League included a creditable .243 batting average, but she was last in the league in fielding percentage at second base. Still, in 1953 the Clowns drew more fans than in any previous season and more than any other Negro League team. "Toni Stone had probably delayed the death of the Negro American League by a season and a half."[54] *The Call* referred to Stone as "the first girl to crack the N.A.L. all-male domination ... the female Jackie Robinson" who would "break down the prejudice against women players in the N.A.L."[55] After leaving baseball Toni Stone missed the game "so bad I damn near had a heart attack."[56] She continued to play the game she loved at the recreational baseball level until she was sixty years old.

After Pollock sold Stone's contract to the Monarchs, he replaced her in 1954 with nineteen-year-old Connie Morgan. He also replaced manager Buster Haywood with Oscar Charleston. Toni Stone initially recommended Connie Morgan to Pollock in 1953 when she tried out for the team.[57] As expected, Haywood was against Morgan. Before signing with the Clowns, Morgan, a versatile athlete, played for five years with North Philadelphia Honey Drippers, a women's fast-pitch softball team,

In 1954, Connie Morgan was signed to replace Toni Stone at second base after her contract was purchased by the Kansas City Monarchs. Known as a superior athlete, Morgan is pictured here with Jackie Robinson (courtesy of NoirTech Research, Inc.).

as catcher, infielder and outfielder. She batted .338. Morgan appeared in several pictures taken during the tryout for the Clowns, with Clowns' outfielder Oscar Charleston and with Jackie Robinson of the Brooklyn Dodgers who was giving her tips on hitting. She was reputed to be an excellent athlete, intelligent, articulate and pretty enough to "have been a beauty contestant."[58]

According to Pollock, "Connie was generally considered the best of the women who played in the Negro American League. In Pollock's view, "the clear consensus is that none would have played based on merit, absent gate value." Morgan batted .178 for the Clowns and she, like Stone, had the lowest fielding percentage at second base.[59] However, this "consensus" was not shared by a sports writer for *The Call* who stated in reference to Stone and Morgan that, "these two ladies prove that we no longer can refer to them as the weaker sex." Connie Morgan's athleticism was given particular note, "Miss Connie Morgan, Indianapolis Clowns' rookie $10,000 female second baseman, electrified over 6,000 fans in the Negro League's opening twin-bill, here on May 16, when she went far to her right to make a sensational stop of a scorcher labeled 'base-hit,' flipped to shortstop Bill Holder and stated a lightening double-play against the Birmingham Black Barons."[60]

Morgan credited Oscar Charleston as her mentor and her brief comments give some indication of the coaching relationship he established with his two women players, suggesting that he was a capable teacher and a respected male authority figure. "Oscar Charleston was my mentor. Once the Clowns hired me and hired him, he took me off-season and taught me all he could about sliding and running the bases and, when it warmed a touch, hitting and fielding. He was a strict manager, not so you couldn't have fun, but stern enough so you knew to get down to business. He had us self-disciplined." Pitcher Mamie Johnson concurred. "With Oscar Charleston, you either played ball or you went home."[61]

Pitcher Mamie Johnson's origin story was structurally similar to the other female pitchers previously mentioned, but her experiences as a player were strongly mediated by race and class. Raised by her grandmother in Ridgeway, South Carolina, Johnson learned to pitch at age ten from her young uncles who taught her to throw rocks wrapped with masking tape. A tree limb or pipe functioned as a bat while a pie plate was first, a broken flower pot was second, a large root was third and the smooth white lid of a five gallon bucket of King Cane sugar was home plate.[62] "There was nothing, really, to do in the country. Whatever the fellas did, I did. And baseball was all we had to do."[63] Johnson, a tomboy, "wasn't interested in dolls or tea parties and such like the other girls."[64]

After the death of her grandmother, Johnson moved to Long Branch, New Jersey, where she first encountered the bifurcation of the sport into softball for girls and baseball for boys. Like Stone, Johnson refused to play softball and totally rejected feminine athleticism. "Girls, Aunt Dorothy kept telling me, were supposed to play softball. Softball? I didn't even like the sound of it. When I go to pitch a ball, ain't nothin' soft about it.... I had to unlearn everything I loved about playing hardball. For one thing the ball was the wrong size — it felt like a big old cantaloupe in my hand. And the coach wouldn't let me wind up and pitch the way I liked. Instead, I had to pitch underhand, like I was throwing feed to a bunch of dumb chickens instead of striking somebody out. I stuck with it as long as I could — three whole games before I up and quit."[65] To Johnson pitching underhand was pitching like a girl, an inferior skill to overhand pitching like a boy. "I liked standing up tall. The looking the other fella in the eye. The sizing him up for a change-up or fastball. And then the pitch. And I didn't pitch like a girl either. Not an underhanded fling of the ball. But a surefire windup, coming-right-at-ya pitch smack dab over the plate. One that let him know I meant business.... Grandma said the pitcher's mound was no place for a girl ... but baseball was what I liked."[66]

Johnson consistently preferred baseball and convinced a White police officer in Long Branch to give her a tryout with the Police Athletic Clubs where she was the only Black and the only girl on the team.[67] In 1947 she moved to Washington, D.C., where she played semi-pro ball with the all-male Alexandria All Stars and St. Cyprian's sandlot team.[68] Johnson's aspiration, unfortunately, was to play for the AAGPBL whose popularity was peaking at the time. Although the League was all White, Johnson admired them as pioneers and believed she had the ability to play for one of their teams. "Those gals had busted the door wide open and changed a lot of people's minds about girls and baseball. It was a door I was ready and willing to walk right through."[69] She hoped that the integration of major league baseball would spread to the League, but her hope was in vain. White women could claim opportunities that Black women could not. Johnson and a friend who played first base for the Cyprians attended a League tryout in Alexandra, Virginia. The result was total rejection: "they looked at us like we were crazy. They wouldn't even let us try out."[70] When Mamie pleaded their case as skilled ballplayers they were told bluntly that, "Just because that colored boy Robinson and a few of his buddies wormed their way into the majors doesn't mean we want colored gals playing next to our girls."[71]

There were no written League rules against hiring African American women players. Instead, fabricated differences relating to athletic abilities, motivation, and the assumption of social isolation justified their exclusion. On November 14, 1951, at a postseason League board meeting, the question of hiring "colored players" was discussed at length, to ascertain the views from different cities. "The consensus of the groups seemed against the idea of colored players unless they could show promise of exceptional ability. That in the event a club did hire one of them that none of the clubs would make her feel uncomfortable."[72] AAGPBL pitcher Jean Faut recalled that Black players had tried out with the team but her impression was that they did not appear to take the trials seriously. Bill Madden, author of the AAGPBL record book, stated, "more than one person ... told me they just weren't up to speed. They said black women at the time weren't really involved in softball, which is where they got most of their players." Some Black women ballplayers like Stone and Johnson rejected softball, and those who wished to play softball in the Midwest would have faced racial segregation. Carl Winsch, manager of the South Bend Blue Sox 1951–1954, admitted, "If the league tried harder, shook the bushes more ... we might've come up with someone."[73]

The League's loss was the Indianapolis Clowns' gain. Johnson, age nineteen, was spotted by Bish Tyson, a player for the Clowns. Johnson had accompanied the Clowns on a barnstorming tour when her pitching impressed Syd Pollock. Tyson introduced her to Bunny Downs, business manager of the Clowns in 1953 who hired the 5'3", 120-pound woman, who was "no bigger than a peanut," to pitch every five or six days over the next two seasons. When she pitched, she "pitched nine innings just like everybody else." Although "some fellas acted ugly," she did not experience the degree of resentment or sexual harassment faced by pioneering Stone.[74] "After I proved I was a ballplayer and not a gimmick, it went along very smoothly. Most of the fellas were very very nice."[75] "If you're out there doing what you're supposed to be doing, your teammates give you the respect you deserve."[76] Johnson's solution to sexual harassment was, "You have your gentlemen, and then you have some out there in left field somewhere. So what you do, you deal with the gentlemen, and then after you do that, then the gentlemen will tell the dummy something, and then it'll all come pretty good."[77] Johnson and Morgan also had the support of their manager Oscar Charleston and Bunny Downs, who set the standard for gender-appropriate conduct by the male players on and off the playing field. "The girls are the money

In 1953, the Indianapolis Clowns signed pitcher Mamie "Peanut" Johnson. She became the first woman to pitch in a major league baseball game (Courtesy of NoirTech Research, Inc.).

makers here. I want you to treat them like ladies or you can be replaced. If anyone messes up, I'll walk you to the bus station and buy you a ticket home."[78]

Like Stone, Johnson's dreams of empowerment centered on baseball. "Playing ball was something that I dreamed about so long. And it was in the back of my mind to say, 'I won't be able to do this because I'm a girl.' But then it happened and it was a tremendous thing for me."[79] "I saw things I never could have seen. It was a tremendous thing to look out the window and be 500 miles from where you were before. It was gorgeous. I enjoyed it. They were the three best years of my life."[80] Johnson "always felt that women can do anything they want to, or are big enough to do."[81] Johnson was released from the Clowns in June 1954. "I had a baby to take care of at home, and just couldn't stay on the road."[82] She still makes appearances, coaches Little League and encourages female athletes to "just try harder" if someone tells them they cannot achieve.[83]

As African American women baseball players, Stone, Morgan and Johnson experienced the double marginality of racism and sexism prior to the Civil Rights and second-wave feminist movements in the 1960s. According to Alan Pollock, these three women were the best female baseball players in the country, each one good enough to help their Negro League teams survive in the declining years after 1947. However, as African Americans, despite their talent, they were rejected as potential recruits for the AAGPBL. They were largely ignored by mainstream sports journalists, and as the Negro Leagues contracted after the integration of organized baseball, coverage of them in the Black sports press also declined. Finally, despite Stone and Johnson being the first women to play and pitch for men's major league teams, recognition for their accomplishments was ignored until recently. As women playing on all men's baseball teams, they had to struggle to be taken seriously as athletes rather than be reduced to novelties hired only to increase paying spectators. Since all women were assumed to be inferior athletes, Stone, the woman first to play second base for the Clowns, faced overt hostility from teammates and managers. Some resented her replacing a man who was "naturally" presumed to be a superior position player, some resented her salary and some subjected to her sexual harassment, a common form of intimidation faced by women entering traditionally male occupations. Both Stone, a married woman, and Johnson stated that establishing clear sexual boundaries between themselves and their teammates was essential to maintaining relationships with men based on respect.

Double marginality also created space for Stone, Morgan and Johnson to reject the dominant construction of feminine athleticism in the 1940s and 1950s. Since Black women were outside the boundaries of hegemonic femininity, they had more freedom to define their own athleticism and image. While it is evident that many White baseball players in the AAGPBL paid only lip service to the hyper-emphasis given to feminine image, League players could not refuse to wear the skirted uniform, don a mannish haircut, or otherwise reject the codes of appearance and behavior on and off the field. If Stone had played for the Chicago Colleens or if Johnson had successfully tried out for one of the AAGPBL teams, they too would have had to conform to League rules. Morgan and Johnson playing in the segregated Negro leagues, following Stone's refusal to wear shorts, rejected the controlling representation of themselves as sex objects by wearing the same uniform as their male teammates. Stone was a married woman and Johnson a mother, statuses that insulated them against being labeled lesbian, despite their athleticism, androgynous appearance on the field and socialization experiences as young athletes who played baseball with boys rather than engage in feminine activities.

Stone, Morgan and Johnson also insisted on one model for athleticism, the dominant male model that set standards for success in baseball at all levels. Stone and Johnson had played on boys' and men's teams all their lives and were clear about gaining access to this male preserve for themselves and for other women. Although the Negro League teams were barnstorming teams, thus eliminating close connections between locales and teams, the three women players enjoyed the enthusiastic support of women fans. Given widespread discrimination against Black men, working outside the home performing physically demanding tasks was not new for Black women in the post–War period. They experienced racism differently from their Black male teammates and faced sexism differently from their contemporary White women baseball players. Like other African American women, these players created "a way out of no way."[84]

6

"Do Something Momentous": The Florida Sun Sox (1984) and the Colorado Silver Bullets, (1994–1997)

After Allington's All Americans folded in 1958, there were no professional women's baseball teams for over thirty-five years, despite the passage of sex equity laws, including Title IX, enacted in 1972, which gave women a legal basis to push for equality in sports at the high school and college levels. Two attempts to open the door to women's professional baseball teams — the failed Florida Sun Sox and the short-lived Colorado Silver Bullets — were made by Bob Hope, a public relations and marketing specialist for the Atlanta Braves.

Hope first considered the idea of women playing professional baseball in 1999 when he worked for Coca-Cola. Bill Veeck of the Chicago White Sox approached the company about funding national tryouts for a woman to play second base. Hope rejected the proposal. "I thought it wasn't reasonable. My thinking was baseball would never stand for that. You have to prove yourself and show you can play at that level. But how can a woman get a chance to play? The only way is have a team at the lowest level of the minor leagues."[1]

In 1977 Hank Aaron asserted that, "Baseball is not a game of strength: hitting is not strength. The game needs a special kind of talent, thinking and timing. Some women as well as some men qualify in that respect.... A ball going 90 miles an hour can be knocked over the fence by anyone sticking a bat out and making perfect contact."[2] Influenced by Aaron's long-held view that women's athletic achievements in basketball, tennis and golf, were sufficient proof that "there is no logical reason why [women] shouldn't play baseball," Hope and his brother-in-law, Major Snow, a real estate developer, tried to take advantage of the 1984 expansion of the Class A Florida State League from ten to twelve teams. Aaron, as a former Negro League player for the Indianapolis Clowns, might also have been influenced by the athletic abilities and achievements of Stone, Morgan and Johnson. The goal of Hope and Snow was to acquire the Daytona Beach franchise and field a team of women players, the Florida Sun Sox, who would compete against men's teams. This minor league opportunity would, they hoped, eventually open doors for women to the major leagues since women faced insurmountable obstacles on their own, learning the necessary skills on a boy's team where they may not be socially accepted. "In baseball a woman will never make it to the big leagues if she has to depend on her own tenacity. 'Hey I want to try out for the boys team.' The pressure is on her as an individual in an awkward situation."[3] Hope wanted to provide a genuine opportunity for women who wanted to play professional baseball. "The only thing I'm concerned about is we do it in good taste, we give them a legitimate chance to play and be comfortable in baseball. No gimmickry."

Following Aaron, Hope contended that, "baseball is the only team sport you can play co-ed with no disadvantage to either party. Baseball is a game of quickness and finesse, not of brute strength."[4] Major Snow summarized their goal: "Our goal is to have several of our players graduate to teams in higher classifications and eventually be responsible for the first woman in the big leagues ... you may see one playing second base and making all the moves and the plays required at that position. Hardly anyone questions whether or not the best women athletes can play Class A baseball. Obviously this is a somewhat awkward precedent that will require a lot of understanding at all levels of professional baseball. None of us knows exactly what women will be able to do in the minor leagues. We simply feel they deserve a chance."[5] While a few front office men in Major League baseball were open to the idea of women playing professionally, Hope and Snow discovered, when the minor league franchise was denied them, that, "people can be cooperative and still keep you out."[6]

The tryouts for the Sun Sox were held at Georgia Tech, organized by Jim Morris and featured an appearance by Hank Aaron, the unpaid

V.P. for player personnel for the team. Forty women attended the try-outs that drew a large media contingent, including a "cadre of lady reporters never before seen at any baseball tryout."[7] Aaron initially offered an enthusiastic appraisal of the tryouts: "This is amazing. A few of them can handle themselves. They're going to have to give them a chance to play."[8] However, his later appraisals of the women players' skills were less sanguine, as were those of Jim Morris. Like managers Margaret Nabel and Bill Allington, who recognized and worked with the physical differences in women and men's upper body strength, Aaron identified pitching as the biggest problem facing the Sun Sox. "I don't think their muscles are ready to throw 120 pitches a game. Even if they could throw an 85 m.p.h. fastball, they'd probably lose their zip after 2–3 innings. We may have to draft men to pitch."[9] Morris, who worked with the women on a regular basis, quickly realized that the gap in skill development between men and women eliminated the possibility for the Sun Sox to play competitively. "Any pro pitcher would no-hit them. They need a strenuous development program for women. Something like the Kansas City Royals Baseball Academy where they can work at the game for long periods of time."[10]

Although the historical context of the tryouts, riding the currents of the second-wave feminist movement and the passage of Title IX, mostly ensured that the players would not be reduced to sexual objects in the media, their athletic capabilities were diminished by many male sportswriters who believed inferior skills justified women's exclusion from organized baseball. Sportswriter Furman Bisher's doubts resurrected images from thirty years ago when AAGPBL players were to be as concerned with their physical appearance as their athleticism on the playing field. "First comes finding a roster of girls who can stand the gaff and play the men at their own game. A Sun Sox player will have to be able to throw the ball hard enough, hit the ball far enough, make it from first to third on the hit and run, or haul down a soaring drive and then crash into the outfield wall without holding up the game to fix her face."[11] Another writer referred to women's need for a league of their own, "Even if some females are good enough to compete in Class A (possible but improbable) and even if the proprietors of the Florida State League were in favor of accepting the franchise as an experiment (which despite some rather naïve reports to the contrary is unlikely) their major league parent clubs are not about to let that happen. Baseball's conservative establishment will reject it ... if they were forming a league by themselves, then that's another matter. But asking these girls to come out and take a beating night after night — that doesn't make sense."[12] Thus, the view that "they" do better amongst themselves prevailed among most. However, Daniel Parker disagreed, echoing Aaron's view, "In baseball I believe a good woman could play major league-caliber ball against men. The key word is 'timing.' Many men are small wiry shortstops, and slender speedy outfielders. Baseball is a universal game as far as physical type goes. Women may not break Aaron's homerun record but may win a gold glove for fielding, steal bases, be effective pitchers. Timing requires hand to eye coordination, speed and reflexes and there is sex equality in these."[13]

Minor League players who would have faced the Sun Sox uniformly agreed that baseball is a man's game. Some were simplistically misogynist in their justifications for exclusion while others were more mindful of the broader sex/gender context. Barry Foote, former major league catcher and manager of the Class A Fort Lauderdale Yankees asserted, "I don't think they can play on the pro level. If they were allowed in, I'd knock 'em on their butt every chance I'd get to see if they're man enough to play a man's game. And I don't want to hear them crying or anything either." Dave Dunlap, third baseman for the Miami Marlins also dismissed women as athletes who could compete against men. "Just the basics of the game — strength, speed — would limit them. Men are just better as a whole. I'm sure a few could play as well or better, but not as a whole.... I'd look at the women like they were just somebody trying to take bread out of my mouth." Relief pitcher for the Vero Beach Dodgers, Mark Rexrode admitted, "I'll be trying twice as hard to get them out. It's an ego thing. You don't want to get hit or get beat by a girl." Tim Richardson, first baseman for the Fort Meyers Royals clearly identified why women were not "physically equipped" to play baseball. "Let's face it, in baseball you learn as you go up — a lot of different things in different levels. Perhaps if they started in Little League and high school and played in college, I'd see things a little differently." Jeff Sellers, pitcher for the Winter Haven Red Sox, focused on the emotional effects of gender barriers. "I think the most difficult part is going to be mental — being able to handle people criticizing and ridiculing you because you're trying to play a game that has been solely for men. The big part will be getting over the social attitudes."[14]

The women players who inspired this lively discourse merely by trying out for the Sun Sox represented a range of occupations, including several nontraditional jobs such as brick mason, coal miner and truck driver. Women's entry into nontraditional jobs has frequently been met with hostility ranging from verbal insults to sexual harassment. The Sun Sox players were aware of making history and eager to be given a chance to play and pave the way for future women. Dolores Owen, a biology teacher, came to the tryouts to set an example for her children. "This is so important — just to have a chance to make history. We have feelings. People forget that. And I say if somebody's good enough to play, you ought to let 'em." Of all the women players, twenty-year-old truck driver Kim Hawkins drew the most media attention because she demonstrated superior skills, was feisty, confident and attractive. "Hawkins with a can of chewing tobacco in the back pocket of her pants, ran, threw and fielded like — well like a baseball player." She could pitch "reasonably hard stuff" and her time of 7.3 seconds to run sixty yards was considered better than some men in the majors. Hawkins was sure that "women can play against men. The men don't think so but I do. I think they're afraid we'd beat 'em."[15]

The decision to deny the franchise to the Sun Sox was, according to Hope, a "vote for tradition" (read exclusion). Although the women proved they could play at the tryouts, "the issue was too controversial to get through."[16] Although Hope reaffirmed his commitment to fielding a women's professional baseball team, sportswriters' opinions on the negative decision in the press were divided. Sportswriter Carol Whittington interpreted the decision as a desire by the general public to preserve "natural," clearly defined gender identities and roles. "The ruling confirmed an underlying feeling of the public that aesthetics and logic outweigh aberrant aspirations. Most people have good reason for not wanting to see women in professional team sports ... although it is a fact that most men can out-run and over-power most women, there are women who could participate in professional team sports against men with the help from special routines and steroids. The question ... is not one of possibility but of aesthetics and role identity ... the world is alive with false images for women. It is reassuring to know that the general public still sees a definite distinction between male and female ideals."[17] In contrast, sportswriter Mitch Albom interpreted the Sun Sox from the perspective of stretching gender possibilities. "If a woman can run, catch, field and hit with the men in the game, if she desired no special treatment, if she'll ride the minor league buses and take all that batting practice and keep looking for another team if she gets cut — then she has the heart for the game. Let's face it. The future of the game ultimately belongs to the big league dreams of a little kid. Even if the kid is named Shirley."[18]

It was a decade before Hope could convince another sponsor to back a woman's professional baseball team. Hope's second attempt was facilitated by the general public's exposure in 1992 to the AAGPBL in the film *A League of their Own*. Hope, now president of Whittle Communications, and Coors Brewing Company announced the formation of an all-women's team on December 10, 1993. Coors fronted $2.6 million to sponsor the team named after its light beer, the Colorado Silver Bullets, and hoped that the favorable publicity would increase the sale of beer to women. Hope announced that the team would be an independent member of the AA Short Season Northern League and play fifty games against men's minor league, semiprofessional and college teams.[19] Players would earn $20,000 for the five-month season, a salary considerably higher than other minor league players, to compensate for the loss of previous employment. Unlike other minor league teams, the Silver Bullets were a barnstorming team. Over 1000 women tried out for the twenty-four-player roster to be managed by Hall of Fame pitcher Phil Niekro, selected by Hope because of his connections with the Atlanta Braves. At first Niekro was unsure about managing the Silver Bullets, but his wife, sister, and scouts convinced him. "So many in the minor leagues and scouts came up to me and said quite frankly they have seen women who could have played minor league ball."[20]

The Independent Northern League had reservations about playing the Silver Bullets, stipulating that the games be exhibition only.[21] The Silver Bullets' inaugural game against the Northern League All Stars took place on Mother's Day, May 8, 1994. Their crushing defeat of 19–0 resulted in a revised schedule to drop some minor league games and add men's amateur teams and a reconsideration of the "battle of the sexes" promotional theme. Niekro stated, "We really had no place playing a team like that. But you've got to try."[22] Although the team fielded fairly well, hitting and pitching were problems. Most of the Silver Bullets had attended college on softball scholarships. As former softball players, most had never encountered curveballs, sliders, and sinkers and they were used to hitting with lighter aluminum bats. According to Niekro, "They're

In 1994 the Colorado Silver Bullets, sponsored by Coor's Beer, became the first professional women's baseball team since the AAGPBL. Front row (left to right): Pam Schaffrath, Julie Croteau, Stacy Sunny, Phil Niekro, Michele McAnany, Michelle Delloso, Charlotte Wiley. Middle row (left to right): Tommy Jones, Joe Niekro, Rachelle McCann, Gina Satriano, Keri Kropke, Allison Geatches, Bridgett Venturi, Elizabeth Burnham, Ann Williams, K.C. Clark, Kim Braatz, John Niekro. Back row (left to right): Jeanette Amado, Laurie Gouthro, Lee Anne Ketcham, Lisa Martinez, Shae Sloan, Toni Heisler, Missy Cress, Shannan Mitchem, Melissa Coombes (National Baseball Hall of Fame Library, Cooperstown, New York).

used to swinging 25, 26 ounce aluminum bats and now swinging 30–31–32 ounce bats. They're just not conditioned physically or mentally to get into this wooden bat."[23]

The Silver Bullets' first season record was poor, consisting of 6 wins and 38 losses, no one hitting above .220 and no pitcher with an E.R.A. below 4.50. Their costly and grueling travel schedule exhausted the players and eliminated an essential base of fan support that grows between a region or community and its team. The women players' lack of baseball experience, the insignificance of losing, and the goal of providing girls with requisite skills and opportunities to play organized baseball in the future were the consistent responses by Hope, Niekro, and the players to media questions about the team's poor performance. Niekro maintained, "If these players had the training that men had, from Little League on up, we might have a woman in the minor leagues by now. The experience gap is many many years. But someday there will be a couple of women in the minors. At that point they will become prospects ... somewhere down the line there will be a woman in the major leagues."[24] Players concurred. "You never like to lose, but what we're doing is bigger than just winning or losing. What we're doing overall — for future generations of young girls is more important. For the kids coming up this will help them achieve their goals."[25] Pitcher Lee Anne Ketcham emphasized the role of the Silver Bullets as cultural trailblazers. "There are several girls on this team who played baseball when they were younger and because of some chauvinistic guy or whatever, they were never allowed to go very far. We've just got to set the precedents, and there will be little girls coming up through the ranks in the next 5 or 10 years who will have had the baseball background, playing right alongside the guys, with the best coaching. They're going to be the ones who will have the best chance, after we change the mentality."[26]

By 1994, the increased visibility and acceptance of women's athletic achievements in the twenty years following the passage of Title IX were reflected in the sports media by sportswriters. The players were not represented as sexual objects or as mannish athletes needing to prove their femininity. "These gals have no desire to be men, only to play a game traditionally enjoyed by them."[27] The reactions of men sportswriters and players to the Silver Bullets were generally positive, with several sharing the view that the team would open doors for women. Dennis "Oil Can" Boyd of the Northern League All-Stars conceded after their debut game that, "They made some mistakes that cost them, but they showed me something ... you don't have to worry about having a girl or boy anymore because girls can play baseball.[28] Although they continued to lose games, Niekro was positive: "I think everybody's starting to realize the talent here. These women are showing that they can play — they're opening doors for others. The men's teams that play us can see it." Men players like Chris Crowder and Pat Terry agreed. "They're not just women baseball players, they're good baseball players. They gave us all we could handle and they earned our respect." "There's a lot of positive things to be had from all this — for women and sports in general."[29]

Coach Tommy Jones explained their criteria for evaluating Silver Bullets' success. "How do we judge success? Not just wins and losses but can we compete on a daily basis. The first time people watch due to the novelty, but why the second time? The Bullets rely on finesse and fundamentals such as bunting and the hit and run. Hitting is a problem. Ninety-five percent of the team were college softball players with less than half a dozen baseball players. We lack baseball instincts. A lot of outstanding female athletes are waiting in the wings to see if this project is successful. If we can prove this is a legit operation, our second and third years will be even better."[30]

Men sportswriters frequently mentioned the skill deficits challenging the Silver Bullets, but these were explained in social rather than biological terms emphasizing the lack of continuous opportunities for girls to play baseball after Little League. Most relied heavily on the perspectives offered by Phil Niekro or Bob Hope who consistently maintained that with sufficient training, women could play baseball at a competitive level with men. Points of interest for men sportswriters included how the players left or took leave from various occupations to try out or play for the Silver Bullets, and how the women were encouraged to play baseball or softball by fathers or brothers who were former major league players. Their origin stories revealed an extraordinary determination to play. For example, Charlotte Wiley, who tried out as a pitcher for the Silver Bullets, grew up playing baseball with her eight brothers, excelled on her Little League and Babe Ruth teams, was encouraged by her parents, and dreamed since third grade of playing for the Mets.[31] "I've never had a problem playing baseball against men ... I grew up with 8 brothers and I was always playing with them. I played Little League from the time I was 7 all the way up 'til high school. And I played on the boys baseball team my junior year. I didn't switch to softball until I was a senior."[32]

Gina Satriano was a favorite for both men and women sportswriters. A deputy district attorney in Compton, California, Satriano earned her law degree from Pepperdine and put her legal career on hold to pitch for the Silver Bullets, where she posted the second-best earned run average on the staff in 1994.[33] Satriano's parents were exceptionally supportive of her desire to play baseball. Her father was a major league catcher for the California Angels and Boston Red Sox and her mother fought hard to ensure that her daughter could play baseball beyond Little

League. "Baseball was in my blood since I was a kid, but I had to think it was an unattainable dream." Satriano brought suit in Malibu, California, to play Pony and Colt League, resulting in phone threats and burning trees in her front yard. She "put up with hassles from coaches and teammates through pony and colt leagues," was forced to play softball in high school and was cut at the end of Fall baseball practice at U.C. Davis. "When I got to high school Mom asked me if I wanted to fight to play there too and I said I'm tired of fighting. I just want to play. So I played softball. I just didn't enjoy the game as much." Satriano continued to play baseball, spending three years with men's semi-pro teams in Los Angeles and New York, often joined by her father and brothers who played with her.[34] Satriano clearly recognized the strong social and economic forces steering girls away from baseball and into softball. "The early teens are a difficult age for any person. To go into something that's not accepted that's not the norm, that's the last thing you want to do. And the other part of it is, there's no future for women in baseball. You figure you need to switch to softball because at least it will get you an education." Several other women on the team also switched from baseball to softball in high school, including third basewoman Shannon Mitchem who as a child pretended to be Hank Aaron.[35]

The reactions of women sportswriters to the Silver Bullets were more dubious, despite their recognition of the players' extraordinary motivation, love for the game and the nonexistent opportunities for continuous training, preparation and play. Some women sportswriters initially thought the team was a publicity stunt by Coors with "women's odds of making the Big Leagues slim to none."[36] Repeated themes included a rejection of the outdated promotional gimmick "the battle of the sexes," an acceptance of the physical differences between men and women, and most advocated strongly for a professional women's baseball league to give women the same opportunities to play competitively as men and to publically showcase their athleticism. Their views relating to whether women could play baseball in men's organized leagues differed. Barbara Walder contended, "You can change psychology, not physiology. So it's a continuing source of wonder to me how some women can still wax lyrically about the day when their daughters will be playing shortstop in the major leagues. What a dumb idea! Little League is fine and even some exceptional college women can compete with men, but at the professional level, it's just not possible."[37] Former AAGPBL pitcher Jean Faut Eastman, who threw out the first pitch at age sixty-nine in the Silver Bullets' inaugural game, liked what she saw but did not think it would last beyond a year. "They are going to get beat a lot.... They have defense, speed, can catch and throw, but men are stronger and will out hit them. The girls can't hit the ball as far." Eastman felt that women should compete in leagues of their own as she so successfully did.[38] Susan Fornoff offered another perspective on physical differences. "The physicality is that woman's natural inferiority in upper body-strength generally limits her ability to hit the ball hard or far, but her lower-body strength and agility may allow her to pitch adequately and field well. Baseball, more than any other team sport, forgives the physically flawed and embraces the short player, the skinny player, the fat player, even the player born without a hand. Someday it will open its arms to a woman, and the only legitimate argument on the point today is over who, when and which position.... The point is, women too can play baseball. And the Silver Bullets are the living breathing emblem of baseball's official 63-year exclusion of women from the game, just as they are also the throwing, catching omen of baseball's ultimate, inevitable acceptance of the first female major leaguer."[39] Finally, Claire Smith argued that the most significant contribution made by the Silver Bullets was cultural — that men and boys were among the paying spectators who enthusiastically watched the first game and after eagerly sought the autographs of "ballplayers who happen to be women."[40] The Silver Bullets improved their record in each of their four seasons and in 1997 they had a winning season (23–22) against men's semi-professional and military base teams.

During the four years, close relationships among manager, coaches and players were formed. Niekro and his coaches were men formed by the homosocial sport of baseball. None had previously coached women and the task of transitioning softball athletes to baseball athletes was arduous, requiring commitment, patience and the ability to translate and teach the essential skills. These players were adult women, not girls who needed socialization to provide them with a set of values, a work ethic or commitment to the team. All were employed, knew how to work hard, were leading independent lives and were grateful to be on the team.

Therefore, the coaches could focus on teaching former softball players the requisite skills needed to play baseball and behavioral norms of baseball, the latter of which required resocialization into masculine modes of interaction among teammates on the field. "Phil [Niekro] was a bit in shock of our on-field behavior.... He said, 'I don't think I've ever seen in baseball a team stand up on the dugout stairs the entire game. And I don't think I've ever seen the entire infield run over and high-5 someone after a great play.... We must act as if we expect to make those plays. Congratulations are done in the dugout. I've never seen the whole team congratulate a runner crossing the plate.... And never, in all the leagues I've played in, ever have I seen a player jump into the arms of the third-base coach after hitting a triple. I think I even heard screaming.'"[41] These women players had to unlearn feminine speech community norms and standards of on-field play that include frequent verbal and physical demonstrations of support and enthusiasm. Since the norms for verbal and nonverbal communication on the playing field were generated by men, women players as newcomers needed to conform to this specific masculine speech community.

How distinct and pervasive these gendered communication norms are was recently illustrated to me at my niece's high school softball game, also attended by my son Julian, age sixteen, who plays baseball for his high school team. After commenting on how small softball diamonds are in comparison with baseball diamonds, he was immediately aware of the gender differences in styles of supportive chatter by the coach (a woman) for the Lacordaire Lions and my niece's teammates. Supportive chatter on all sports teams serves to boost team spirit and provide emotional support and encouragement to players both when they play well and when they do not. On male baseball teams, displays of emotion and encouragement on the field are controlled, reflecting the greater control over emotions expected of males in our culture. Male players will verbally or nonverbally recognize a good play after it happens and a coach will, at times, offer encouragement or advice, particularly to a pitcher in a jam. Examples of male chatter at my son's high school included, "Let's go, Julian. All right, Julian. Good eye. Nice hit. You gotta protect." This effort at impression management serves to convey the message of confidence to the opposing team. In contrast, on the girls' softball team, not only is the effusive positive chatter constant, with lapses interpreted as apathy, but what is said differs: "Wha' da' ya' say, Lacey. You're a hitter, Lacey. Shake it off, Lacey. Nice try. Good effort, Lacey. Let's go, Lacordaire, get that batter outa there."

Julian's strongest reactions related to on-field behavioral norms among teammates. The strong opposing team was coached by a man, who, presumably, as a boy was coached by other men. Nevertheless, he had adapted his coaching style to feminine norms. After every strikeout (there were many) and every successful defensive play (also many) the infielders would quickly congregate on the pitcher's mound to high-five and verbally encourage one another to continue playing well. Julian was dumbfounded, and his incredulous adolescent facial expressions should be visualized by the reader during the following interchange:

JULIAN: "Mom, what are they doing? Why are they all on the pitcher's mound?"

AUTHOR: "They're showing support, team spirit."

JULIAN: "Why? It's delaying the game. Why doesn't the umpire stop it?"

AUTHOR: "The umpire isn't objecting and neither is the opposing coach."

JULIAN: "Are they so insecure that they have to high-five after every strike-out?"

AUTHOR: "They are killing the Lions. They don't appear to me to be insecure."

JULIAN: "My team never does that. I've never seen any other baseball team do that. We show a lot of team spirit. What they are doing makes them look stupid. When I make a good play at short, I get verbal encouragement like 'nice play.' We don't all gather on the pitcher's mound and discuss it. In baseball there's a time and place to gather on the pitcher's mound."

This Mars-verses-Venus dialogue reflects how gender mediates appropriate on-field communication norms among male baseball and female softball players. Although the competitive drive of the girls equals that of boys, girls will freely demonstrate verbally and physically their emotional support and social connections with teammates, thus reflecting the wider latitude given to emotional expression in appropriate feminine behavior. Most coaches for male baseball and female softball teams will instill in their players that sportsmanship and team spirit is as significant as winning games. The significance of relationships among women softball players on competitive college-level teams is illustrated by the recent highly publicized generous gesture of sportsmanship by two players for the Central Washington team. They carried an opposing team member around the bases after she hit her first home run, injured her knee and could not run herself. The coach of the opposing Western Oregon team, Pam Knox, stated: "Everybody was crying. It was an away game and our four fans were crying. We couldn't hit after that." Although all involved denied that gender ("Is there something intrinsic to women's sports that caused this generosity?") mediated the gesture, few would argue that the displays of emotion — crying — fell within the boundaries of normative femininity rather than masculinity.[42] Masculinity requires emotional control and male players learn to keep their emotions in check while on the field, reserving displays of support or tears for the dugout, bench or locker room. Emotional control, from the male perspective, communicates confidence — that players expect to perform well, while frequent emotional display communicates insecurity.

The agents of socialization on baseball teams who teach young boys self-control include vertical agents — adult coaches — and horizontal agents or peers. Beginning at the early stages of Little League, coaches adopt a rational, rule-bound paradigm that subsumes the multiple identities of athletes into discourses of effort, sportsmanship and teamwork. Male athletes are socialized early to control their emotions ("man up"), acquiesce to authority figures, to avoid intimacy and disclosure ("leave it off the court") with their peers, adult male coaches and trainers. Such avoidance boundaries are culturally constructed and understood as professional barriers that maintain the equal treatment of all players. Peer socialization also begins early focusing on controlling aggression, fear, and tears and displaying appropriate emotions such as being tough, the desire to win and the bond of teamwork or unity.

According to Gary Fine's analysis of Little League socialization, boys learn how to shape a self-image that reinforces acceptable masculine behavior: "Such control represents the embodiment of the male sex role; the preadolescent boy is learning through the reactions of his peers, how to channel his behavior; how to control his body, and how to look 'cool,' even when he may be feeling hot."[43] If a boy cries he is acting like a girl, and he will face sanctions from his peers. This link between emotional control and adult masculinity is continually reinforced as adolescent boys mature into young men seeking to play baseball professionally. A significant element of the socialization process of young Dominican baseball prospects by their American coaches is learning to control their emotions, especially when they are not playing well. "We don't show emotion, we pitch emotion. This is the relationship between boy and man."[44] Female athletes and coaches who openly display their emotions by talking intimately, laughing, crying and demonstrating physical affection are interpreted by males as unprofessional and the antithesis of masculinity.

Dave Kindred's portrayal of the coach/player relationship on the Silver Bullets was intimate in the familial sense and demonstrates how men coaches adapted to open emotional displays of affection toward them by young women players. Coaches were able to transcend the gender separation characteristic of the sport partly by believing in the players' abilities and partly by extending fictive kinship terms (daughter, sister) and the accompanying emotional feelings to players who viewed them as role models and father figures. For example, on Father's Day, 1994, the players gave the coaches an array of gifts including "#1 Dad" hats. The coaches responded warmly and were not reluctant to display their affection for the players. "Joe [Niekro] added that if he had another daughter, it would be any one of us. TJ [Tommy Jones] ... said it is hard sometimes to keep the relationships straight because we are like daughters, sisters, friends and players to him."[45] Other sport researchers have demonstrated that one way male athletes handle the presence of women in male sports settings including teams or locker rooms is to fit them into familiar, stereotyped, de-sexualized, feminine kinship roles through the extension of kinship terms such as mother, sister, or daughter, depending on the ages of those involved.[46]

Although the Silver Bullets provide a fascinating test case of negotiating gender boundaries and communication on and off the playing field, given the relatively short period of time that most of the Silver Bullets players exclusively focused on baseball skills, they do not provide us with a sufficient test case for women's baseball potential. A couple of players, including Julie Croteau, discussed below, and Gina Satriano, played baseball with boys continuously during their lives. A few Silver Bullets players were offered opportunities in organized baseball; however, none advanced, as is the case for the vast majority of men seeking opportunities to play at this level. One example is Kendra Hanes, an outfielder who did not make the final cut for the Silver Bullets. Despite having no previous baseball experience, she was scouted and offered a chance by Manager Mike Weisbart to play for the Independent Class-A Frontier League Team. Hanes's contract made her the fourth woman to sign a minor league contract after Eleanore Engle. Weisbart agreed with Bob Hope that "someday there will be a woman in baseball and the best way for that to happen is to start in the minors. There are some very disturbing attitudes in baseball about women, and we think they need to be attacked." Hanes was an addition to the team, not a replacement, and all considered her first year to be a "school year" when she would transition from softball to baseball.[47]

In 1994 two Silver Bullets, Julie Croteau, first base, and Lee Anne Ketcham, pitcher, played for the Maui Stingrays, a team in the Hawaii Winter Baseball League. Despite Ketcham's achievement as ace of the pitching staff with five wins in 1994 and the leader in earned run average, neither was given much playing time, with Ketcham pitching only nine innings. In 1995 Shannon Mitchem, who played third base and right field, and Ann Williams, a relief pitcher, tried out for the New York Mets. Neither made the team. In 1996 Pamela Davis pitched for a major league farm team for the Detroit Tigers in an exhibition game, pitching a scoreless inning.[48] Also in 1996, the Silver Bullets were invited to Taiwan to play exhibition games against major league men's teams, where they lost all five of the games played.

By 1996–1997, attendance at Silver Bullets games dropped and Coors announced it would no longer be a sponsor. Hope-Beckham, Inc., which purchased the team from Whittle Communications, could not find new sponsors.[49] In 1997 Mike Ribant formed the Ladies League Baseball, a professional league consisting of four teams located in California. This League played twenty-six games before running out of money. In 1998 the Ladies League was reorganized and re-named Ladies Pro Baseball with six teams located in the West and East Coasts. After sixteen games financial troubles again closed the league. There have been no women's professional baseball teams since 1998.

Julie Croteau, first baseman for the Silver Bullets with a .990 fielding percentage, was one of the few women baseball players with continuous baseball experience since childhood. Croteau, born in 1970, along with Ila Borders discussed in the next chapter, provides both data and insight relating to what girls/women might accomplish when they have the same opportunities to play baseball as boys/men. Although neither made it to the major leagues, the same is true for 98 percent of men with minor league contracts. They also provide us with longitudinal case studies of the unfolding emotional dimensions and challenges of being the "lone ponytail" in a gender-bifurcated sport.[50]

Croteau was exactly the sort of female baseball player that Bob Hope and others involved with the Sun Sox and Silver Bullets envisioned when they repeatedly identified the core problems facing girls and women motivated to play professional baseball. She began playing baseball with her cousin and joined a local T-ball team at age six. Since this was two years after girls had legally won the right to play Little League Baseball in 1974, about half of her teammates were girls. By age nine, at Fenway Park in Boston, Croteau announced to her parents that she intended to play professional baseball.

However, by age twelve Croteau was the only girl on her Little League team. Because Croteau was a talented player, she was treated well by most of her teammates. Although she was not sent to the All-Star team during her first season, coaches sent her to the All-Stars the following season. Selection of Tournament or All-Star teams is made by players, team managers, coaches, umpires and Little League officers. Each group submits a list of players at a meeting of the League Board of Directors. The names are read and counted from each group and players in order of total votes become eligible for the All-Star team. Croteau was the first girl to make the Little League All-Stars in Virginia, with a batting average of .300.

Croteau continued to play baseball in the Major Leagues for thirteen- to fifteen-year-olds, in a Fall league for fourteen-year-olds, and in the Babe Ruth Leagues for sixteen- to eighteen-year-olds where she maintained a fielding average of .975 at first base. In the off-seasons she attended clinics and baseball camps, practiced routinely in batting cages and lifted weights despite decreasing encouragement from her coaches. A baseball coach at Catholic University who worked with Croteau at a winter clinic said, "She has average high school ability for boys. She's a line drive hitter and she makes good contact. I'm seeing 70 to 80 high school games a year, and she has enough ability to make most high school teams."[51]

Nevertheless, serious problems for Croteau began in high school. As a freshman she did not make the Junior Varsity baseball team and the coach encouraged her to play softball with the girls' team. She replied that softball was "not my sport." "I was very angry. The coaches didn't call the boys and suggest that *they* change sports.... Softball is an entirely different game." As a sophomore she made the Junior Varsity team but was benched for most of the season, despite outplaying a boy for the first base position. "I felt like the coach was embarrassed having a girl on the his team. Having a girl who could start would be a putdown on the school."[52] As a junior she played for a supportive coach, but was cut from the team due to interference from the Varsity coach. "Every year they've done something to knock me down." As a senior she was cut from the Varsity team despite her achievements on the Babe Ruth League outside of school where she outplayed many of the boys. Both the Varsity coach and school principal were against girls playing on the boys' team. Consequently, she and her parents in March 1988 decided to sue for sex discrimination.[53] Croteau was the third girl to take legal action to play on a high school baseball team.

The first was Jo Ann Carnes, an eighteen-year-old high school senior from Wartburg, Tennessee. In 1976 Carnes sued her high school for sex discrimination. Carnes was among thirty-five students who tried out for the baseball team at Central High School. After trying out she was accepted on condition that she cut her hair to conform to team rules. Carnes complied and was also prepared to wear a chest protector specially designed for women. Although her coach considered her to be "baseball material and ... knew of no physical reason why she could not play on the team," she was barred from play because the Tennessee Secondary School Athletic Association did not permit girls to participate in contact sports. Because Carnes was not eligible to play on the baseball team, Central High School might be suspended from the association if she was permitted to participate.

Carnes won her case. The District Court ruled that Carnes was discriminated against for two reasons under the legal provisions of Title IX. One, Central High School had no women's baseball team. "Consequently, plaintiff either must play on Central's only baseball team or not play at all. Thus, rather than foster equitable competition, TSSAA's rule operates as a complete bar to plaintiff's opportunity to compete solely on the basis of her sex." Two, Carnes' vulnerability to injury as a female was not seen to be greater than that to which the male players would be exposed. "She appeared physically suited to play baseball.... She has actively engaged in other sports without suffering any serious injuries." Thus the Court rejected the frailty myth as a basis for exclusion. Carnes intended to play baseball in college.[54] The second girl to play on a varsity high school team was Linda Williams, who played right field for her high school team in Houston, Texas, in 1978. The University Interscholastic League attempted to prevent her from playing due to her sex, but a judge ordered her to be reinstated.

Croteau, however, did not win her case, although her former Little League and Babe Ruth League coaches testified that she was skilled enough to play on a high school varsity team. Their positive evaluation of her athletic skills was supported by two male high school players who had played with or against her on these teams. One boy contended that she "could hold her own with the team." Another, a pitcher, who competed with and against Croteau said he would rate her as an eight on a scale of one to ten as a first baseman. "She's also hit off me. I don't think I ever struck her out." Still, her high school coach and teammates insisted otherwise. They stated that she could not hit, run or throw; "she doesn't fit into our speedy team."

The court determined that Croteau failed to prove that the decision to cut her from the varsity baseball team was tainted or motivated by gender bias. The court was convinced that she had received a fair tryout and that the decision to cut her was made in good faith and for reasons unrelated to gender. "Although there was no persuasive evidence here of discrimination, there was abundant evidence ... that plaintiff is a fine athlete and a dedicated baseball player. But the competition for a place on the Osbourn Park varsity team was keen. For reasons wholly unrelated to gender, plaintiff did not succeed." The judge dismissed the case, stating that there is "no constitutional or statutory right to play any position on any athletic team. Instead there was only the right to compete for any position on equal terms," which he concluded had occurred. "The coach and team cheered and jumped around like they had won the World Series."[55]

Despite the anguish and ostracism endured by Croteau during and after the trial, a sympathetic reporter covering the trial, Mike Zitz, had watched video tapes of her skills at first base and hitting. "When I went up there, it was evident what was going on. The players were snickering in and out of the courtroom. When I saw the tape in the courtroom with her footwork around first base and her bat work, it was obvious she could play at that level. The boys' problem was rooted in something other than her ability." Outside of the courtroom after the trial, Zitz interviewed Croteau whose anguish moved her to tears. Her anguish moved Zitz to invite Croteau to practice with his semi-pro men's team, the Fredericksburg Giants. "I thought it was wrong that someone should love the game and have the ability and be booted out."[56]

Croteau took full advantage of the opportunity, driving forty-five minutes each way to practice with the team. She was the first to arrive and the last to leave, impressing manager Zitz with her dedication. Zitz evaluated her skills: "fundamentally she is one of the best players we had."[57] At age seventeen Croteau joined the Giants, making her the first woman to play semi-pro baseball in Virginia. Croteau batted ninth and her batting average was low. Croteau was "a line-drive single-type hitter.... At 5'7" she's expected to draw a lot of walks. Obviously because of her size, she's no big power hitter, but she has a good swing."[58] Croteau felt that the team was "really positive toward me and I'm learning a lot."

Zitz considered her to be a solid player with the ability to concentrate, focus and handle the pressure on the field and in the media. Handling intense media attention was one of the consequences of crossing gender or race boundaries. Zitz was criticized in the press for having Croteau on the Giant's team, claiming that it was merely a publicity stunt, another common consequence of crossing gender or race boundaries. Two of his players — a pitcher and an outfielder — switched teams, refusing to play with a woman. Still, Croteau was able to have her moment, batting in the winning run during the team's final game. She continued to play with the Giants on and off for six years. According to Zitz, Croteau was the team's best first baseman in its fifteen-year history.[59]

Croteau's ambition was to play baseball in college. In 1988, after working hard through fall training, she became the first woman to play men's NCAA Division III baseball for the Saint Mary's Seahawks in Maryland as the number-two first basemen and defensive replacement. Again at the opening game and throughout her first season when she was eighteen, Croteau was the object of intense media attention, with fifteen television cameras focused on her during the first game. Her defensive play (5 errors in 92 chances) was better than her offensive with a .222 average at the end of the first season. Coach Hal Willard considered Croteau to be "tough" and several opposing coaches considered her to be a legitimate Division III player. As the media attention decreased during her second and third seasons, so did her playing time, with much of Croteau's third season spent on the bench.[60]

Although Croteau's teammates at Saint Mary's were largely supportive, she faced hostility from opposing pitchers who would often walk her rather than face the humiliation of giving up a hit to her. She also found it difficult to adjust to the highly sexualized and misogynistic speech community of her male teammates who would frequently use obscene slang to refer to female genitalia. Such experiences parallel women's entry into other non-traditional occupations, including law enforcement, construction, mining, and branches of the military, where they are frequently exposed to a sexually charged, hostile and intimidating atmosphere by male coworkers. On bus rides players would read aloud from Penthouse magazine "a very specific degrading article about women's body parts. I don't think they were directing it at me, but I was the only one on the bus with those parts." Their discussions of an end-of-season party included pornographic videos and graphic descriptions of sexual acts, resulting in Croteau declining to attend. When questioned about these incidents, the team coach responded, "It was just guys being guys.... Julie has as rotten a mouth as any of the guys." Croteau, feeling angry, decided to take a semester away from the school. She stated that she "has spent more time fighting and being emotionally destroyed by baseball than enjoying the game. It's not fun anymore."[61]

Nevertheless, Croteau remained dedicated to playing baseball. Her pioneering achievements, her anger directed against the overt sexism that she experienced, her critique of the patriarchal organization and culture of baseball and her future-oriented recognition that her actions affected other girls and women who wanted to play baseball were acknowledged by leading women's organizations including N.O.W., the Women's Sports Foundation (where she was discovered during an internship the AAGPBL and appeared as an extra in *A League of Their Own*), and she was the subject of many magazine articles. "I've been through things people shouldn't have to go through to play a game. I've had people spit on me, call me names, and call me in the middle of the night."[62]

In 1991 she began to give baseball clinics for young girls to encourage their participation and in 1992 she became the first woman to coach men's college baseball as an assistant coach at Western New England College in Springfield, Massachusetts. As an assistant coach at University of Massachusetts, Amherst, Croteau was once again the "lone ponytail," but this time she was in a position of power as a former professional player and teacher. Still, negotiating gender was an issue, affecting her acceptance by the all-male team. Since ability is partly a cultural construct, it is important for boys/men to play with girls and be coached by women, as Croteau realized. "Men coach half of women's teams. In these cases we accept that the coach's gender does not hinder their ability to do their jobs. Why wouldn't the same logic apply to women who wish to coach men's teams?" A pitcher coached by Croteau stated, "I think at first we were all on edge, not knowing what to expect. She played professional baseball, which is more than any of us can say." Croteau astutely linked her acceptance with men's level of self confidence: "I've found out the better the player, the more confidence they have in their ability, the easier it is to accept me. I'm always asked what's it like to be the first coach. To be honest, I'd rather be the 200th."[63]

In 1993 Croteau was invited to try out for the Colorado Silver Bullets and, after making the team as first baseman, was the only player who had never played baseball with girls or softball. The next year she and teammate Lee Ann Ketcham were offered an opportunity to play with the men's professional Maui Stingrays. When she returned to the Silver Bullets in 1995, Croteau injured her shoulder, requiring surgery. That ended her career as a player. She continued her connection with baseball as a broadcaster, an assistant coach at University of Massachusetts in Amherst, an NCAA Division I team, and promoted baseball around the world for Major League Baseball.

Croteau, who experienced firsthand the inequities for girls and women in baseball, continues to work toward the elimination of gender barriers in sports through baseball clinics for girls and by promoting baseball at the high school and college levels.[64] Mike Zitz explained Croteau's intensions: "She is trying to reach out to younger girls who love baseball and have people who try to stop them from doing it. She hopes what she's doing makes a difference."[65] Croteau's efforts were rewarded when she was selected as the coach of the 2004 Team U.S.A. women's baseball team that competed in the Women's World Cup Tournament in Taipei, Taiwan, against women's national teams from Canada, Australia, Taiwan, Hong Kong, Japan, and Cuba. Although Team U.S.A. won the gold medal, the game was ignored by the U.S. sports media.[66]

The women trying out for the Sun Sox and playing for the Silver Bullets were mostly former softball players who faced enormous difficulties switching to the different sport of baseball. The field dimensions were larger, the ball smaller and harder, and they were not used to the heavier wooden bats. Consequently, if the franchise had been granted to the Sun Sox, they probably would not have been able to field an all-women's team and the Silver Bullets lost the majority of their games.

Hope and all of the coaches were aware of the disadvantages women baseball players faced due to the deficit in skill development. It is to their credit that these men rejected the ideology of physical inferiority to

In 1994, Colorado Silver Bullets first baseman Julie Croteau and Lee Ann Ketcham played for the men's professional winter league team in Hawaii, the Maui Stingrays. Croteau is pictured here in uniform (National Baseball Hall of Fame Library, Cooperstown, New York).

explain why women did not play baseball at a competitive level with men. The fact that most girls did not share in the continuous development of their baseball skills was repeatedly emphasized by Hope and the other men who organized and coached the women's teams and by some sports journalists.

It was Hope's goal that these teams would inspire an infrastructure for young female talent that would feed into organized baseball, such as exists for boys. Baseball provided nothing for girls after Little League ended at age twelve, depriving them of critical stages of skill development since girls then usually switched to softball. Hope and Snow sought to provide a legitimate opportunity for the "many twelve year old girls who were the stars of their Little League teams because they are physically and mentally committed to baseball and ... then there is no place to go."[67]

Unfortunately, Hope's promotional background influenced his decision to "do something momentous" — organizing a minor league team of adult women, who were just transitioning from softball to baseball, to compete against professional men's teams who had the benefit of a lifetime of baseball experience. Thus, the consensus of opinion among advocates for women's professional baseball is that Hope unwittingly set the women's teams up for failure by eliminating a long-awaited opportunity for women to be judged on their own merits and missing a key opportunity to promote a new women's league. A women's league would have drawn public attention to women's athletic capabilities and generated an infrastructure for young female talent to develop after Little League. This farm system would generate a pool of female talent, some of whom could compete at the college, minor league or even major league level with men. Minor League Class A is not the place to begin learning and playing baseball since the gap in skills and experience is too wide.[68]

The Sun Sox and Silver Bullets were the first attempts to establish an all-women's professional baseball team since the demise of the AAGBPL. The teams are socially significant because they clearly illustrate the consequences of the bifurcation of baseball for boys/men and softball for girls/women: creating a structure of inequality for girls that denies them equal access to opportunities in sports. The difficulties faced by former softball players in transitioning to baseball, particularly with hitting and pitching, and the lack of success by the Silver Bullets against men's teams served to reinforce prevailing assumptions that women's bodies were inferior and they could not and should not play baseball at a level competitive with men. These assumptions were voiced by some of the men players and some sports journalists, both men and women. Since there has been no change in the gender-defined power structure of baseball since the Silver Bullets, all of the issues negatively affecting women's potential to play baseball remain.

The Silver Bullets were a homosocial team comprised of women coached by men, as were the AAGPBL. However, after forty years and the gains made by the second-wave feminist movement, Silver Bullets players wore appropriate uniforms, were not sexualized either on the field or in the media, and were viewed as responsible, autonomous adults. Unlike the women who played alone on all-men's teams, like Croteau, they did not face sexual discrimination or sexual harassment and teammates formed close social bonds.

Croteau's experience as a high school and college player on men's teams illustrates the forms of hostility men resort to when reminding a woman that she has transgressed a gender boundary. Girls are tolerated in baseball only when they are young. After Little League they are pushed into softball. It is significant that boys who played with Croteau on Little League teams did not construct her as feminine "other." Rather they saw her as a teammate who contributed to the success of the team. They also supported her during her lawsuit.

However, Croteau refused to switch to softball after Little League and she faced years of humiliation and isolation beginning in high school. This "othering" entailed being constructed as an inferior player, being benched, being cut from the Varsity high school baseball team, losing her sex discrimination case to the delight of her teammates, and being subjected to a sexualized, polluted atmosphere by her college teammates. Still Croteau continued to choose baseball because, like other girls who persist in playing baseball, she realized that softball is not an equivalent sport. "If it's an equivalent sport, why aren't the guys playing?"[69]

The Silver Bullets were aware of their agency as instigators of cultural change, challenging by example exclusive gender ideologies excluding girls and women from baseball. However, their tenure was too short to have a major impact on the gender exclusive prestige structure of organized baseball, despite the dedication of individuals like Julie Croteau who continued to work toward increasing opportunities for girls to play.

The plan to establish a farm system for young female talent and a women's league to showcase women's talent did not materialize.

It is significant that during the four years of the team's existence, their fans and spectators included boys and men who watched women playing baseball, thus recognizing that women could play the sport competently. Little boys sought their autographs as baseball players who were also women. Women and girls enthusiastically watched them as fans, and the Silver Bullets hoped to inspire some of these girls to play baseball.

Because the Silver Bullets played against men's teams, they had to conform to rather than change the masculine-scripted verbal and nonverbal communication norms on the playing field. Since the players were socialized as women athletes playing on homosocial softball teams, they were used to demonstrating emotions and support on the field using normative feminine codes. However, because they competed against men's teams, they had to be re-socialized by men coaches to adopt male norms for displays of emotions and support during games so as to communicate confidence in their skills and self-control. Players and coaches also had to negotiate gender differences in verbal and nonverbal communication norms on and off the field. The feminine socialization of the young players created greater latitude for emotional expression in the social interactions with men coaches, but displays of emotion needed to be coded in comfortable familial terms to diffuse potential sexuality.

7

"But Ila's for Real": Ila Borders, 1985–2000

During the barnstorming years of the Silver Bullets, another woman in 1993 was awarded the first college baseball scholarship and later pitched three seasons (1997–1999) for men's minor league baseball teams in the Independent Northern League. Southpaw pitcher Ila Borders' origin story is reminiscent of the others in that she developed her throwing and pitching skills from age three in a supportive family environment created by her committed father, Phil, a former minor league player. Phil Borders was thrilled that his daughter was left-handed and envisioned her as a pitcher from the time she was a baby. "My first thought was left-handed pitchers don't grow on trees." By age seven she was able to throw a softball from third to first base. At age ten she rejected softball after attending a Dodgers game where she announced that she wanted to be a pitcher. Her father supported her decision and practiced pitching skills with her for hours on weekends.[1] Borders, like several other "lone ponytails" was motivated enough, talented enough and supported enough to play baseball with boys and men continuously. Although other women players such Alta Weiss, Jackie Mitchell and Toni Stone were also given formal opportunities as children to develop their baseball skills with boys and continuously played with men, Borders, like Julie Croteau, was a child of the post–1972 Title IX era. She was the only girl on her Little League, Little League Majors, junior high school, high school and college teams prior to pitching in the all-men's professional Independent Northern League.

Because Borders played baseball with boys continuously from 1985 to 2000 she provides another longitudinal case study of the unfolding, complex, existential dimensions of gender dichotomy in baseball. Borders could also have been one of the Little League stars that Bob Hope had referred to in connection with creating opportunities for continued development for girls. During her initial years playing Little League and in the Little League Majors and Majors All Stars, Borders was accepted by her boy teammates and coaches, who viewed her as a valuable asset to the team rather than as female "other." Borders' Little League coaches were impressed by her strong pitching arm and powerful hitting.

However, similar to other gender or race pioneers in baseball, she was treated with hostility by opposing teams who threw pitches or rocks at her and she faced hostility from spectators, principally the parents of boy players. "The Little League mothers were the toughest on me" for challenging gender norms by playing a male sport instead of dolls or tea parties. An example of the hostility was: "Go back to Barbie dolls. Stick with your tea party. Who the --- do you think you are." As a result of these confrontations with parents, Phil Borders became a protective "coach, mentor, friend and agent" to his daughter. He advised her to keep her long hair, told her that she would have to work harder than the boys and attempted to place her in supportive, quiet school environments.[2] Like Black players before her who "turned the other cheek" to racial slurs, it was through sports that Borders learned the value of discipline, motivation, and hard work while ignoring hostile negative comments and playing environments.

At Whittier Christian Junior High School, Borders was the only girl to try out for the baseball team in sixteen years and the first girl to make the team. Her coach Rolland Esslinger recognized her talents and encouraged her aspirations to pitch in the minor leagues. "For that age, her speed was above average, and she had a really good curve ball. She spotted her pitches well, and her slow pitches were wicked — hard for hitters to hit. She was smart and knew where to throw the ball and what would get hitters out."[3] Esslinger's support of Borders was significant in her development and she maintained a correspondence with him for many years. She worked hard, practicing overtime. He worked hard to keep the spotlight off his shy player. Borders was also accepted by her teammates and their parents as her talent contributed to the success of the team that was undefeated for two seasons. "She had proved herself such a good player that she wasn't viewed as a joke." Borders earned MVP honors and set records.[4]

Puberty is a liminal or transitional time in the life cycle when many girls abandon their tomboy aspirations and behavior and when boys often construct their oppositional masculinity through participation on homosocial sports teams. Borders did not abandon her aspirations to play baseball and male acceptance boosted her confidence, allowing her to experience an androgynous athleticism. "It was still cool to be an athletic female." Boys playing against her, however, did not find it cool to be struck out by a girl.[5] Through dedicated participation Borders learned commitment to the team and experienced the satisfaction of athletic competence and competition. Borders also played Little League Senior Division, played on a town league team, and joined an adult men's semi-pro team to toughen her resolve.

At Whittier Christian High School, the coach, Steve Randall, already knew of her and many of her teammates had played either with or against her. Her presence on the mound was familiar, smoothing her freshman year transition. Still Randall questioned whether she would be accepted by her teammates. Borders' athleticism was respected by her coach and teammates who commended her mental toughness and work ethic, rising at 5 A.M. to run and to weight train. Randall called her "warrior." "I often think if more of the guys in the minors had her determination and commitment, they'd make it."[6]

However, playing baseball on a boy's high school team represents a more significant violation of male privilege than junior high school teams since college and minor league scouts are present, looking for talent to recruit. Randall's integrity was questioned by other coaches who viewed Borders as a publicity gimmick, a familiar stigma plaguing Borders (and other women baseball players) throughout her career. Parents criticized the Borders for allowing their daughter to play with teenage boys and adult men. Still, in spite of these negative comments, Borders excelled, winning MVP honors her senior year and achieving a winning record of 16–7.

Unfortunately, Borders' athletic achievements did not increase her popularity among her female peers as they usually do with boys. Although one study of adolescents' attitudes toward gender transgression by males into female-dominated sports suggested greater tolerance among girls, this was not Borders' experience.[7] Borders confronted social isolation among her peers and the denigration of her athletic abilities. Although Borders characterized herself as "an introvert" she was bothered by her social isolation from high school girls who were preoccupied with boys and their appearance and from the camaraderie of her teammates off the diamond. While some girls encouraged her, others questioned why she persisted in playing a man's sport. The negative treatment she received from girls, a pattern that continued throughout her career, permanently damaged her trust in women. "Girlfriends and mothers of opposing players are the worst.... They're the ones who've threatened her life, told her she'd better watch her back, and forced her to seek a kind and willing soul after the game to help her get to her car safely."[8]

College scouts were indeed watching Ila after the local newspaper reported on her accomplishments. She was the first woman to be awarded a college scholarship to play baseball for Southern California College, a small quiet Christian college in Costa Mesa. Coach Charlie Phillips stated: "I had her pitch against my top lineup. She only gave up one run in three innings. She was tough mentally on the field."[9] Although Borders' first coach, Charlie Phillips, a former southpaw pitcher, was a supporter and eager to sign her ("She's something special"), college-level baseball exposed her to the full range of sanctions for violating gender separation in sports and to a deluge of media attention. Both were difficult for her emotionally. This time Phillips was accused of signing Borders as a publicity gimmick. He countered, "I don't sign anybody who cannot pitch. I'm not in the game for publicity. If she can get outs, who cares if she's male or female?"[10] Many cared. At her pitching debut in front of 500 spectators and the full spectrum of sports media, the first batter spiked his bat when he flied out. Borders threw 104 pitches during nine innings, winning 12–1. "With this game, the pony-tailed athlete made history. Ila became the first female to pitch a complete game for a men's college team. When the game ended, Ila had several strike outs and many new fans."[11]

While some opposing team players respected Borders, others continued to subject her to abusive names and profanities during games. Her own teammates resented the media attention she received during her freshmen year and repeatedly threw balls at her back during workouts. "Before games, opposing coaches would corner Phillips and whisper, 'You're not throwing Ila today are you?' Privately, not a single coach or player could stomach losing to a woman pitcher." Opposing players "were very abusive. They were calling Ila names and using profanities throughout the game." Her teammates could be abusive also due to their resentment of the media attention she received. Borders, who never strongly identified as a woman athlete, or as a feminist, discovered that to everyone else her gender was paramount. She also experienced social rejection from her former college friends and isolation from teammates, resulting in her feeling "completely alone."[12]

After returning to Southern California College from playing summer baseball in Canada, where again she felt lonely, Borders learned that Coach Phillips was fired. He was replaced by a coach who was unreceptive to women on the team and she lost her place on the roster as a starting pitcher. After spending most of her time on the bench she transferred to Whittier College in her senior year and pitched regularly.[13]

While at Whittier in 1997 owner Mike Veeck offered Borders a tryout with his Saint Paul Saints of the Independent Northern League. Although the season was sold out, Veeck still had to defend his decision to sign Borders as a player rather than as a publicity stunt. "Borders' only interest is playing baseball, just like the 26 men who will emerge from the home clubhouse next Thursday morning. But they will be presumed competent until their skills prove otherwise. Borders will be a sideshow in the Saints' circus until her skills prove otherwise."[14] Borders' first preseason game for the Saints was watched by Jim Wadley, owner of the opposing team, the Duluth-Superior Dukes. He recalled: "She struck out our first batter. It went from a joke on the bench to a very serious pitcher who was throwing strikes. I watched her for two days — her conduct, posture, handling of the press and the crowds. I told the Saints manager that if he doesn't sign her, I'm interested." Within a month Ila was traded to the Dukes.[15]

When Veeck's manager Marty Scott approved her, two other managers of Northern League teams responded in negative ways, reminiscent of Eleanor Engle in 1952. Doug Cimunic threatened to pull his team from the field if she pitched and Ed Nottle referred to her as "that thing." Borders was further objectified by teammates and fans of both sexes who asked her out.[16] However, she was also very popular with fans who chanted her name when she appeared on the mound. When Veeck traded Borders to the Dukes his young daughter was furious.

Unfortunately Borders' appearances for the Saints were few (six innings) and her earned run average high (7.50) and in June she was traded to a last place team, the Duluth-Superior Dukes. She was mostly used as a relief pitcher when a win or loss was certain. The Dukes called her "Paws" since her hands were large. On her new team she initially drew media attention, but more significantly, in this less pressured environment, she enjoyed tremendous fan support, especially with young girls who emailed and wrote to her. She also became the first woman credited with a win in a men's regular season minor league game. Unlike the barnstorming Silver Bullets, Borders established a strong fan base in Duluth as revealed by a local journalist and photographer: "I submit that the game is more than wins and losses, more than individual and team statistics, but about investing in the fans and communities who support the game. Ila invested her talent and heart in our community, and the fans appreciate it."[17]

In her second season with the Dukes, Doug Cimunic again complained that Borders' high ERA could "taint the quality of the league."[18] She still threatened the oppositional masculinity of male players and her pitching coach Steve Shirley had "psychological" work to do with her teammates to accept her, an experience that remained elusive.

Several factors contributed to Borders' difficulties fitting in with and being accepted by her teammates: their resistance to her presence as a player; her exclusion from bonding in the dugout, locker room and bus; her own inclination to keep to herself; and her Christian faith. Locker rooms are key settings for social interactions among players. As a woman, Borders obviously changed and showered elsewhere, rarely entering the locker room. "So much happens in here, like when guys talk. This is where the bonding takes place. Its hard for her to bond with us because she can't really come in here."[19] She knocked on the locker room door and called out "housekeeping" to forewarn her teammates before team meetings, read on the bus, and avoided partying. When invited by the manager to watch television in the locker room with her teammates she refused. In the bullpen, where she spent most of her time, she listened to endless stories about sexual encounters. During her second season she began to join in for post-game beer and pizza and she became friends with men who had also experienced marginality: a Jew, an African American and a closeted gay man.[20]

Opposing batters still dreaded the humiliation of facing a woman on the mound and striking out. Larry See, the Duke's manager in 1999, had faced Borders. "Coming up against her is a no-win situation ... if you get a base hit; you're expected to off a woman. And if you don't ... you look like a fool." Catcher Chris Coste stated, "It's almost unexplain-

In 1997, left-handed pitcher Ila Borders was signed by the Duluth Superior Dukes, an independent league team. On July 9, 1998, Borders was the first woman named as a starting pitcher in a regular season minor league game (courtesy of Saint Paul Saints).

able, the feeling you get when you look up at her and she's coming for her wind-up, her hair's flying around."[21]

Ila Borders was put on revocable waivers by the Dukes in her third season and retired from the Zion Pioneerzz of the Western Baseball League in 2000 after playing baseball for seventeen seasons. Her pitching philosophy was summarized by Jean Hastings Ardell: "as you would expect of a 5-foot-10, 165-pound pitcher, is to pitch with her head. 'I change speeds and keep the ball low. I'm a close observer of every batter. During batting practice, I'll watch to see how he pumps the bat. Does he pump it high or low?— that's a natural preference. What are his strengths and weaknesses? Is he double-play material, tending to hit ground balls? When I throw the curve, does he flinch. I watch the little things.'"[22]

Borders' case poignantly illustrates the complex intersectional divisions that exist among women as many were hostile to her attempts to deviate from established gender norms and transgress into the male preserve of baseball. Her case also illustrates how emotionally complex success can be for girls and women. Similar to other adolescent girls who exhibit outstanding academic, athletic or artistic achievement and intense commitment to their chosen interests, Borders was faced with a difficult dilemma: achievement and affiliation are often mutually exclusive. Affiliation or social acceptance, particularly among adolescents, is often based on conformity to norms or expectations and these are deeply permeated by gender ideologies.

When girls choose to participate in sports classified as male — baseball, football, wrestling — they risk losing their girlfriends. One such athletic girl who played Little League baseball and tackle football, Sharon Lennon, stated, "They liked me when we spent time alone. We could act, naturally, without fear of being judged. However, in the clique I was 'weird' and often shushed or simply told to shut up because I was detracting from their group statement. They were girls who knew how to fit in, and I was not." Lennon gradually withdrew from her friendships with girls ("They were exhausting me") and hung out with boys in her neighborhood who were willing to play street hockey or football with her.[23]

Girls also receive contradictory messages about success. On the one hand we encourage girls to aspire to do whatever they choose, yet on the other hand there are structural constraints that limit girls' aspirations and their ability to achieve. These include constructions of femininity that preclude girls being too competitive, being too assertive and achieving success at the expense of other girls and boys which separates them from solidarity with their peers. Girls often do not fear success itself but rather fear the social isolation they associate with success.[24] In Borders' view, "My personal opinion about it is that we're taught to be victims ... when women see other women out there being successful, they're threatened. Whereas I think many men, like my boyfriend, like to see a strong woman."[25] Thus, both women and men breathe the polluted air of sexism.

Borders' experiences as the only woman playing on men's professional teams are remarkably similar to earlier players, revealing the persistent challenges associated with pioneering individuals who cross gender boundaries and are exposed to the stress created by intense media attention. Borders struggled against being regarded as a gimmick rather than a competitive athlete; with hostility from female peers, male teammates, opposing players and occasionally coaches and fans; and with emotional abuse, sexual harassment, exclusion from camaraderie with teammates in the locker room and after games, and she dressed in gender-neutral clothes to avoid being sexualized. Nevertheless, like the other "lone pony-tails" Borders enjoyed her athletic competence and emphasized the positive support she received from spectators: "I've been spit on, had beer thrown on me and been sworn at and was hit 11 times out of 11 at-bats while in college. But the memories I have are the ovations when I would run in from the bullpen."[26]

The women players — Stone, Johnson, Croteau, Borders — who played on men's professional teams had remarkably similar experiences since the structure of power relations governing sport is remarkably persistent. All accepted the masculine merit-based criteria for defining athletic ability and success, coped with the sexually charged speech norms of their male teammates, assumed an androgynous persona to blend into the team by wearing men's uniforms, sought no special treatment or favors as women and desired only to blend in and be judged on their merits as ballplayers. They and other women athletes confronted and continue to cope with the paradox of hegemonic feminine body types, demeanor and dress visually displayed everywhere in the visual media and their own athletic counterparts that are more androgynous or masculine. Although one of Borders' male teammates wished that "she'd look more like a girl and wear a dress sometimes," Borders rejected this attempt to feminize her and set her apart from her teammates. "Wear a dress on a bus with twenty-five ballplayers? I don't think so. During the season, I want to blend in as much as I can. I live in my uniform, my warm-ups."[27] Toni Stone would have agreed.

8

He-Sport and She-Sport: The Origins and Infrastructure of Gender Exclusion in Amateur Baseball

The dearth of professional women baseball players is a direct consequence of an absent infrastructure to support girls' continuous development of baseball skills beginning in childhood. It remains in this section to trace and analyze the cultural assumptions and structural barriers that produced and reproduce this phenomenon. Historically, the identification of baseball as a "He-sport" and softball as its "She-sport" alternative had its roots in the golden era of baseball and the Progressive Era of the 1880s in the United States.

Merrie Fidler locates the origins of softball or indoor baseball in late-nineteenth-century urban Chicago where outdoor baseball needed to be modified to meet the specific ecological and built environmental conditions of that city. Not only was the weather a deterrent to outdoor baseball, the eradication of large open spaces, due to the unregulated expansion of capitalist development of the built environment and the rapid influx of European immigrants and southern African Americans moving to Chicago, who needed housing, made outdoor baseball impractical. By 1892 there were 100 indoor baseball leagues in Chicago, whose spectators and players were gentlemen "of the best classes." The lower classes played baseball in sandlots and increasingly on smaller diamonds as indoor baseball moved outside as a viable modified substitute.[1]

Modified baseball, indoor baseball, "playground ball," or softball with its larger, softer ball and smaller diamond dimensions was first played by urban children on settlement house playgrounds such as the Hull House playground in Chicago. The institutional expansion of softball began on these settlement house playgrounds in the Midwest and was the result of the efforts of social reformers including Jane Addams, founder of Hull House in Chicago, Jacob Riis of New York and Joseph Lee of Boston, who were concerned with improving the living conditions, health and assimilation of poor immigrants and their children in their expanding cities. These reformers were leading advocates for the establishment of playgrounds for urban children across the nation to bring healthy recreation, light and fresh air into poor, working-class neighborhoods. According to Fidler, although settlement house athletic programs focused on boys, it is likely that interested girls also began to play indoor baseball or softball on playgrounds with their brothers and neighborhood friends.[2] At first softball went by the names of women's baseball, playground baseball, mush ball, and kitten ball, each played with somewhat different rules. The sport was eventually named softball by Walter Hakanson, a Denver YMCA official.

While playgrounds and their associated forms of recreation were initially seen as an educational tool to mold the social and ethical character of urban boys, by 1910 this concern also included girls. As the first-wave feminist movement spread during the Progressive Era to extend the franchise to women, it became more accepted that girls also needed to learn the democratic values of cooperation and loyalty. Further, the benefits of exercise for girls were gaining increasing acceptance among educators. By 1899 indoor baseball was gaining popularity in various Chicago high schools, and by 1917 the sport was a regular playground activity for girls. By 1926, in response to growing class antagonism, employers also began to sponsor recreational activities for their employees, including women's softball teams that grew in popularity throughout the 1930s and 1940s. In the 1940s there were approximately 500,000 men's and women's softball teams in the United States.[3]

Despite the rapid growth of softball teams, the norms governing athletic conduct for women in educational institutions differed considerably from those governing softball tournaments played in public parks. The position of professional physical educators and the National Amateur Athletic Federation about women's athletic endeavors still reflected Victorian constructions of gender roles and presumptions of women's biological frailty. They discouraged extramural sports and competitiveness since athleticism presumably posed threats to women's physical and reproductive health and served no domestic purpose. In contrast the rules governing highly competitive women's public softball tournaments were the same as those governing men's. The National Softball Association and the Amateur Softball Association encouraged public intercity, regional and national championships which were advertised and charged admission.[4]

With the number of softball teams for men and women growing rapidly in the decades before World War II, the necessity to standardize rules of play became apparent. The National Amateur Playground Association began establishing a set of standardized rules for modified baseball in 1908, but the process was not complete until 1923 when Joseph Lee, president of the Playground and Recreation Administration, appointed a committee to standardize the rules of playground ball. This committee grew into the Joint Rules Committee on Softball by 1934. Representatives from a number of organizations including the Amateur Softball Association formed in 1933 and National Softball Association standardized rules for softball teams that numbered 760,000 by 1935.[5] In 1926 Gladys Palmer also published a modified set of rules for girls' baseball. She believed that a modified, less strenuous version of baseball with smaller base paths had educational merit for girls. Girls were encouraged to play modified baseball or softball in schools, and on smaller playground diamonds, while boys were encouraged to play baseball. By 1933 the Amateur Softball Association made the term "softball" official. It was a game distinct from baseball and accepted as an appropriate female sport.[6] Nevertheless, the Amateur Softball Association stressed that softball was a game that everyone could play and it sponsored tournaments for amateurs. Its first tournament with fifteen women's teams was in 1933. The National Softball Association was a semi-professional organization.

This process of standardization clearly distinguished the rules of play for baseball and softball creating different games. During these years amateur baseball also expanded. By the 1850s in New York, adult baseball teams were so plentiful that dozens of affiliated junior clubs for boys were formed. Baseball was promoted as a means to solve social problems since school classrooms were considered not to be a sufficient outlet for young masculine energy. Baseball could maintain physical health, keep boys out of trouble, and develop sound character and morals. Schools began organizing athletic programs and by the 1850s baseball was a part of the curriculum. By 1900, when millions of children attended public schools, most American boys were exposed to baseball. At this time girls in public schools also had the opportunity to play baseball. Schools were joined by the YMCA, local businesses, churches and colleges that sponsored local baseball teams for boys.[7]

While softball was promoted as an inclusive sport that was well suited for women, amateur baseball in these years was intent on formally codifying gender exclusion. In 1914, the National Amateur Baseball Federation set the standard for baseball as a boys' sport. American Legion Baseball modified their handbook to exclude girls after 1929, and Little League Baseball was conceived as a sport for boys from its inception, formally excluding girls between 1939 and 1974.[8]

One of the most significant moments in the establishment of codified barriers to exclude girls from amateur baseball centered around Margaret Gisolo of Blanford, Indiana, a close-knit coal mining community. In 1928 Margaret Gisolo, a second basemen and pitcher on the newly formed National Junior Baseball program of the American Legion, was barred from play due to her sex. The American Legion junior baseball program was begun in 1925 and conceived from its inception as a boys' program designed for players through age sixteen. Its goals were to extend "athletic competition to more boys in America" and to "forward physical development, teach good sportsmanship and make boys better American citizens." The program spread rapidly and had the enthusiastic support of major league baseball that recognized it as a source of potential talent. Under the Commissioner of Baseball, Kenesaw Mountain Landis, $20–50,000 a year was contributed to the program, partly to finance regional and national championships. By 1946 over 161 professional players were produced by the program. No explicit thought was given to girls playing on these teams.[9]

Margaret Gisolo was taught to play baseball by her older brother, a semi-pro and minor league player. Unlike her two older sisters, Margaret loved playing baseball, and she excelled. She pitched for her school team and played sandlot games after school. When the opportunity to play for the American Legion junior team arose in 1928 when she was fourteen, she jumped at the chance. Margaret's team, the Blanford Cubs, played regular games and qualified for the Junior World Series. A photograph of Margaret and her brother depicts them side by side in identical uniforms with no apparent gender distinctions other than Margeret's smaller size.

Representations of Gisolo's athleticism in the sports media are ambiguous. Due to her talent, some descriptions were relatively free of dichotomized gender constructions and focused on her flawless play at second base or as a hitter. Her competent baseball skills and her androgynous appearance enabled her to easily blend in with the other boys on the team. The following recollection suggests this was Margaret's intention: "It was an unusually good team. We worked so well together. There was a feeling of cooperation." After Gisolo contributed the single that drove in the winning run in the twelfth inning of the first game of the county championship between the Blanford Cubs and the rival Clinton Baptists, she was a sensation in the local newspapers. The press was well aware that the novelty of a girl player would sell papers as the following headline reveals: "Girl Player Wins Game in 12th with Single." Unfortunately, some writers constructed her talents in terms that were certain to instigate defensive and divisive responses from the opposing boy's team. The Clinton Baptist team was described in the press as "the first ball club to ever be beaten by a safe hit off a girl's bat in a championship affair."[10]

The losing Baptist team protested the game on grounds that American Legion regulations stated that "any boy was eligible to play" thus inferring that girls were excluded. When the Cubs defeated the Baptists a second time, Robert Bushee, Indiana American Legion state athletic officer, suspended Margaret for six days. During this time Bushee met with Baseball Commissioner Kenesaw Mountain Landis, and it was ruled that Margaret could play for the Cubs since there was no explicit rule barring girls from the teams and "in view of the services of our women in the World War and The American Legion and the American Legion Auxiliary."[11] The Cubs defeated the Baptists in the third game. Margaret's contributions to the Cubs' win included excelling as a second baseman who could easily turn double plays, stealing bases, and driving in runs as a hitter. The team continued to win and move up the tournament ladder. Commissioner Landis sent Margaret an autographed baseball: "To Margaret Gisolo, With my very good wishes."[12]

Margaret Gisolo continued to play well in the tournament games and the novelty of her gender and talent was featured in newspapers across the country. Sportswriters supported the Commissioner's ruling allowing her to play. They followed her progress and celebrated her achievements. "Covering the keystone sack adeptly, the Gisolo girl stabbed one out of the air to start a double play that retired the Baptist nine in the fifth frame, the only inning in which the Clinton nine was threatened."[13] Although Gisolo's athleticism was highlighted in the press by references to her as "Girl Babe Ruth," "Girl Slugger," "prima donna of the diamond," her talent was also constructed as disruptive, a challenge to the masculinity of the boys, rather than as beneficial to the sport since it was assumed that boys would suffer emotionally if beaten during competitions with girls. "The little Italian maid is the cause of considerable disruption in the ranks of the tourney just because she can hit, field and run better than most of the boys her age."[14]

The Blanford team continued to win. In the sectional tournament championship Margaret won the sportsmanship award for her play. After winning the Indiana state title, 14–12, her play was summarized in glowing terms: "It was a powerful hitting attack unleashed by Sungali, Taparo and Margaret Gisolo that carried the Cubs to their margin of victory.... Margaret Gisolo shined with unusual brilliance around the keystone sack, making two sensational catches of line drives, and featuring in one double play. The girl star has not made an error in seven games of tourney play." In seven games of tournament play Margaret was nine hits for twenty-one at bats, a batting average of .429, made ten putouts and twenty-eight assists with no errors.[15]

The Cubs advanced to the national championship in Chicago, and was "probably the biggest thing that ever happened to Blanford." Players and coaches on the team were local celebrities. Although the team lost, Margaret played well. *The New York Times* stated: "Margaret starred in defeat." In her four at-bats she singled, walked, sacrificed, scored a run and batted in a run. In the field she played errorless at second base. "Margaret Gisolo, scintillating girl second baseman on a championship team in a boys' tourney, electrified the Chicago fans with her sensational playing around the keystone bag." Margaret had become a national celebrity featured in newspapers and a short movie sketch was made about her by Movietone News that appeared in theaters. One sportswriter was inspired enough to suggest, "Perhaps it won't be long before some young lady will break into the lineup of a professional baseball team." Her achievements and those by two other young women who excelled at baseball, however, led this journalist to forge a dangerous link between women's suffrage and baseball as evidenced in the headline. "Girls Usurping National Sport: Suffrage Now Extends from Ballot Box to Baseball Diamonds."[16]

Although the small mining town of Blanford was delighted with the team, and Margaret had become a national celebrity, in 1929 a new rule was written excluding girls from playing on American Legion teams. The ruling shocked Gisolo, her team and the Blanford community. The reason given was financial — since more girls wanted to play they would need separate dressing rooms, hotel rooms and chaperons. These were expenses the Legion could not afford. Everyone involved accepted the decision. This rule barring girls from American Legion teams stood until after 1972 when Title IX made such discrimination illegal. Although Gisolo continued to play baseball for another five years for the American Athletic Girls Baseball Club and for Maud Nelson's All Star Ranger Girls Baseball Club, American Legion teams ceased to provide a structural opportunity for girls interested in developing their baseball skills, while they continued to serve this function for boys.[17]

The social and historical context for the emergence and expansion of softball during the Progressive Era and in the 1930s and 1940s was multidimensional. As a sport suitable for urban settings with limited open park spaces, its advocates include progressive activists such as Jane Addams, who were concerned with the welfare of immigrant children in rapidly industrializing American cities like Chicago where open spaces were disappearing in the crush to invest in the city's built environment. This new playground baseball was deemed suitable as an alternative to baseball for women whose bodies were presumed to be inferior in athletic capabilities. The new sport spread rapidly, attracting many women players and men. For men, softball became another sport that they might choose, whereas for women, channels to play baseball were eliminated, restricting their choice to softball.

This restriction solidified when American Legion baseball banned Margaret Gisolo and, thereafter, other girls from participation on their teams for the next 43 years until Title IX was passed in 1972. Since American Legion teams were a significant source of future talent for organized baseball, they received support from the Commissioner of Baseball and major league team managers and scouts. At fourteen, Margaret Gisolo was a player with considerable talent, and acknowledged by all who played with her to be one reason why her team continued to win during tournament games. While it was the novelty of her gender that drew public attention to her talent as a baseball player in the sports media, her talent was genuine and she played at the same level or better than her male teammates. It is unknown how far she might have advanced in organized baseball if given the chance. Instead, after being barred by Commissioner Landis, she joined mixed gender baseball teams operating on the periphery of baseball, such as Maud Nelson's Bloomer Girls team.

The media often treated Gisolo fairly, focusing on her talent as a fielder and pitcher rather than on her feminine charms. However, at times, sportswriters stoked the fire of what Don Sabo has labeled the "myth of coed catastrophe" by inflaming male sensitivity and presumed loss of self-esteem over losing to girls who were/are presumed to be inferior players. This myth assumes that athletic competition between or among both sexes will physically and emotionally harm participating girls, because as physical inferiors they do better amongst themselves, and harm the boys who face humiliation and lose self-esteem when they lose to girls. The evidence suggests that Gisolo thoroughly enjoyed playing on the Blanford team partly because of her talent and partly because she was accepted by her teammates, coaches and community. The stated reason for barring Gisolo was the financial burden on the American Legion organization posed by the need for separate facilities for girl players. Although this reason was accepted by all, it is reasonable to assume that during the tournament games, the privacy issue was successfully handled by Gisolo and her coaches. Excluding girls was a premature move since it was uncertain how many girls would seek to join boys' American Legion teams. The "myth of coed catastrophe" resurfaced in the 1970s to justify the rationales for excluding girls from Little League Baseball.

9

"It's Baseball Lib": Little League Baseball and Public Americana, 1939–1974

The most significant organization globally dedicated to the development of baseball skills in children and adolescents is Little League Baseball. Little League Baseball was established in the small lumbering town of Williamsport, Pennsylvania, in 1939 by Carl Stotz, who adopted the existing American Legion structure for organizing local teams and tournaments. For the first thirty years the organization and its teams were male with no thought given to girls as players and no need for rules specifically barring girls from playing. According to founder Carl Stotz, "When we started the Little League the idea of a girl playing baseball, even with other girls, was simply unthinkable."[1] Although girls and women had been playing baseball for decades, when Stotz was asked in 1944, one year after the establishment of the AAGPBL, to organize a baseball league for girls in memory of his daughter, Little League Baseball for boys was all that he could handle. "I regretted not being able to organize baseball for girls."[2] The end of World War II led to an expansion of Little League with parents playing gender-appropriate roles — fathers teaching their sons to play and mothers assisted by their daughters running concession stands, painting fences and joining ladies' auxiliaries. For Little League the issue of girls playing baseball did not emerge until after the program expanded beyond Pennsylvania. In 1951 a single line made its first appearance in the Little League regulations. "Girls not eligible under any conditions."[3]

In the 1950s and 1960s, under the leadership of Peter J. McGovern, Little League Baseball was an overtly ideological organization, serving as a platform for Cold War conservative political and economic commentary promoting "Americanism." For example, J. Edgar Hoover stated in a 1950 letter to Little League management that "a clean healthy body begets a clear healthy mind and the two are absolute essentials to good Americanism." Herbert Brownell Jr., Attorney General of the United States, was quoted in a 1954 Little League World Series Official Program: "The young Americans who compose the Little League will prove a hitless target for the peddlers of godless ideology."[4]

This fusion of masculine sport with patriotism at the height of the Cold War led to Little League becoming the only sports program granted a federal charter. On the silver anniversary of the organization in 1964, President Lyndon Johnson signed Public Law 88–378 granting Little League a Congressional Charter of Federal Incorporation. Since the organization is a quasi-governmental agency, all revenue is tax-exempt. Its mission and values should support those of the United States government and an annual financial and philosophical report must be filed with the Judiciary Committee of the House of Representatives.

The Congressional charter charged Little League with didactic responsibilities beyond teaching baseball skills. The original objectives of the organization were: (1) "to promote, develop, supervise and voluntarily assist in all lawful ways the interest of boys who will participate in Little League"; (2) "to help and voluntarily assist boys in developing qualities of citizenship, sportsmanship and manhood"; (3) "Using the discipline of the native American game of baseball to teach spirit and competitive will to win, physical fitness through individual sacrifice, the values of team play and wholesome well-being through healthful and social association with other youngsters under proper leadership." Little League games were "moral events" where "character, courage and loyalty are central moral values."[5]

Sports were recognized as a significant socializing agent in teaching Americanism as a set of positive values to promote responsible citizenship. These values were gendered masculine, and were to be learned by boys through participation in homosocial sports. Further, the Little League organization at the local level is enmeshed in an institutional network including education, government, local businesses, houses of worship and law enforcement that support and further legitimize the link among sport, gender and political ideologies. Local businesses and government agencies are asked to sponsor teams and local politicians are invited to throw out the ceremonial first pitch.

Despite the firm policy of Little League Headquarters to "preclude the feminine touch," girls continued to play on Little League teams in the 1950s and 1960s.[6] In 1950, a year before the rule barring girls from Little League, Kathryn Johnson posed as a boy and used a nickname to try out and make a Little League team in Corning, New York. She tucked her short hair under her cap and used the name "Tubby." After making the team, she revealed her sex to the coach and played on the team since the manager considered her good enough to play and it was a novelty.[7] In 1958, a Little League All-Star team traveled to Puerto Rico to play the sons of naval officers stationed there. The "skinny pitcher" was a girl, Donna Terry, who struck out the first three batters. When her ponytail betrayed her sex she was declared ineligible and barred from playing baseball with boys.[8] In 1963 eight-year-old Nancy Lotsey played for the New Jersey Small-Fry League as a pitcher. According to *Life* magazine, in her debut game Nancy "hit a home run, struck out three opposing batsmen and was the winning pitcher. And thanks to Nancy's fastball, the team went on to chalk up a 10–1 record for the season and, with it, the league championship."[9] Nancy lived next to the playground where the team practiced. Interviewed in 1974 by *The New York Times* during the heat of the suits brought against Little League Baseball by girls seeking to play on boys' teams, Nancy reflected: "I loved it. There was no psychological damage. I could play better than most of the boys on the team."[10]

Girls were keenly interested in playing Little League Baseball. During the 1960s Robert H. Stirrat was Director of Public Relations for Little League Baseball. In 1968 he received a cogent letter from Norma Young, a girl who wanted to play and challenged him to clearly explain and justify the rule barring her and other girls from playing on Little League teams.[11] "I understand about going by the rule, but who makes the rule and why can't it be changed. In the last letter you didn't give me a good answer. All you said was that it was the rule. I just want a direct answer instead of just by the rule. The least you could do is consider starting a girl's Junior or Little League. If you can't do this, why? If you don't think enough girls want in it, I can start a petition. Please! Try to work out something. Over fifty girls are depending on me and you. Please! Send a letter back telling me why. A few years ago you had a girl on the Little League and she played fine. Consider about the Junior League."

Stirrat's reply to Norma is equally remarkable, revealing the persistence of fabricated cultural constructions of female bodies as physically inferior justifying their exclusion from baseball. "I am sorry that we must tell you once again that Little League is a boy's game and while I am sure that it comes as a disappointment to you, the rules which govern Little League are made by a committee of about 500 men who meet once every two years and only they can make changes which they believe best for Little League. One of the reasons that girls should not play baseball is that it is a game which requires unusual strength, talents which girls do not have and all doctors advise against permitting girls to participate in this kind of strenuous activity. I hope you will try to explain this to the 50 girls who have asked you to write about this. And I am sure there [are] many, many activities in which girls may participate on an equal basis with boys such as swimming, golf and tennis, but sports such as baseball and football are not among these. I know how disappointed you must be if you are a baseball fan but I know you are old enough to understand why rules are made in the best interest of all young people, boys and girls alike." One can only imagine what individual responses the many women previously discussed who already had played baseball with unusual talent would make to Stirrat and Norma.

However, six years later social forces intersected to challenge the legality of the rule barring girls from playing Little League baseball. These included the organized strength of the second-wave feminist movement (referred to by many at the time as Women's Lib, or disparagingly as Libbers) who brought to public attention the multilayered social and cultural affects of institutionalized sexism in our society, the passage of Title IX in 1972 barring discrimination against girls and women in educational institutions and in sports and changes in public opinion regarding the meaning of femininity and roles of women in the public sphere.

Before 1974, it was the standard practice of Little League Headquarters to threaten the revocation of the charter of any local league team allowing girls to play. Revocation of a team's charter meant the team could not call itself a Little League team; the players could not wear the Little League uniform or designation patch on its uniforms, stationery, fund drives etc.; the team would have its uniforms, equipment, bank accounts taken away; the team could not enter Little League championships or All Stars tournaments; and the team could not apply for group accident insurance through Little League.[12]

For example, in 1973 Little League Baseball Inc. revoked the charter of a Ypsilanti, Michigan, Little League team when it allowed twelve-year-old Carolyn King to play on the Ypsilanti Community American Little League "Orioles" team. King and the City of Ypsilanti responded by joining as plaintiffs in a sex discrimination suit filed against Little League Baseball Inc. Since there was no Little League Baseball team for girls, King tried out for the boy's team and was accepted strictly on the basis of her ability. She practiced with the team and was designated by her coach to start in the opening game. One month later Little League Headquarters informed the Ypsilanti Little League that if King remained on the team roster, appeared in uniform with the team, or continued practicing with the team, its charter would be immediately revoked. The community responded by calling a special meeting of the local Little League Board of Directors where they initially decided to drop King from the team so as not to jeopardize the program for about 220 boys. However, at the second special meeting held the next day they decided to reverse their decision and retain King on the team. The city further supported King by withholding the use of city parks and baseball diamonds from organizations that practice any form of discrimination. Little League revoked the charter and the plaintiffs brought suit. The case was dismissed by the U.S. District Court for the Eastern District of Michigan for lack of jurisdiction and the U.S. Court of Appeals ultimately affirmed the dismissal.[13]

Although this case was not precedent setting, it is of considerable social interest for several reasons. First, Carolyn was not marginalized by her teammates or the community. The community viewed her as an athletic child who wished to play baseball rather than a girl seeking to usurp male privilege. She was fortunate to enjoy the support of her team since she "proved herself one of the team's best all-round performers." She also received the support of city officials who joined with her as plaintiff in the case and whose broad support for social justice was demonstrated by their non–discriminatory policy regarding the use of public space. After the case was dismissed the city's officials decided to set up a baseball league of their own with no gender discrimination. Carolyn King, of course, played on the team. Ironically, these inclusive actions by city officials undermined the appeal case. The Appeals Court ruled that no court intervention was necessary since the discriminatory situation that existed in the past had been radically changed by the city prior to appeal.[14] Rather than using the law to further the goal of integration at the societal level, the Court's passive position sidestepped the controversial societal issue of sex discrimination in sports by supporting an individual-level community response.

The second reason why this case is significant involves the comparison with race discrimination. The case law cited by the District Court Judge included a suit, *Statom v. Board of Commissioners*, "wherein two Negro boys were afforded relief after being denied membership in a boy's club on account of their race." Judge Freeman commented: "If the present case were concerned with racial discrimination, defendant Little League, like the boy's club in Statom might well be deemed to have acted under color of law. But the state action is found more readily when racial discrimination is in issue than when other rights are asserted." Other rights, of course, refer to sex discrimination. Judge Freeman rejected that parallel legal responses by the state should exist in cases involving sex and racial discrimination, again inhibiting the law from serving a progressive role in social change. The Appeals Court did not adopt Judge Freeman's opinion, but relied on the actions previously taken by the city to eliminate sex discrimination to affirm the dismissal of the case. "In Statom the plaintiffs sought to enjoin the use by the club facilities until it admitted Negro boys to non–segregated participation in the club activities. This is precisely what the plaintiffs have already done in this case, and without the necessity of court intervention."[15]

Finally, the King case is significant because in legal footnote n1 the Appeals Court mentioned that following oral arguments, published reports indicated that Little League Baseball intended to drop its boy-only policy. It "has eliminated and no longer enforces its former rule which rendered girls ineligible to participate. It has petitioned Congress for an amendment to its charter to declare that girls can play." Although Little League was beginning to read the writing on the wall, they stridently resisted these changes until after the precedent-setting loss of the legal suit filed one year later by N.O.W. (National Organization for Women) against Little League Baseball in 1974.[16]

The precedent-setting case against Little League Baseball that did set in motion progressive social change involved Maria Pepe of Hoboken, New Jersey, the "Birthplace of Baseball." Pepe was represented by Judith Weiss of the Essex County N.O.W., and the 1974 ruling in her favor by Judge Sylvia Pressler broke the gender barrier in Little League baseball. Maria Pepe, then age eleven, was encouraged by her male friends to sign up for a local clubhouse Little League team, the "Young Democrats." The Young Democrats was a social and athletic club in Hoboken whose athletic participants were entirely male. Maria was only five when she started hanging out with boys in her densely populated apartment complex in Hoboken playing baseball, stickball, and wiffle ball with the numerous children living there. Although neither of her two brothers played baseball, like many of the girls described above, Maria was an androgynous "buddy" of the local boys who fully accepted her as a ballplayer and treated her like a sister. "If you'd have asked me what I wanted to be when I grew up, I'd have said a Yankee or Met."[17] She preferred to play baseball with boys since her athletic abilities were superior to most of the local girls and she thoroughly enjoyed the competitive game.

At this time, Hoboken and the surrounding area (known as District Seven) had a population that supported twelve sponsored Little League teams. If one team dropped out, it could be replaced by another, such as the Young Democrats. Team members were provided with schedules, uniforms, equipment and even eyeglasses for children who could not afford these. By word of mouth the community learned of the new team and interested children came to the Club to sign up. A group of local boys who were Maria's friends came and told the team manager, Jimmy Farina, age twenty-five, that there was a girl with them waiting outside. According to Farina, Maria, a sixth grader, looked the part; a tomboy wearing a baseball cap. Her friends told Farina that Maria could play as well as they could and possessed varied skills. "She could not only pitch, but hit and field too." Maria appeared nervous to sign up because of her sex, but Farina encouraged her. He asked her if she could play and if she wanted to play. She did and was given a permission slip to take to her parents.[18]

Several days later at the tryouts Maria demonstrated her skills at pitching, catching and throwing. Farina described her as "overqualified" to make the team, hitting better than most of the boys. After trying out Farina signed her as a starting pitcher, third baseman, and left fielder. Farina stressed that Maria was very focused, knew the game and was committed. Every day after school Maria practiced her fast overhand pitching and her batting precision with her friends.[19] According to Farina, the boys on the team accepted her as a competent team member and opposing team members did as well. The boys just wanted to play, as she did.[20]

For the opening game coach Farina selected Maria as starting pitcher, subjecting him to the opposition of other coaches, parents and Hoboken town officials who argued that he was breaking Little League rules. Farina was oblivious to the rules and ignored the opposition. His attitude was simple and never changed: if she had the skills to play, she could play on his team. When local officials, such as District Seven Little League President Carmine Conti, verbally informed him of the Little League rules concerning girls, he ignored him as well. The Mayor of Hoboken was concerned over the possible revocation of the team charter and the controversy that had ensued in Hoboken, but he also supported Farina's position without openly taking sides. Farina wanted a statement in writing from Little League Headquarters. Prior to the opening game Farina had written to Little League officials to question them if playing Maria was legal. The reply letter stated that it was the opinion of the Eastern Region that it was not recommended that girls bat against hard-throwing boys.

Hoboken recreation supervisor Joseph Polano attempted before the opening game to dissuade the Young Democrats from playing Maria, arguing that the team would lose its Little League charter. Farina stood by his decision and chose to worry about the consequences later. He and his assistant coach James Ryan insisted that Maria was playing because of her skills: "We're not using her to break the sex barrier." Polano announced that the game was illegal and was being played under protest. Coaches insisted on obeying the Little League rules. The opposing Elks team catcher complained, "This is supposed to be a boy's sport." Others felt that if Maria could play other athletic girls they knew should be allowed to play. Parents, many of whom opposed Farina's position, did not confront him openly, but were talking behind the scenes.[21]

Maria played only three games with the Young Democrats before the letter arrived from Little League Headquarters threatening to revoke the team's charter for breaking the ban on playing girls. By this time the local press and the national press had begun to publicize the story and Maria's parents were concerned about Maria's name and their names appearing in the newspapers. Farina and the team stood by Maria with Farina willing to let her stay even if the team lost its charter: "I wasn't no women's libber, but if she was good enough to make the team, I just couldn't see why she shouldn't be allowed to play." Farina offered to let Maria stay with the team and keep score, but she refused, feeling isolated and desiring only to play. Maria knew that others felt something was wrong with her playing baseball, but she also knew she was good enough to play.

Farina came to Maria's house to tell her parents about the Little League decision. He told her parents that he would continue to support her: "I don't know where I was going, but I was with her all the way."[22] Maria cried and turned in her uniform. "I think the hardest part was when they took my uniform away. I didn't feel I was doing anything harmful." "I was stripped of my uniform because I was a girl, not because of an inability to play. As a twelve-year-old, I couldn't stand up for myself and that really hurt."[23] Despite her grief, she did not "want 200 kids mad at me. I'd never come out of my house again." Maria, an innocent child, was hurt and confused. "I used to think either God made a mistake and gave me ability even though I was a girl or everybody else was wrong. Why would He give me a skill if I wasn't allowed to use it?" Maria, whose only desire was to play baseball, was deeply hurt and felt that Little League had "interrupted her childhood way of being." Children are "free spirits" whose talents and interests should be encouraged not encumbered by the gender boundaries constructed by adults.[24]

After Maria's dismissal, Hoboken's Little League charter was reinstated and Little League Headquarters considered the incident closed. Farina continued to manage the team as he did for several years. However, Hoboken is a small community, one square mile in size, and the incident had received national press coverage. The New York Yankees had honored Maria and her family with "Yankee for a day" at Yankee Stadium where they sat close to the dugout and received a Yankee jersey and players' autographs. Fifty Yankee and Mets players were polled by the *New York Times* and 61 percent of Yankees and 70 percent of the Mets supported girls being allowed to play on Little League teams.[25]

As a result of the publicity, the Essex County N.O.W. chapter approached the Pepe family to champion the case. Although her parents could not afford legal fees and were fearful of suing an organization as large and powerful as Little League Baseball, they agreed, knowing how strongly Maria wanted to play. During the case Maria's mother often asked her if she wanted to read the press coverage of the case. Maria always refused, as she was only interested in whether the case had been settled in her favor so she could resume play. Maria also never went to the court, although she wanted to show Judge Pressler that she could play baseball.

It took two years before a favorable ruling was handed down on March 29, 1974, from Sylvia Pressler of the New Jersey Division on Civil Rights. Maria was by then fourteen and too old to play Little League. Although Maria could have attempted to play in the Babe Ruth League, she was too "winded" and decided to leave that fight for someone else.[26] "After the ruling came out, I was too old to play, but my Dad said, 'You have to think about all the girls that will follow.' I don't think I really understood." An understanding of her pivotal role in the evolution of girls' sports came later as an adult. "I'm very sentimental about my youthful experience because it was a little hurtful. It took me a while as an adult to kind of reconcile it. I got caught up in the controversy and I wasn't judged as an individual."[27]

The responses of the Hoboken community toward Maria and her family during the case were more mixed than those in Yipsilanti, Michigan. Farina was not asked to testify in the case but remained supportive, encouraging her to ignore negative comments. Maria, a quiet child, and her family were acutely aware of creating a "commotion" in Hoboken and attracting media attention. Even N.O.W. was unprepared for the media frenzy. Mothers, concerned that their sons would be prevented from playing, stopped Mrs. Angelina Pepe to ask, "Why do you let your daughter play baseball?" "Don't you think your girls ought to be home with you instead?" Some neighborhood children and adults taunted Maria and a man in her apartment building elevator yelled at her: "you're causing all this trouble in town." Letters from priests were sent stating that Maria should not play baseball since it was damaging to the mental health of the boys. They did not voice similar concerns for Maria's mental health.

Maria felt social isolation and disappointment. She was scrutinized and judged both physically and psychologically by the experts testifying at the trial and worried that something was wrong with her for wanting to play baseball. Although Mrs. Pepe regretted causing trouble, she supported her daughter's and other girls' desire to play baseball. Mr. Pasquale Pepe initially told Maria that baseball was a boy's sport, but fully supported her after she made the team. He insisted that his fellow longshoremen in Hoboken also supported Maria. "They all wish they had a daughter who would do the same thing."[28]

It took Maria years before she could visit the Hoboken Little League field and she also kept her distance from Little League Headquarters. "What upset me the most was how hard Williamsport fought to keep girls out."[29] Maria was, however, allowed to keep her baseball cap. Her cap and glove were on display at the Little League Museum in Williamsport, Pennsylvania, and the cap is currently on display at the Baseball Hall of Fame in Cooperstown, New York. In 2004, thirty years after the 1974 ruling, Maria was invited by Little League Baseball to celebrate the decision during the Little League World Series. Maria and her mother, whose attitude she described as "a little reserved," accepted. Maria was escorted to the pitcher's mound by two girls, current players for their Little League teams, where she threw the ceremonial first pitch. She also met Dr. Creighton Hale, a key expert employed by Little League Baseball during her trial who argued against girls playing baseball with boys. After Hale told Maria that "my granddaughters play," she felt closure for the first time.[30]

Between 1972 and 1974 fifty-seven lawsuits were filed against Little League Baseball, prompting concerted efforts by management to defend its boys-only policy. Little League correspondence from these years reveals the organization's defensive strategy. "Little League Baseball has been in existence for thirty-five years and suddenly finds itself overnight accused of being a monster — a parasite and an enemy of womanhood."[31] The perspective of Little League Baseball was that expert evidence confirming greater female susceptibility to injury was being overlooked by feminists to advance their own agendas. "Sitting in the background is the ever present and ubiquitous N.O.W. whose ambitions have launched a crusade against Little League Baseball and who apparently would be willing to destroy it if they do not get their way."[32] Groups opposed to the women's movement agreed. For example, the San Francisco–based International Anti-Women's Liberation League, who described themselves as "an organization for those who believe Women Should be Women and men should be MEN — Ah — MEN," stated that Little League teams had the right to discriminate as did other private clubs.[33]

The evidence and rulings in the two pivotal legal cases against Little League Baseball Inc. — N.O.W./Maria Pepe and Allison "Pookie"

Fortin — both argued in the spring of 1974, will be analyzed since they illustrate a changing social and legal climate for athletic girls and women after the passage of Title IX. They also illustrate how cultural changes in gender ideology can lag behind legal precedents and how real and fabricated biological "facts" can be used to justify ideologies for the exclusion or inclusion of women in sports. At issue in the two cases was the construction of children's bodies under age thirteen and the underlying assumption that because the female body is inferior to the male body, girls need to be protected from inevitable injury. Robert Stirrat, Director of Public Relations for Little League Baseball, consistently reiterated, "our directors have taken a firm stand that there is no place for girls in the Little League."[34]

In the N.O.W./Pepe case several experts on physiology and psychology were sought to provide supporting evidence for their position to exclude girls. Dr. Thomas Johnson argued that although women have long participated in athletics with and without men, baseball is an exception. Johnson, a former Little League player, coach, umpire and physician, justified the exclusion of girls from boys Little League teams for the following reasons:

1. The reaction and movement time of males is faster, providing them with advantages when attempting to avoid being hit by a pitch when batting. "If girls were permitted to play in Little League two mounds would be necessary. Boys would pitch to boys from one mound (46 feet) and to girls from another mound which would be greater than 46 feet from home plate."

2. Males have greater muscle mass than girls due to male hormones. The number of muscle cells in the male body increases fourteen times between the ages of two months to sixteen years, where as for girls the increase is ten times. Males are stronger than females.

3. At puberty there is a marked difference in bone strength, with the length and mass of bone greater in males meaning that the breaking load of compact bones, long bones, and vertebrae is less for females.

4. Male metabolism is higher with more red corpuscles, hemoglobin, and higher specific gravity of blood, resulting in the superior athletic ability of the male.

5. "Females are more emotional than males and there is an innate basis for a sex difference in emotionality. Women's greater affectability is based upon differences in physical make-up, physiological functions

and the effect of the standards of society upon emotions. Environmental influences and pressures increase the emotional instability of women."[35]

Johnson concluded that girls would sustain more injuries in baseball than boys due to slower reaction times and lesser strength. Their breast tissue was particularly vulnerable to injury and the risk of cancer, and a special protective brassiere must be developed since none to date would sustain the impact of a baseball. Although Johnson welcomed increasing opportunities for girls and women, he lamented the decline of single-sex activities. We should not "overlook the importance of providing some islands of separation between grade school boys and girls." These are years when gender identity is consolidated, when children are more comfortable with same-sex adults as well as friends. "Same sex organizations provide a sense of security through group strength and identification which prepares them for later boy-girl relationships of adolescence. Girls share their own 'slang,' problems, feelings of equality and superiority over boys while boys discover their masculinity and handle their anxiety over dealing with more mature advanced girls." Johnson rejected bisocial sports teams because they are largely negative experiences for girls and boys.[36]

At Maria Pepe's trial, Johnson's evidence of sex differences favoring males along with other studies relating to comparative bone strength, muscle strength and reaction time were presented by Dr. Creighton J. Hale, physiologist, executive vice president of Little League and its director of research. Hale argued, based on Japanese studies of cadaver bones of persons aged eighteen to eighty, that the risk of injury to girls was greater. The State's expert witness, Dr. Torg, a specialist in pediatric orthopedics rejected Hale's conclusions, noting that between the ages of eight to ten the weight and height of boys and girls is about the same with girls surpassing boys between ages ten to twelve. Although Dr. Torg agreed that boys' muscles have more fibers, other factors were more relevant than strength in eight- to twelve-year-old children affecting safety. These include "general systemic physiologic maturation," in which girls aged eight to twelve are ahead of boys, levels of training, experience, motivation, nutrition and home environment. Dr. Hale acknowledged that some girls would have the skill to play baseball with boys, and he testified that Little League has various leagues graded according to the ability of the player, so that girls could be rated to play with their peers of either sex. He was still concerned that the less-skilled girls would be more apt to suffer injury even when playing with less-skilled boys. Torg concluded that a significant proportion of girls eight to twelve years old were physically capable of playing Little League with boys, but that after age thirteen there is a widening gap in athletic abilities. Prior to age thirteen the physical performance of girls is equal to boys.[37]

Finally, following Johnson, Hale argued that it is psychologically beneficial to provide "islands of privateness" for same-sex children to socialize. Little League Baseball teams could serve this purpose for boys with girls served on separate softball teams. The State's psychiatric expert disagreed with the need for sex-segregated activities at ages eight to twelve. He thought sex-integrated baseball would contribute to the mental health of children of both sexes.

Hearing Examiner Sylvia Pressler of the New Jersey Civil Rights Division, taking the initiative to forge comparative links between gender discrimination and rationales for race and religious exclusion, agreed with the State psychiatrist: "I have no doubt there are reputable psychologists who would agree with the birds of a feather theory. However, the extension of that theory is that whites like to be with whites, blacks like to be with blacks, and Jews like to be with Jews. That whole theory is in contradiction with the laws of this state.... We must start somewhere in reversing the trends in this society. Girls should be treated no differently than boys. The sooner that little boys realize that little girls are equals and that there will be many opportunities for a boy to be bested by a girl, the closer they will be to better mental health."[38]

The Appeals Court concurred that "the psychological testimony on both sides was too speculative to rest any fact-finding on it ... we are clear that there is no substantial psychological basis in the record to warrant a conclusion that the game is reasonably restricted to boys in this age bracket."[39] The Appeals Court also concluded "that girls of ages 8–12 are not as a class subject to a materially greater hazard of injury while playing baseball than boys of that age group." The court's position stressed the "underlying purposes of sex discrimination legislation as a current social phenomenon ... to emancipate the female sex from stereotyped conceptions as to its limitations embedded in our *mores* but discordant with current rational views as to the needs, capabilities and aspirations of the female, child or woman."[40]

N.O.W. had argued that Little League as an organization was under the legal jurisdiction of the new Title IX because it used public recreational facilities and in some cases received town funds. The court agreed, ruling that Little League baseball fields are places of public accommodation because the invitation is open to children in the community at large to play at them. Similar to the American Legion before them, Little League was concerned about the privacy of the girls, stating they would need separate accommodation. This concern was also bogus since children changed their clothes for play at home. There was "no significant hazard of breach of privacy in the context of bisexual Little League baseball."[41]

Finally, the court rejected that the goals of Little League Baseball to develop "qualities of citizenship, sportsmanship and manhood" would be impaired by the admission of girls. "Assuming 'manhood' ... means basically maturity of character, as does 'womanhood,' we fail to discern how and why little girls are not as appropriate prospects for learning citizenship and sportsmanship and developing character, as are boys.... We note the justified characterization by the hearing officer of Little League as a 'piece of public Americana.' It has become synonymous with children's baseball—a sport which the Little League handbook proudly claims as America's national game. The record evidences the fact that substantial numbers of young girls want to partake in it and are qualified to do so competitively with boys of the same age. The logic of the statutory support for their aspirations is compelling."[42]

While this ruling eliminated the gender barrier for girls wishing to play Little League baseball, the dissenting opinion of J. A. D. Meanor was prophetic as to how the gender barrier would be permanently reconstituted by bifurcating Little League sponsored programs into baseball for boys and softball for girls. Meanor focused on the emerging physical differences between the sexes after age thirteen: "There is virtual concession in this record that from puberty females cannot successfully compete with males in this contact sport. There may be a few isolated females of exceptional athletic ability who can, but for classification purposes they safely may be ignored. Generally, then, it will be true that females, after reaching adolescence, will be unable to capitalize upon baseball skills acquired during childhood unless they do so in all-female competition which is not now available. Males, on the other hand, may continue in the sport until the approach of middle age and perhaps thereafter. There is nothing unreasonable in the position of Little League in desiring not to teach girls a skill that is only temporarily useful.... One may consider the impact upon the girl who devotes several years to baseball only to find that upon the onset of puberty she can no longer play.... It seems to me reasonable to have a policy, which considering today's available athletic resources, tends to channel female childhood sports into areas that will provide recreational skills susceptible of long-term enjoyment."[43]

After the initial State Division on Human Rights ruling (which was appealed and upheld by the Appellate Court), at the urging of Little League Headquarters, most of New Jersey's 2000 Little League teams continued to refuse girls and suspended operations. Such actions were reminiscent of the Massive Resistance movement led by Virginia Senator Harry F. Byrd in 1956 against the Supreme Court decision in *Brown v. Board of Education of Topeka* 347 U.S. 483 (1954) where racially segregated public schools were viewed as inherently unequal. Rather than integrate, schools in counties throughout the State of Virginia were closed. Little League District Administrator R. B. Alexander in a letter to President Peter McGovern similarly recommended "that we suspend operations in the state of New Jersey and revoke the charters of all the New Jersey league teams on the basis that we cannot and will not be a party to the willful violation of our Federal Charter."[44]

A petition with 50,000 signatures protesting the decision was sent to the State legislature. A Bill allowing Little League teams to operate without girls for one year regardless of the ruling was introduced by Assemblyman Christopher Jackson who warned that if girls played they might get "hurt in their vital parts."[45] It was narrowly defeated after intense debate in the Assembly by a 39–38 vote. Eventually the New Jersey teams complied with the ruling so that the interests of boys (not girls) would not be penalized by losing their opportunity to play baseball.[46]

Sports Illustrated devoted a lengthy article in 1974 to the issues and intense emotional responses raised by the lawsuits brought against Little League baseball, especially those voiced after the N.O.W. ruling in New Jersey. A Ridgefield, New Jersey, counsel for the Ridgefield Boys Athletic Organization stated that rather than admit girls the RBAO "would take its ball and go home, also denying 251 boys a chance to play." The presiding judge was incredulous: "I don't understand. What's the big deal?" Judith Weiss, a local N.O.W. official was also astonished:

"My God, this particular issue is as fraught with emotional backlash as any I've ever seen. We're seeing the same hostility and fanaticism on behalf of segregated baseball as from the right-to-lifers."[47]

Frank Deford, journalist for *Sports Illustrated*, ruminated that the uproar was about much more than girls infiltrating an institution "as American as apple pie." Men's childhoods were at stake. "So swiftly do girls steal boys from their first love that American men still use the argot of the diamond to express themselves romantically. It begins, simply enough, with the *pitch*, but the man who is rejected by a woman has *struck out*— although, probably, he will protest that *she threw me a curve ball*. Most revealing is the very precise universal language of teen-age boys to communicate, in the most familiar way they know, their sexual probing. *Getting to second base* for the first time is an enshrined male adolescent achievement as momentous as obtaining a driver's license or a beer over the bar."[48]

The devoted middle-aged director of the RBAO for twenty years was "baffled, disoriented" by the verdict to admit girls. "Can't people understand? We've had boys getting broken noses, smashed teeth. Boys can get along real fine in that way, but girls are disfigured for life. And you feel like you're wasting your time with girls. They get to be 13 or 14 and they become amorous and lose interest. Now we have nothing against little girls, but we set this program up for the boys all the way down the line. If we have to accept one girl it will degrade the whole program. What is it when a group of supposedly free men, can't help the boys of their town?" [49]

A woman law student and mother was not concerned that the ruling would subvert women's sports as more boys seek to play girls sports such as softball or field hockey. She agreed with Judge Pressler's decision in the N.O.W. case that bisocial sports teams will generate cultural as well as structural changes regarding women's equality. "In the end, these verdicts will mean more people playing more games. And you've got to get the little girls playing with the little boys. Sports are vital in determining aggressiveness and competitiveness in life, and of course the men want to buy us off with separate but equal. We will not accept that. The failure to compete with men in sports infiltrates every facet of our lives."[50]

In April 1974, one month after the precedent setting ruling in N.O.W.'s favor, another sex discrimination case was filed in U.S. District Court of Rhode Island where plaintiffs Allison "Pookie" Fortin and

her father Robert Fortin filed suit against Darlington American Little
League, defendant, of Pawtucket, Rhode Island. Pookie Fortin was a
ten-year-old girl who was denied participation on the Darlington Little
League team on the basis of her sex. The decision to exclude her was
again justified by adhering to Little League rules that prohibited girls
from playing Little League baseball on the basis of physical differences
that pose greater danger to the safety of girls.

District Court Judge Day agreed with this reasoning and stated in
his decision:

> The expert testimony presented during said trial convinces me that there are
> material physical differences between boys and girls in the 8 to 12 age
> bracket regarding musculature, bone strength, strength of the ligaments and
> tendons, pelvic structure, gait and reaction time, and that these differences
> could undoubtedly result in serious injuries to girls in said age bracket who
> participated in contact sport such as baseball. This Court takes judicial
> notice that baseball is a contact sport and that at times such contacts are vio-
> lent. Witnesses for the defendant, who have a great deal of experience with
> Little League baseball, expressed the opinion that girls in said age bracket
> would suffer personal injuries of a possibly serious nature as a result of such
> physical contacts.... It is my opinion that sex is a rational distinction where a
> contact sport is involved.... I find and conclude that the defendants have not
> illegally deprived either of the plaintiffs of any of their constitutional
> rights."[51]

The following year the U.S. Court of Appeals for the First Circuit
reversed the District Court's decision, rejecting the argument that physical differences would inevitably lead to more girls being injured as a convincing rationale for excluding girls from playing Little League Baseball
with boys. The judges cited constitutional law relating to equal protection for sex and gender. "A sex-based classification denies equal protection in the constitutional sense unless shown to rest on a convincing
factual rationale going beyond archaic and overbroad generalization about
the different roles of men and women. A burden rests upon the propo-
nent of any sex-based classification to demonstrate that there is a convincing reason, apart from convention, for its existence."[52] Although it
is difficult to draw absolute distinctions between facts and their culturally situated interpretation, the Appeals Court judges focused attention
on an important link between power structures and knowledge by insisting on a distinction between empirically grounded knowledge and ideologies that justify social exclusion. "Convention" or dominant gender

ideologies can and do color how biological "facts" are interpreted either as a justification for discrimination or inclusion.

Expert witnesses — medical doctors — testified in this case as they did in the N.O.W. case, offering anatomical "facts" to support their positions. Evidence to support the defendants' position to exclude Allison was provided by Dr. Crane, an orthopedist, who had considerable experience treating male athletes and who had coached Little League teams. However, he had no experience coaching girls and little experience treating female athletes. He stated that the average girl could not safely compete with boys since they are more sedentary and, therefore, more likely to be in poorer physical condition. Also, due to the design of their pelvis, girls walked with a more unstable gait. Girls lacked the capacity to throw overhand and girls' bones would be more vulnerable to fracture since they grew faster than boys during the 8–12 period. Dr. Crane's evidence relating to skeletal differences in boys and girls was refuted by a radiologist for the plaintiffs.

The plaintiffs' principal expert, Dr. Mathieu, was a pediatrician and medical director for the City of Providence public schools. She stated that girls could play baseball safely with boys since girls between the ages of eight and twelve are generally larger and stronger than boys of a similar age. Further, girls are no more subject to fractures, no more unstable on their feet and are neurologically similar to boys. Girls do have a lesser respiratory capacity, but she felt this should not affect their ability to play baseball.[53]

The Little League program in Darlington sponsored three tiers of teams to accommodate players of different levels of maturity and ability. Younger boys, ages eight and nine, played on the minor league teams, of which there were eight. There were also several instructional league teams for boys of lesser ability. Boys ages ten to twelve were drafted into the seven Little League Teams, although some older boys never reached that level if they lacked the ability. Darlington also had a policy of accepting physically handicapped boys, placing them in teams and positions suited to their ability. "Even Dr. Crane believed that a few girls could compete at the level of boys, and it is reasonable to suppose that handicapped and unauthentic boys would be less proficient than many girls. Girls found to lack conditioning or ability to play safely could, like similarly situated boys, be retained on instructional or junior league teams rather than advanced to little league teams."[54]

Since Dr. Crane did not present statistical data showing greater female than male susceptibility to injury in the eight-to-twelve age group, the court found it "difficult to tell how much of Dr. Crane's deposition rested on personal views, to which he admitted, that it was normal activity of a young lady to keep off the baseball fields and play with dolls and how much on science ... even if Dr. Crane's testimony were not entirely without empirical support, it represents the sort of gender-based generalization which cannot suffice to justify the categorical exclusion of girls." The judges also concurred with the decision in the N.O.W. case that girls should be allowed to play Little League Baseball even if they will not be able to compete with boys after age thirteen.[55]

The intensely emotional discourse generated by these suits against Little League in the press suggests that the social implications of changing gender conventions in sport and potentially in other social institutions were broad — challenging the cultural assumptions of male superiority and privilege posited to be grounded in biology. Edward Wood, writing for *The Providence Sunday Journal* about the Pookie Fortin case, recognized the "swirl of sociological unrest" caused by allowing girls to challenge a masculine domain. After highlighting the "chaos" wrecked in New Jersey after the ruling in Maria Pepe's case when many leagues threatened to close down rather than accept girls, Wood stated, "The American sporting world is the zenith of the machismo spirit. And baseball is the zenith of the American sporting world."[56]

The President of the Providence Little League argued that girls would degrade the game by dampening the boys' competitive zeal during play. He argued that it is natural that males, the stronger sex, should want to protect the weaker female sex from injury. "Boys naturally and correctly would not throw an inside pitch when a girls was at bat, would not slide as hard into a female second baseman and would give way if a girl attempted to upset them with a slide at home plate. This is the way boys should react. Protect the weaker sex. A Little League boy can get hit in the face with a pitched ball and wear the broken nose like a bade of honor for the rest of his life, but it could ruin a girl who depends upon her looks." Pookie Fortin disagreed: "If they hit me in the mouth, I'll hit them in the mouth."[57]

This theme of girls degrading the competitive level of play continued with Homer Metz, sportswriter for the *Providence Journal*. His son, a baseball player who was hurt when sliding at second base, asserted that if a girl was the base runner he would not have blocked the bag: "She would have been killed if she tried to take me out." Metz, overflowing with paternal concern for Pookie, asked: "Does even the most liberal Women's Libber want to see little Pookie with a shiner or a strawberry on her rearend?" If girls play with boys, according to Metz, the quality of baseball will decline to the level of softball or the absurd: "It would reduce the play to the level of a Sunday School picnic softball contest and definitely end the value of Little League as training schools [for Major League baseball]. Can you imagine Raquel Welch pitching for the Red Sox or Mama Cass catching?"[58]

Other sports writers against the ruling in the N.O.W. case also focused on the "incontestable" athletic superiority of males, a fact that females would just have to accept and adapt to. Jack Kofoed of the *Miami Herald* said: "Why don't the dolls face it? Men can't have babies and even transvestites will frankly admit it. Nature hasn't armed and engined the female to compete with males in strictly physical sports. Even the most extroverted libber must admit that there are certain things both sexes like to do with no interference from the other. Yet ladies who poke their noses into things that don't concern them have taken the case of Little League Baseball to New Jersey Appeals Court and those dim-eyed sitters on the legal bench have decided that it is illegal to keep girls off of a boy's team. They should be told one thing. There's nothing in the Constitution or Bill of Rights that says a team manager must play a girl if a male candidate for the job can out hit and out field her."[59]

Bob Allison of the *Gazette Sports* in Phoenix agreed: "But why do Mommy and Daddy want little Jane to play Little League baseball when her best chance is to be a little better than the worst boy on the team and even that not for long? It is possible to imagine a 10 year old girl being as good a baseball player as some 10 year old boys. It is not possible to imagine an 18 year old girl being a good enough baseball player to have any place on a respectable boy's team of that age level. So why doesn't Jane play girls' softball from the start and find her place in a sport where she can hold her own as long as she wants to compete."[60]

Finally, a mother's view was quoted in the *Sun Gazette* of Williamsport. "The boys and girls are not on the same teams. Why should they be? The boys have their own league just as they always have and the girls have theirs. The girls play softball (slow pitch) and have their own set of rules. The girls' teams play against each other as the boys do.... I do not want to see my daughter on a boys' team.... I don't think most girls have the experience, the patience or the stamina to make it on boys' teams.... I'd like the boys to remember that my girl is a girl even though she may be the most tom-boyish girl ... she won't always be."[61]

Those supporting the ruling in the N.O.W. case included Phoebe Schan, a member of Women's Rights in Tenafly, New Jersey, who actively sought to sign up girls for Little League. "What boys in Little League are learning is to be leaders. They're also learning that only boys are leaders of this country. It is important for children to look at each other as individuals, not as a class which reinforces stereotyped thinking. It makes it very hard for boys growing up not to feel they belong to a superior group. The real unspoken reason for barring girls is not their safety, but that a male preserve is being threatened."[62]

Richard Seltzer, a Maryland-based sportswriter, agreed. "Every time one is just about satiated with claims and demands of more militant women's liberationists, it seems there comes along an incident to remind us men — or at least those of us who think we have open and fair minds on the matter — of just what women are unfortunately still up against. The controversy over whether little girls should be allowed to play Little League or T-ball League baseball is ridiculous ... if there are girls good enough to play, what possible legitimate reason can there be for barring them? Certainly no enlightenment was added by the Public Relations Director for the Little League who is quoted as saying that participation by girls (under 12 years old!) 'In a contact sport such as baseball is hazardous.' If that is really so, one wonders about the safety of boys under 12 years old."[63]

A West Virginia mother whose daughter pitched on a boy's team agreed: "I was against it at first. If some boy had to sit on the bench because a girl was playing I'd rather the girl not play. I have three older sons who play baseball and I don't like to see them sit on the bench. But now since I've seen a few girls play, I know they enjoy it just as much as the boys. She has been 'upended' running to third. I told her she has to be able to take that." Her daughter Bunny considered playing with boys to be "a lot of fun, especially when you strike out the boys." She had been upended by her brother and "it didn't hurt a bit."[64]

In 1973, the year before Little League Softball was established, an increasing number of girls were joining Little League baseball teams, threatening these "male islands of privateness." To one sportswriter who recognized the vital role Little League played in the training of future major league players, it appeared to be "just a matter of time" until a woman would play major league baseball. His humorous sexualized portrayal of the first woman to play on a major league team focuses as much on her physical appearance as her athletic skills, demonstrating the writer's inclination to objectify this fictive woman in humorous sexual terms. "By 1985 a player will be linked romantically with another player, 22–25 years old, 5' 5"-5' 8", 120–138 pounds playing shortstop. She will tell reporters how her father started playing with her because he wanted a boy. Her ancestry will be Italian, Lithuanian, African. She will, as the first of her kind, be a gimmick attraction, somewhat more important than Bill Veeck's midget pinch hitter. She will have small breasts (teammates and opponents when asked about her statistics will stammer, well she has kinda small waddyacallems, yeh breasts) and slim legs. Her hair will be brown and she will wear it in a long ponytail, not because she considers the style attractive but in tribute to the women who broke the barrier for her, the first female jockeys. She will be a pinch hitter. She will bat from both sides. She will have excellent range at shortstop and a better throwing arm than three quarters of the males playing the position ... prepare yourself. She is on the way. After her will be many others of varying sizes and shapes."[65]

After the ruling, the girls who wanted to play Little League baseball continued to face resistance and alienation. While they could not be denied membership on a team due to their sex, teammates might or might not accept a girl player and the coach (still usually a man) could determine how much playing time a girl had and her positions. Many who opposed integrating boys teams justified the exclusion of girls due to assumed violations of modesty or propriety. "Before each game coaches must look into boys' trousers to check for protective equipment. A man can't very well do that to a girl."[66]

In her 1975 recollections about playing Little League Baseball, Sharon Lennon recalled how her teammates routinely "called my strength and intelligence into question" and how her coach never permitted her to try out for catcher. When she asked her coach if she might try out for catcher he responded with a "cool, amused smirk" that she could, "but you'll have to wear a cup like everyone else."[67] Another eight-year-old girl from Michigan who was asked to wear an athletic cup refused considering it "a ridiculous thing." The umpire ordered her to knock on her cup. When he heard silence the umpire ejected her, instigating a fight between the girl's parents and her local Little League officers.[68]

Responses by children playing Little League Baseball to girls joining boys' teams were also reported in the press. As we might expect, the girls who wished to play stated that girls can play as well as boys, and were able to handle the risks of injury. "They say we might get hurt. So what? So do the boys. We aren't little babies who fall apart when we get hurt. We're as tough as they are." The boys' responses when asked if girls should be allowed to join their teams were more complex. Some boys by age ten or eleven had already accepted that girls were inferior players and assumed they were more concerned with physical attractiveness than athletic skill: "I wouldn't mind of they could do their job, but I'm against it because I know they couldn't." Again: "No girl around here is good enough to make the team." "I don't think they should 'cause if they're practicing and they miss a swing the coach'll ask 'em why and they'll say my make-up smeared or something and they're always too flimsy. They can't play very good." Others boys felt that "if the girls are good enough, they should play. But they shouldn't be given any advantages because they are girls." Finally, one who played with a talented girl pitcher stated: "She's better than a lot of us. If we didn't have her, we'd lose. It's kind of embarrassing sometimes."[69]

Little League teams are small-scale social groups characterized by context-specific sets of symbolic interactions and behavioral norms. Sociologist Gary Fine's analysis of these norms, based on ethnographic research of six Little League teams, took place between 1975 and 1977, the years immediately following the lawsuits. Although his book unfortunately makes no mention of the impact of these sex discrimination suits on the coaches, families or team members, it is a rich source of evidence for the role played by homosocial sports in the development of masculinity as a dichotomous gender identity. For some coaches, the male adults charged with the moral responsibility of teaching masculinity along with baseball skills to preadolescent boys, girls and softball teams were negative reference groups used to motivate boys to act or perform at a superior masculine level. "Hey, you're not girls out there. You're baseball players. Play like men."[70] Preadolescent boys, wishing to conform to the hegemonic model of masculinity, attempted to control their emotions, particularly crying, and to act tough or stoic even when intimidated or injured. The stigmatized gendered labels for "immature" babyish boys who did not conform included "wuss," "queer," "faggot," "fairy," "gay," "girl," all of which reflect a dichotomized "othering" of the feminine.

Boys learn impression management early through interactions with their peers, particularly regarding masculine sexuality. Since sexual prowess is a mark of maturity, boys need to convince their peers that they are sexually active and knowledgeable. Strict codes of conduct prevailed between players and their girlfriends to manage the image of the boy as not too intimate or attached to his girlfriend. "The problem is that such a deep relationship implies an equality in power and commitment between the sexes, contrary to the male sex role." Girls should not replace other boys as the focus of their attention. The sexual and romantic activities of players were frequent topics of discussion or insult, enabled or discouraged by individual coaches, with speech again reflecting the development of a deeply homophobic and misogynistic world view where males "expect each other to be sexually aggressive and females await their attempts with undisguised arousal."[71]

Unfortunately more recent anthropological or sociological studies of Little League teams do not exist for longitudinal comparison. It would be useful to know if the passage of thirty years has diminished these gender biases among Little League coaches and team players. Brett Stoudt's ethnographic data on reproducing hegemonic masculinities in an elite boys' school suggests otherwise. Exclusive masculine sports culture is still normative, structuring patterns of social interaction in school outside of sports, including its dichotomous misogynistic (pussy) and homophobic (gay/faggot) elements.[72]

The responses of parents to the ruling allowing girls to play baseball on boys' teams varied. The trailblazers—Pookie Fortin and Maria Pepe—were prevented from playing baseball for their local Little League teams and never again played baseball on teams with boys. Both, however, were fortunate to have supportive parents and sufficient support from their communities. While their daughter's case was being argued in court, the Fortins were determined that girls wishing to play baseball should have the opportunity. In 1973 they joined with other local parents to form a separate girls baseball league, appropriately named the Darlington Pioneers, for local girls ages ten to sixteen. Many girls joined, seeking an alternative to baseball on boys' teams and to softball. Two years later the league changed its name to the Slaterettes in honor of Pawtucket's historic Slater Mill. The Slaterettes thrived over the years and are one of the few girls' and women's baseball leagues in the United States.[73]

The reactionary response by Little League management was to implement a program that harkened back to the separate but equal logic of *Plessy v. Fergusson* 163 U.S. 537 (1896). Little League acted on Creighton Hale's 1973 proposed pilot program "to determine the feasibility of incorporating a parallel activity for girls of the local little league community.... The program would provide a softball activity for girls ages nine to twelve and thirteen to fifteen organized and chartered under the same basic provisions and regulations as now govern the parent Little League. Teams would be fully uniformed, managed by women (with the option of male coaches), played on existing Little League fields with modified pitching distance."[74] Drs. Thomas Johnson and Creighton Hale had earlier proposed that girls be accommodated by establishing their own separate league with a 35–40-foot pitcher's mound, 60-foot baselines, chest protectors, no sliding into bases, no profanity, and a larger, softer ball delivered underhand.[75]

Since girls or women playing baseball competently with boys or men was regarded as infeasible, the logical step was to exclude them and segregate them into a sport requiring less athletic prowess — softball. "Ironically or perhaps by design, Little League Baseball this year for the first time in its 35 year history has recognized little girls and has encouraged its 9000 member leagues to organize girls softball divisions." Little League Baseball stated, "We could have easily said go ahead and open Little League to girls. Not many of them will be able to make the teams anyway, but we don't feel that's the proper attitude. We feel its best to serve all the girls and this softball program is the answer."[76]

Such preservation of "islands of privateness" has consistently been the path chosen by Little League Baseball. While Little League initially lost the battle over excluding girls from boys' teams in 1974, it won the war by institutionalizing the sexual bifurcation of the sport into softball and baseball. Such strategies of offering different sports for boys and girls or establishing sex-segregated teams with different rules of play within the same sport are powerful means toward the institutionalization of sex segregation in sports generally. The 2003 Little League Baseball logo, a powerful symbol of youth baseball worldwide, features a boy, reinforcing the perception that baseball is a male sport. Similarly the 2006 Little League Softball logo worn by hundreds of thousands of children features a girl. In 1974 Little League Softball for girls was established and promoted without asking "the girls which game they wanted to play."[77]

The percentage of girls playing Little League Baseball was highest just after the 1974 decision, numbering approximately 30,000.[78] However, girls who were thereafter steered toward softball have never comprised more than one percent of players.[79] Most of the girls who play baseball are children participating at the instructional and T-Ball levels. According to John Kovach, "girls wanting to play on the Minors level and up are subjected to the Little League 'don't ask, don't tell' policy," meaning if girls and their parents don't ask about playing baseball Little League will not tell them that girls can play on these boys' teams. "At almost every Little League season sign-up if you are female you are sent to the softball line and never told you have a choice. The choice is made for you."[80]

Similarly the softball program was intended as an all-girl program. Some boys have challenged this rule, which was dropped in 1995, and all settlements of suits were out of court.[81] In 2003 Little League began implementing a Boys Softball Division, reflecting the choice of 500 boys playing Little League Softball by 2000. Although boys comprise a very small proportion of the vast number of children playing Little League Softball, a separate boys' division was organized, including a Boys Softball World Series. No such parallel program exists for the small proportion of girls playing Little League Baseball. "One can make a case that an organization such as Little League still harbors resentment in having to admit girls to baseball."[82]

Through 2003 only ten girls have played in the Little League Baseball World Series held each summer in Williamsport. The first girl appeared in 1984. Only one woman had coached a Little League team in the World Series in 1993, and two women were umpires in the World Series, one in 1989 and the other in 2002.[83] In 2005, when eleven-year-old Katie Brownell pitched a perfect Little League game and was honored by the Baseball Hall of Fame in Cooperstown, she was still the only girl in her upstate New York Little League.

Today local Little Leagues teams continue to discriminate against girls as the recent case of Irina Kovach illustrates. Irina, a twelve-year-old pitcher, was one of two girls chosen to represent the United States at the 2006 World Children's Baseball Fair in Japan. When she attempted to sign up for the Rolling Prairie Baseball Association's twelve-to-fourteen Intermediate Division she was turned down because of her sex and offered softball as an alterative. The initial decision to deny Irina the opportunity to play was "made after the athletic director of a local high school suggested that letting her play now would only fuel her drive to play at the high school level, which he did not want." Both the Women's Sports Foundation and Irina's father have functioned as advocates for her to be given the opportunity to play baseball. Still, despite verbal confirmations that Irina would be allowed to play, she has not been granted formal permission. Irina's confusion and embarrassment mirrors the confused, hurt feelings of Maria Pepe thirty years before her who was also denied her childhood desire to play Little League Baseball due to her gender. "Our town is small and pretty much everyone knows I play baseball. When they ask me how I was doing this year, it was hard to tell them I wasn't allowed to play this season because I was a girl. I hope that doesn't happen to other girls who like to play baseball."[84]

Little League Baseball does not keep accurate yearly statistics on the number of girls playing baseball or the number of boys playing softball. They learned their discrimination lesson well. In 2004, when Maria Pepe threw the ceremonial first pitch at the Little League World Series, 500,000 girls were reported to play Little League Baseball and Softball.[85] Although occasionally a talented girl will number among the Little League players at the World Series and be publicly showcased, and although Berlage states that between 1990 and 1998 there was a 20.5-percent increase in the number of girls playing Little League baseball, the gender regime of their institution premised on male athletic superiority has been maintained.[86]

Steve Keener, Little League president and CEO, concerned about tournament play when an all-girl softball team meets a bisocial team, voiced this enduring perspective. "I find it odd that a male, particularly when he gets to be fifteen or older, would get any real satisfaction out of being on a team or appearing to excel against a team of female participants. Conversely we all seem to marvel at a female who can compete and excel in a program that is predominantly a male program."[87] Until baseball offers continuous opportunities for interested girls, female athletic talent will flow into the sports where such opportunities exist, such as basketball and tennis. We will never know what proportion of girls and women might play baseball at a level where opposing males would feel real satisfaction when excelling against them.

Conclusion: "Islands of Privateness" or Islands of Privilege

In the United States baseball is a core sport in the institution of sports at the amateur and professional levels. It is also a sport with strong and growing significance in North, Central and South America, in Southeast Asia and in Australia. As a core sport it is characterized by efficient systems of production and distribution of baseball talent sold as entertainment to millions of spectators. In this country and elsewhere the sex of this human athletic talent that is profitably sold worldwide is male, forging a strong connection between sport generally (and baseball particularly) and ideologies justifying the unequal sex/gender system in professional sports and in our society.

Softball and women's baseball are peripheral sports at the amateur and professional levels in the United States and elsewhere in the world. In contrast to organized men's baseball, these sports are characterized by underdeveloped and relatively inefficient systems of production and distribution of athletic talent, despite the passage of laws seeking to equalize access to resources and opportunities. Although Title IX eliminates formal barriers to girls choosing to play baseball rather than softball, girls still have to contend with a relative absence of structural support from educational and recreational institutions, and with the social isolation and psychological stress associated with deviant behavior.

Title IX has been ineffective in integrating baseball since intersecting power and prestige structures are firmly entrenched that control the settings for recruitment, talent development and opportunities for team play. Sex segregation in all sports is still the norm beginning in childhood. However, baseball, America's national pastime, has been the most consistent and persistent in constructing obstacles to the female half of the population. Title IX has not addressed the negative implications of institutionalizing-sex segregated sports such as softball as the alternative to baseball for girls. The South Bend Blue Sox Women's Baseball in Indiana is an organization that advocates for girls and women denied opportunities to play baseball and promotes opportunities for them to learn and play the sport. They astutely and succinctly summarized the current challenges facing girls and women: "Opportunity does not always mean equality."

Although Title IX can protect softball here in the United States, the International Olympic Committee recently ruled to eliminate softball along with baseball after this August's Summer Games in Beijing. Don Porter, president of the 130-nation International Softball Federation, is lobbying hard to get softball reinstated for the 2016 Games. As George Vecsey argues, the loss of Olympic baseball is far less significant than the loss of softball. "The unfair part is that the softball and baseball constituencies are vastly different. For the women, the Olympic gold medal is as big as it gets. Baseball doesn't need the Olympics the way the women do."[1]

Today opportunities for young girls under age twelve to play T-ball or Little League are available and many young girls join bisocial teams. However, when they reach their teens, girls are pressured to switch to softball. While most junior high and high schools have baseball teams that girls could join if they qualified, few girls choose to do so. According to the Women's Sports Foundation, approximately 1,015 women played high school baseball during the 2004–2005 academic year.[2] The persistent reason given by girls for their departure from baseball is pressure from boys and men coaches seeking to exclude them from baseball teams and peer pressure from girls who seek conformity as the key to including them as friends.

For example, a woman player on the New Jersey Nemesis team in 2006, a traveling team that plays baseball tournaments across the country, stated: "They don't want girls to play. I felt it all the time. Regardless of where I go. You're a girl, you play baseball? You're a lesbian.... You get all the stereotypes that come with it. It has changed a lot, especially with Little League. Girls are getting the opportunity to play, but where it hasn't changed is once they become teens. Even though technically the opportunity exists for them to play on a lot of the men's teams, they're definitely steered towards softball, and then there's peer pressure. I think there needs to be a stronger structure in place, especially at the high school level."[3]

A second example from Montclair, New Jersey, involved Vanessa Selbst, a pitcher for the Montclair High School team. Encouraged by her mother, who played baseball and softball recreationally, Vanessa played baseball on all-boys teams as a young child, beginning with T-ball at age five, Little League teams with her brother and on travel teams in the summer. She began to pitch at age nine after thinking it would be fun to try. Although she was the only girl, Vanessa was accepted by her teammates and supported by her coaches because she was good.

However, like many of the girls previously discussed, Vanessa began to face strong resistance in high school when she entered in 1997. She was not the first girl to play for the boys' team at Montclair High, and although the freshman coach was supportive, her teammates were not, subjecting her to homophobic remarks, talking behind her back and ostracizing her. As the other boys on the fifteen-member team became friends, they would socialize after games without inviting Vanessa to join. Even the three other pitchers excluded her, making it difficult for her socially to be on the team. When a few male players made friendly overtures towards her, they were subjected to intimidating peer pressure and drew back.

As one of four pitchers, Vanessa rated herself as third. She therefore worked hard during the summer after freshman year to improve her pitching skills before the junior varsity team tryouts. Vanessa worked out with friends, throwing the ball nearly every day between her freshman and sophomore seasons. At those tryouts she was the only girl. Despite the freshman team's poor record, despite the need for pitchers and assurances by other athletes, Coach Groh, described by Vanessa as "sexist and misogynist," would not give her an opportunity to pitch during the ten separate tryout sessions. Consequently, Vanessa was cut from the team. When she spoke with the coach to complain, he claimed that she had been given the chance. He also justified his decision to cut her based on her performance during freshman year. Vanessa brought her complaints to the high school athletic department and after a series of meetings about the situation, the coach resigned.

Vanessa chose not to press the issue further since the season was already half over and she had switched to softball. Vanessa did not pitch for the Montclair High softball team. She played third base and tried to adjust to a game she considered to be very different. "I didn't really enjoy the game. Baseball was really important to me and I couldn't mentally adjust to the switch." Her own negative experience influenced Vanessa's perspective on girls playing on boys' teams. "You have to pick your battles." If a girl wants to have fun, to play the game just for the enjoyment, she may be better off on an all-girls team where she does not have to "pave the way for women's liberation."[4]

Although Title IX will protect those girls and women with athletic talent seeking to play on men's middle and high school teams, Vanessa's case, like those of Ila Borders and Julie Croteau, demonstrates that there are clear emotional costs associated with being the "lone ponytail." One social benefit of team sports is being able to form strong same sex bonds that are absent when girls play on boys' teams.[5] When girls and women play on all-male teams, they encounter "with-then-apart" interactions with male teammates: with teammates when on the diamond, apart from them when in the locker room and after the game. As Ila Borders' and Julie Croteau's cases illustrate, the younger the players, the more socially accepted the girl is, particularly if she is talented. As oppositional masculinity develops and competitive stakes advance with age, the girl/young woman is subjected to increasing isolation and hostility. Thus the "choice" made by most girls to play softball, a sport that is less privileged than baseball in every respect, is spurious since real choice is premised on real options.

With the exception of professional tennis, where women athletes have achieved parity with men, women's sports such as softball remain under-financed and enjoy less prestige and support from the media and spectators. In the sport of golf, women are still barred from men's tournaments that exclude them from "the tradition of men's tournaments on morning weekends, events that are woven into the fabric of golf life at private and public courses." In the past two decades many women have brought suits against private golf clubs and even municipal or public courses over access to weekend tee times, membership, access to men's groups and dining rooms.[6]

Title IX suits have evolved from the establishment of opportunities at local recreational baseball leagues or educational institutions for girls and women to play sports, to seeking parity in resources such as improved fields, locker rooms and equipment for middle or high school softball teams that are comparable to those afforded to boys' baseball teams. They also include women coaches at universities who are discriminated against on the basis of sex. Some jury awards at the university level have been large enough to encourage others to implement preventative changes. At the high school level, Title IX suits are often initiated by fathers, who as a category have been referred to as the "angry-dad phenomenon."

The most common Title IX complaints involves the disparity between the playing fields and facilities for softball and baseball. Amateur and professional baseball games are public spectacles. With amateur sports like baseball or softball, spectators are much closer to the players, enabling them to see and hear much of what is happening on the field. The playing field is the physical background for the activity and therefore its physical condition is part of the baseball experience, contributing to the spectators' satisfaction or lack thereof. Amateur fields should duplicate certain characteristics of the professional fields, including care of the grass, foul lines and base paths. Although young players might not care about the upkeep of the baseball fields, involved adults often do.[7]

For example, in Alhambra, California, the softball team must change into their softball uniforms in a tin shed alongside the school field. There were no working toilets at the field and the weedy, bumpy playing surface was poorly maintained. In contrast, the boys' baseball team plays in Moor Field, locally referred to as the "Field of Dreams," a city facility that Alhambra recently spent more than $900,000 to renovate. Angry dads have themselves already experienced the benefits of men's high school athletic programs and when they have daughters who are not treated equally, they become angry and file Title IX suits. While Title IX suits at colleges receive more publicity, the middle and high schools are the real battleground. "It's about providing a grass-roots gateway to sports that benefits millions."[8]

The position of the Women's Sports Foundation in the United States regarding co-ed participation in sports follows the legal precedents set by decisions in Title IX cases, such as those involving Little League Baseball. Their position is similar to that of the Canadian Association for the Advancement of Women and Sport and Physical Activity. Prior to puberty there is no gender-based physiological reason to separate the sexes in sports competition. Competition groupings should be organized around skill and experience. Girls and boys of equal skills should not be prohibited from playing on teams consisting primarily of the opposite sex. While separate-sex teams are not appropriate in instructional leagues, in some competitive youth sports leagues it is recognized that girls may not have had the same opportunities to develop skills compared to similarly aged boys. In these situations, separate-sex leagues may be appropriate, grouping according to skill rather than gender, when engaging in competitive play. After puberty boys will develop more muscle mass, and less fat-free body mass than girls, enabling them to be stronger and faster and to throw farther. After puberty for most girls single-sex competition will be appropriate, but for some girls co-ed competition is still desirable, since some will be able to compete with or against boys.[9]

The physical differences in size and strength between men and women that justify the exclusion of girls and women from baseball have frequently been used to establish bone fide occupational qualifications that justify excluding women from various non-traditional jobs. Since the passage of Title VII in 1964, the courts have critically evaluated whether these qualifications are in fact related to the performance of an occupation or simply function as a means to discriminate against women in employment. A relevant example pertaining to baseball involved an adult woman, Bernice Gera, who sought employment as an umpire, an occupation within the sport of baseball that is even more overtly gender exclusive than baseball teams. In 1967 Gera, using the first name "Bernie" and concealing her sex, made an application to the Al Somers School for umpires, stating her age to be thirty-five, her height to be 5' 3" and weight 144 pounds. Gera was a former high school softball player, a Little League coach, and had experience umpiring numerous baseball games for various organizations including American Legion, Catholic Youth Organization, YMCA, and the New York Police Department.

The Al Somers School was approved, supervised and subsidized by the Baseball Umpire Development Program, which was organized under major league sponsorship in 1964. Umpires hired by the various major league presidents were subject to the approval of the Baseball Umpire Development Program that established qualifications for umpires. These included an age limit of thirty-five, minimum height of 5'10", minimum weight of 170 pounds, graduation from high school and from an approved umpire school. Although Gera did not meet these physical criteria, the Al Somers School initially was willing to accept her until she informed them that she was a woman. Somers then informed Gera that her sex raised an important policy matter to be discussed with the administrator of the Baseball Umpire Development Program and that she would be further advised regarding the application. Gera did not receive any further communications from the school.

In 1968 Gera wrote to the president of the New York–Pennsylvania Baseball League requesting an application as a woman but without listing her physical qualifications. The application was rejected because of her sex. "It is our professional opinion that it would be unwise to expose you or any other lady to situations such as those stated previously above." During Gera's suit before the New York State Division of Human Rights, the New York–Pennsylvania Baseball League asserted that being of the male sex was a bona fide occupational requirement for an umpire. It was the opinion of the New York State Division of Human Rights that insufficient factual evidence was produced to support that women are not qualified for the job of a professional baseball umpire. Although Gera clearly did not meet the established physical requirements, the court recognized that "such standards bar all but less than one percent of women for consideration of employment as professional baseball umpires. Our concern therefore is with whether ... these standards bear a reasonable relation to the requirements of the job. Testimony was given that these standards were 'born of the judgment of men with long experience in professional baseball,' that an umpire 'must be a person who commands respect of big fellows, big men,' also to the increased size of professional baseball catchers, the possibility of confrontation with big athletes, physical strain, travel conditions, and length of games." While these conditions were to be taken into consideration when hiring an umpire, it was the opinion of the hearing officers at the New York State Division on Human Rights that none of these justify an inflexible standard of height and weight. Thus, they concluded that the qualifications were inherently discriminatory against women and that Gera was, therefore, discriminated against on the basis of her sex.[10] Despite the ruling in Gera's favor, there have been very few women attending umpire academies, only three women have reached the ranks of baseball umpires in the minor leagues (Pam Postema, who also filed a sex discrimination suit in 1992, Ria Cortesio and Shanna Cook) with none officiating in the major leagues.

While physical differences, real and fabricated, have questionable relevance to umpiring baseball games and perhaps to playing certain infield positions (small professional players such as Brian Roberts or David Eckstein who field their positions well enough), strength does play a role in hitting home runs. Today, there is greater pressure on both minor and major league players to hit home runs — a known fan pleaser — and this emphasis strongly favors males, especially those males whose hitting power is improved by performance-enhancing drugs. The media plays a key role in constructing masculine bodies emphasizing size and strength. Measures of masculine athletic performance in the media highlight exceptional baseball players who are power hitters or power pitchers who throw fastballs above the mid–90 m.p.h. range. Very few women indeed will fall into this select category. Very few men genuinely do as well, without the help of performance-enhancing drugs, as the recent publicity on this widespread problem in baseball suggests.

In 2005 Michael Lewis examined the hyper-emphasis on strength in the minor leagues and how it is changing recruitment and development of talent in baseball. One of the featured young players, Steve Stanley, a small-boned man at 5'7" and 155 pounds, is particularly relevant to a comparison with talented women baseball players and their potential to advance to the minor or major leagues. Steve Stanley was born to hit singles, beat out infield hits, and steal bases and was a fine defensive center-fielder for Notre Dame. In college his statistics in all of these areas were outstanding. His supportive father recognized that Steve's size would pose a problem for pro-scouts and "shaped his game to minimize the costs of what he couldn't do and to maximize the benefits of what he could do": hit and run.[11]

Despite his talent and achievements, "baseball scouts looked at him and saw a body unlike any in the big leagues. Scouts from two major league teams told Stanley that, if he was lucky, he might be selected in the 15th round of the '02 draft, which is to say he'd be handed a thousand bucks, a plane ticket and a recommendation letter that told everybody in baseball not to pay him any mind." Although Stanley was picked by the Oakland As, advanced to Triple A in the minor leagues and was described by scouts as a "prospect," he did not advance into the major league. Stanley also felt "like a freak. He could live with being the least likely player on the field to hit the ball over the wall; what drove him nuts was the thought of a bigger player using drugs to widen the power gap even further between him and them."[12]

The relevance of Stanley's experience for potential women baseball players today is unmistakable. Prior to the media-driven, statistics-driven, fan-driven emphasis on power in baseball that encourages drug use, there were opportunities for smaller men who were skilled at getting on base, stealing bases and fielding their positions. These opportunities are shrinking fast, further eliminating the chances for women to advance through the minor leagues. If we "don't see many guys who look like Stanley in the big leagues" talented women of Stanley's size will be invisible.

A consistent argument made here and by others analyzing the problem of excluding girls from baseball is that if girls were given the same opportunities as children and adolescents to consistently play baseball and develop their skills with and against boys, some women would emerge as players who can compete with or against men at the minor league or major league level. The barrier erected by Little League Baseball after 1974 consisting of the gender bifurcation of baseball as a He-Sport and Softball as the She-alternative has proven impermeable and is a formidable obstacle to this development.

Another new structural barrier for girls' development as baseball players is the increasing significance of elite travel baseball teams that are coached and financed by parents with the help of a handful of local sponsors. These teams are technically under the jurisdiction of Title IX ensuring that a talented girl wishing to play would be allowed to join. A small number of girls have joined boys' travel teams and, recently, a girls' team of the Chicago Pioneers has joined an elite boys' travel league, the North Shore Baseball League. Nevertheless, this separate and rapidly evolving structure of baseball teams are overwhelmingly male and focus on providing talented boys with a fast track to advancement into organized baseball where there are no opportunities for women. The majority of girls who have played on elite travel baseball teams have been under age twelve, when the physical differences between boys and girls are not pronounced. Given the elite travel teams' emphasis on developing above-average athletic talent, these talented girls were accepted by their teammates and supported by their coaches.

In 2006 Sara Corbett discussed this new phenomenon in the *New York Times Magazine*. She highlighted the extraordinary dedication and sacrifice of parents who enable the extraordinary dedication and sacrifice of their talented male children. "There was a time when being a baseball parent meant little more than playing catch in the back yard and cheering through 15 or so Little League games in the spring and summer. But by all accounts, the level of play in youth baseball, as well as the degree of competitiveness and the investment of time and money required of parents, has escalated dramatically in the past 10 years or so — primarily owning to the rising popularity of tournament-oriented travel teams." Parents provide the money for team membership, tournament and travel expenses and structure the time investment (including time taken from their various occupations) to play baseball for ten months of the year. Some boys play more than 120 games a year, a schedule not unlike a major league player. As expected, many of these teams are located in "sun-drenched states" where outdoor sports can be played all year and where retired professional players live and offer private lessons, such as Florida, California and Texas. Young players and their families travel to various states, some by plane, to "slug it out against other elite-level, baseball-obsessed kids in weekend tournaments where the winning teams are sometimes required to play up to eight games in a single 48-hour stretch." When they enter high school baseball teams they are "finished products."[13]

Although Corbett argues that "baseball ... remains governed by the great American notion of sports democracy: any determined kid with a ball, a bat, and a sandlot to play in stands a chance of making it big," this slice of quintessential Americana has always excluded determined female kids. Parents form elite travel teams so that their exceptional children can compete with and against other exceptional teammates and be rescued from "rec-ball hell," presumably meaning local recreational Little League teams. "Taking the field with children who were just learning to play — who couldn't field a zinging line drive or get their glove around a crisp throw from third base — had become troublesome. 'He was going to end up hurting somebody. We couldn't get out of there fast enough.'" Little League teams operate on "populist principles" where any local child can sign up to play. Travel teams use the major league model of holding tryouts for boys who are "unhindered by matters of geography."[14]

Elite players and their teams are carefully ranked and these rankings are posted on websites such as Travel Ball Select, along with news updates on their performances at tournaments and tips from coaches and scouts relating to developing skills and exposure to college and pro scouts.

The criteria for ranking and choosing specific players as winners or honorable mentions depend on the age of the player. Older players are judged on ability and what they have achieved in the field. In the younger age groups winners are judged on potential and performance at major national and international competitions.[15] Travel teams seek to provide talented players with opportunities to play in tournaments, to attend specialized baseball camps, exposure to scouts and publicity, all essential to giving a talented boy a competitive edge.

While the Little League World Series is still the most prestigious event for eleven- to twelve-year-olds, particularly given its expansion to sixteen leagues, its international pool of players, and the games being televised by ESPN, it is only one of about 200 national championships staged annually for baseball players of all ages. Today there are an estimated 30,000 teams and over two million boys playing travel ball, which is entirely separate from Little League and its rules of play. The Little League World Series may not even be the most competitive event in its own age group (twelve and under) as the Cooperstown Dreampark's National Tournament of Champions and the U.S. Specialty Sports Association Elite 24 World Series are currently drawing a greater number of the nation's elite players in that age group. The dominance of elite travel leagues over the widespread local recreation leagues is also becoming pronounced in the thirteen-to-seventeen age groups as talented, privileged teenage players above age twelve seek the "best competition" and opportunities available. Thus, in baseball "the elite is also the mainstream."[16]

Participation in elite travel baseball is costly (as high as $20–30,000 a year) and the odds against a boy making the major leagues are overwhelming. If parents and children are going to make the financial and time sacrifices, structural barriers, such as sex discrimination, blocking their gifted child's advancement into organized baseball cannot exist. To date such barriers are impenetrable for girls, even the gifted ones like Katie Brownell whose perfect game in 2005 was honored by the Hall of Fame. Although the unbalanced sex ratio of Little League teams is a persistent problem, "rec-ball hell" will include some girls, whereas elite travel teams usually perform in a pristine all-male heaven where girls and women (girlfriends, sisters, mothers) are usually spectators. While the occasional girl will try out, make and be encouraged by supportive travel team coaches, only boys can dream about "baseball for life."

While "baseball for life" dreams are denied to girls, they are increasingly shared by boys from countries outside the United States. The "strip-mining" of cheap male talent from Central American countries, particularly the Dominican Republic, is another structural barrier to developing female talent since girls and women are excluded both as "raw material" in baseball academies and as "finished commodities" to be sold to major league teams in the United States. Although women's baseball is in its infancy in the Dominican Republic, with a women's national team formed and ready to compete at the Women's World Series, in 2005 one out of every seven players in the major leagues was born in the Dominican Republic. This is the highest number from any country, including thirty percent of players in the United States minor leagues. All thirty teams now scout what baseball owners commonly call 'the Republic of Baseball' with several operating multi-million dollar baseball academies. These academies are exclusively male since the channels for recruiting and developing young talent at every level are limited to males as are opportunities to play professionally in the United States.

Baseball, linked as it is with the underdeveloped impoverished Dominican economy, is most popular in the Southeast where generations of males were and are involved in the sugarcane industry. In the off-season, sugarcane factory owners would encourage their young male work-forces to play by providing financial support for the teams. Since 1955 North American baseball teams have developed "working relationships" with a specific Dominican team. The American partner team was always dominant, offering higher salaries and better resources for developing skills. While some few American men played on Dominican teams, the larger flow of talent was from the Dominican Republic to North American teams. Often, poor boys quit school at age twelve or younger to play baseball full time at the academies. As in the United States, 98 percent of these children will never make it to the major leagues. Dominican players, however, face additional barriers including racism, language and cultural differences and emotionally grapple with the enormous expectations of their families to lift them all out of poverty. Unlike in the United States, where most athletes who do not make it have at least a high school diploma, those in the Dominican Republic, especially those who have dropped out of school, have no fallback skills and return to lives of poverty.[17]

In the United States in the last decade an alternative organizational structure to Little League for girls and women has emerged at the local and national levels where they can learn baseball skills and play. According to the American Women's Baseball Federation, in 2007 there are thirty-nine youth and women's baseball teams in the United States that play in nine leagues and independent tournaments throughout the year. Local leagues follow the lead of the Pawtucket Slaterettes formed in 1973 during the Pookie Fortin suit against Little League Baseball.

Until 2006 the Slaterettes were the only girls and women's baseball league in the United States and serve as the model for emerging girls' leagues elsewhere in the country. Its four divisions are also a model to incrementally develop baseball skills for girls. The league consists of four divisions: Instructional for ages five to seven, which is comparable to T-ball; the Minor Division for ages eight to ten, comparable to modified Little League with a 35-foot pitcher's mound; the Junior Division for ages eleven to thirteen comparable to regulation Little League and the Senior Adult division for ages fourteen and older that uses a field with 80-foot base paths, a 54-foot pitcher's mound and Major League Baseball rules.

The Slaterettes draw approximately 200 girls and women from the surrounding area and aim to expand into southern New England. Since this league is homosocial it attracts girls who want to play with and against other girls and avoid intimidation by boys, as evidenced by the experience of Vanessa Selbst. It also draws girls who wish to play baseball rather than slow or fast pitch softball. However, given the lack of opportunities to play baseball at the high school level, most of the talented young baseball players end up playing fast pitch softball in high school.[18] The Slaterettes compete in national tournaments against other teams from the United States and Canada and its players are eligible to compete for the Women's National Baseball Team.

At the National level there are several organizations dedicated to providing opportunities for girls and women to play baseball. The American Women's Baseball Federation was formed in 1992 to "organize and promote baseball as a mainstream and lifetime opportunity for women." Since that year the AWBF has organized seventeen regional and national tournaments and in 2004 the Federation joined with international teams to organize a Women's World Cup Tournament. The Federation maintains a database of women players interested in trying out for Team U.S.A. A second organization is the Women's Baseball League founded by Justine Siegal in 1999. Its mission is "creating opportunities for the daughters of the world" to ensure that girls have a place to play baseball. In 2002 the WBL conducted tryouts for Team U.S.A. in Doubleday Field in Cooperstown, New York. They also traveled to the Dominican Republic in 2003 to provide a baseball clinic for interested girls.

One example of a new progressive baseball league for girls is the Chicago Pioneers Girls Baseball league formed in 2006. The Pioneers currently organize baseball for approximately eighty girls who were preparing to play for local Little League teams, or had played for several years on community teams, on travel teams, or, in one case, for her high school freshman baseball team. The Chicago Pioneers petitioned a boys' travel team, the North Shore Baseball League, for an opportunity to play as a team in their league. The petition was accepted and in June 2007, sixteen Pioneers ages twelve to fifteen became the first all-girls team in the United States to participate in a previously all-boys travel baseball league. They are hoping to field additional teams with the NSBL. The Pioneers also compete in national women's baseball tournaments and for positions on the Women's National Team. The Chicago Pioneers Program is currently working with Little League International in Williamsport in the hopes of starting a girls baseball pilot program across the United States. Although the Pioneers have launched a successful program, their costs are not defrayed by powerful institutions such as Little League International. Consequently, their website ends with a plea for donations: "Currently it is not easy or convenient to play baseball on an all girls team or in an all girls setting. The Pioneers are looking for sponsors to defray the costs...."[19]

In 2007 the Carolina Miners Girls Baseball league formed to provide opportunities for girls to play baseball in that southern state. The name reflects North Carolina's historic gold and gem mines and the teams also compete in national tournaments.[20]

The young women playing in the sixteen and above division in these independent leagues can compete for Team U.S.A., a team that competes at the World Cup level against international teams from Canada, Australia, Japan and Taiwan, Hong Kong and Cuba. There is a three-stage national tryout for selection for the national team. Other countries including Korea, Venezuela, Dominican Republic, India, and Argentina have organized national women's baseball teams but have not yet competed in the Women's World Series. Competitive international women's baseball began in 1999 when Japan sent an all-star team, Team Energen, to play in the South Florida Diamond Classic tournament organized by the American Women's Baseball Federation. The following year the United States team flew to Tokyo to play and in 2001 the Women's World Series, including national teams from Canada and Australia, was played in Toronto. The Women's World Series has continued each year with the number of teams expanding to eight in 2004, creating an international network of countries and organizations that develop women's baseball programs.[21]

Although Team U.S.A. has been successful in its competitions, the team reflects the underdevelopment of women's baseball in the United States. Few in this country know about girls' baseball leagues and the national team receives no press coverage. In 2004 Team U.S.A. formed only two weeks before the start of the tournament. This is in contrast to Japan that has a nationwide women's program beginning in childhood and extending through college, supported by the Baseball Federation of Japan. While most girls in Japan play softball or "kenko" which is a rubber ball, some girls play hardball in high school and college. Most of the members of the Canadian team play together all year and the Australian team practiced for five months before the tournament began. In Canada, women's baseball is also supported by a national governing body, the Canadian Federation of Amateur Baseball funded by Sports Canada. This federation is made up of provincial and territorial associations with over 400,000 players organized into three levels of all-girls teams: Peewee (ages eleven to thirteen), Bantam (ages fourteen to sixteen) and Women (ages seventeen and older). At the Bantam level almost every province in Canada has a team to develop talented players for their Women's Invitational Championship and their national team. Although most Canadian girls play on homosocial teams, a girl who is qualified to play on a boys' team would be supported.

The experiences of the women on Team U.S.A. reveals their determination to play a sport that persistently excluded them. For example, Lilly Jacobson was a member of the 2004 Team U.S.A. when she was eighteen. She played baseball with boys all her life, resisting the switch to softball. Coaches and parents after Little League encouraged her not to waste her talent, but Lilly preferred baseball and excelled at the skills the sport demands: fielding agility, base-running and hitting. She was well aware that women are excluded from the "fame and fortune" promised to talented boys who play professionally. Still, Lilly switched high schools to escape a coach who told her she was not good enough to play on his team and to work with a coach who encouraged her to play. Many of the players on Team U.S.A. faced similar resistance to their choice to play baseball in high school.[22]

While these amateur developments in the United States and elsewhere are encouraging, it is significant that no women's professional baseball teams have formed since the Silver Bullets in the 1990s. Women's semi-pro baseball teams form, but face considerable financial difficulties. For example, those women who live in proximity and wish to play baseball can join the Eastern Women's Baseball Conference, currently in its eighteenth year, with players ranging in age from 24 to 64. While these women play with determination, as do those women playing in the Independent Women's Football League, these teams operate on the outlying fringes of these male-dominated sports where there are few paying spectators[23]

All of these women's baseball leagues and teams are homosocial, competing against other women's teams. Sexual bifurcation and segregation in sport both produces and reproduces exclusive gender differences. Messner and Sabo suggest that breaking the sports/masculinity link is necessary to reconstructing masculinity as a less exclusive category. Breaking this link on homosocial (or racially segregated) teams is obviously more difficult, as is teaching gender tolerance and respect. They argue that bisocial athletics creates a social context where boys and men can cooperate with and compete with girls and women as equals.[24] The process of creating dichotomous categories and their exclusionary consequences can be countered in sport by both increasing the opportunities for girls and women to play on teams with boys where they will be evaluated by the same criteria as their male teammates, and by allowing for female homosocial sports where girls and women can construct their own norms of social interaction among teammates and coaches. On bisocial baseball teams, children, adolescents and young adults who have similar physical capabilities will learn to play with and respect one another's abilities and varied contributions to the team. According to Ilana Kloss, World Team Tennis CEO and commissioner who oversees the eleven-team WTT pro league and nationwide recreational league programs: "It's amazing how much more the men respect the women when they've been on a team with them, and have to rely on them. Anybody can come through under pressure and anyone can choke — it's not gender specific."[25]

These teams will also serve as a source of young female talent who have benefited from years of skill development like their male counterparts. As they grow older fewer girls will play baseball at the level of boys, but some exceptional girls who can remain on the boys' high school or college baseball teams should be able to do so as long as their abilities justify their retention. Although Title IX has protected girls who seek to play on boy's teams, the ideologies justifying their exclusion creates social isolation that is emotionally draining for many. This will change only when it is more common to have girls on boys' athletic teams. For the majority of young women who will not play baseball at the men's level, there should be high school and college baseball teams of their own, in addition to softball, equally financed, where women's talents and relationships can flourish. To offer and finance softball as the she-sport alternative to baseball only reproduces gender dichotomies that justify exclusion. Real inclusion for women in sports requires widespread recognition of the cultural assumptions that support institutionalized segregation and concrete strategies that will promote athleticism as gender neutral.

Three recent examples of girls playing traditional men's sports, one for her Little League team and two on boys' high school teams, are of interest in this regard. The first example relates to baseball. In May 2005, Katie Brownell, a 5' 8" eleven-year-old pitcher on her Little League team, pitched a perfect game, striking out every batter and instigating media attention. Katie's origin story is similar to the other women pitchers discussed in this book. She began to love baseball at age six and learned the game from her two older brothers. Katie's strikeout pitch is her fastball that she can "place just about where she wants." In the season's first game she allowed only one hit and struck out fourteen batters in five innings. Her first year as a "lone ponytail" was difficult: "her teammates sometimes told her she should play softball with the other girls." Nevertheless, she persevered deciding not to switch to the girls' softball league. The manager of Katie's Little League team was "glad she stayed with us." Like Ila Borders, Katie is fortunate to have a supportive coach and family. Unfortunately, since it is still very rare for boys to face girl pitchers, the resistance by male batters that Borders repeatedly confronted remains strong. Manager Sage stated that players on other league teams might find it unnerving to be overpowered by a girl on the pitcher's mound. While adult men viewed Katie's pitching prowess from the perspective of its presumed negative affect on a boy's self-esteem, "I can't imagine being a boy that has to face her at the plate," her teammates "think it is great that she is on our side."[26] Katie's perfect game was recognized in 2005 at the Hall of Fame in Cooperstown where her Number 3 jersey is displayed. It will be interesting to follow this talented pitcher if she continues to play baseball.

The second relates to a 5'9" and 310-pound back-up offensive line player Holley Mangold, the sixteen-year-old younger sister of the Jets' center, Nick Mangold, who plays football for Archbishop Alter High School in Ohio. Although her brother, father and coach all agree "football is not a sport for girls," only football has held her passion. "I like to hit people." Although Mangold receives more attention than her teammates due to her gender, the article suggests that she is not a regular player, playing only twenty downs in the season. To date Holley is merely a presence on the team, not yet a real factor in winning games. Still, she has learned to distance herself from negative comments that isolate her from prevailing images of femininity, particularly those relating to her size: "so many people judge me that I don't even care any more." She spends most of her time with her male teammates.[27]

The article suggests that Holley's teammates accept her presence, but have symbolically distanced themselves from her by nicknaming her Den Mother. Extending the desexualized parental kin term "mother" to a sixteen-year-old peer, includes all the "emphasized feminine" cultural symbolism associated with a role stereotypically assigned to women (i.e., nurturing, protective). Although Holley accepts the label and feels included in her "second family," she refers to them as "brother," another desexualized sibling kin term associated with her own generational status.[28] Other studies have shown the same symbolic response by male athletes coping with the presence of women in male space.[29]

The third example is particularly relevant since it concerns the ultimate contact sport: wrestling. In this case, the girl, fifteen-year-old, 103-pound Jessica Bennett, is a regular on the all-male team at her high school in Montville, New Jersey, with a winning record: 23 of 35 matches in 2007. Her teammates who wrestle with her at practices do not focus on her gender. Rather they recognize that she is good, and "cheer wildly" when she wins. Those boys on the opposing teams, however, do notice her gender since, "there is still some pain in watching a teammate being beaten by a girl." Some boys will forfeit rather than wrestle a girl and others are intimidated by the intimate physical contact with a girl's body in a match. Women's wrestling is now an Olympic sport, and some states (Hawaii, Texas, California) have girls' wrestling teams. Although most consider the expansion of all women's teams to be a positive step in the sports' popularity, the few girls who are excelling on all-boys teams are directly challenging the biologically-based justifications for excluding women from male-dominated sports.[30]

This case study of women and baseball highlights persistent divisions in feminism along race/ethnic and class lines and between liberal feminists who seek equal access to resources and opportunities reserved for men, but leave unchallenged the patriarchal ideologies and norms that protect male privilege, and radical feminists who seek to transform patriarchal conceptions while creating and maintaining spaces, including sports teams that are exclusive to women. While marginalized groups, such as women athletes or women in nontraditional jobs, have benefited from Civil Rights laws such as Titles VII and IX, the structure and culture of both employment and sport remains masculine. To succeed and be accepted as legitimate or professional athletes, women must conform to masculine standards of success and behavioral norms governing social interactions on the playing field.

Crenshaw points out that identity politics, based as it is on membership in a single oppressed category such as women, can ignore or conflate intragroup differences.[31] The present analysis of women's participation in baseball confirms this view. Gender is the central axis of oppression denying all women access to opportunities in amateur and organized professional baseball. However, as the experiences of many women baseball players confirm, girls and women were as likely to reject as to support them as female athletes. Clearly intense anxiety can be aroused in women as well as men when entrenched gender constructions and roles are challenged.

The stigmatized category "lesbian" creates intersecting identities and additional persistent negative social and political consequences for women athletes. However, subordinated people can and do display their agency by "subverting the naming process in empowering ways."[32] The category "tomboy" and the shifts in its meaning over time is one example with particular relevance to girls and women playing baseball with boys. Adopting the ambiguous gender label "tomboy" was for many of the women athletes an act of resistance during their childhood and adolescence against the limiting oppressive construction of hegemonic femininity. Sexuality has been a persistent, albeit silenced, identity for women athletes. For over a century, there has been a consistent attempt to script the sexuality of women athletes in heteronormative terms. Nevertheless, baseball, like other sports, provided an alternative for tomboys and lesbian players who could find and define spaces conducive to sociability and athletic achievement.

Further, race, class and ethnicity produced intersecting differences among women athletes. In the nineteenth century, class was significant as respectable women athletes played on elite, secluded, homosocial teams while lower-class women exposed their bodies and their reputations to the male gaze and comment. Class remained important on the Bloomer Girls teams, where managers sought to protect and insulate the reputations of their players, thereby reproducing middle-class constructions of femininity. Women players persistently confronted sexual harassment as a hostile reminder of their transgression and evidence suggests they also faced hostility from the wives of male spectators who perceived them as morally questionable. From the earliest days until the mid-twentieth century, baseball teams in the United States, whether male or female, were racially segregated. Although Black Bloomer Girls teams existed, access to the most prestigious teams such as the New York Bloomer Girls was restricted to White women. The AAGPBL excluded Black women, including those like Mamie Johnson and Toni Stone who were talented enough to play in the men's Negro League. The Latina players were constructed as White by the League although they perceived themselves as breaking color barriers. Men's organized baseball remained racially segregated until 1947 and, thereafter, the Negro Leagues declined. It was only then that White, male owners of Negro League teams, such as the Clowns' owner Syd Pollock, briefly opened the door to three Black women to boost attendance. More recently, the Colorado Silver Bullets were predominantly White, with Black female athletic talent flowing into other sports.

Baseball has a long history of constructing power structures and supporting legitimizing ideologies that exclude categories of people from participating as players, umpires and sportscasters, including African

Americans, women and Jews. This book has addressed race and gender. A recent editorial by Murray Chass suggests that religion was and is another structure of inequality. Minor League umpire Josh Miller, a Jew, was forced to endure Baseball Chapel services every Sunday in the small locker room where evangelical chapel leaders preached about the glory of Jesus. Last season there were four Jewish umpires in Triple AAA; this year there is only one since three have served the maximum number of years with no prospect of promotion. Miller, who umpired the last three seasons in the International League, continued to face anti–Semitism: "One umpire I worked with last year called me Jewie, and I said I wasn't comfortable with it. It took a more senior guy to get him to stop."[33]

Finally this study has argued that the media has been and remains a powerful agent in the construction of women's bodies, sexuality and gender categories that function to limit or facilitate girls' and women's transgression into male sports and other traditionally male occupations. Visual images of girls and women's bodies and sexuality in the media are increasingly used to filter out "clutter" and stimulate demand for a bewildering array of commodities. These visual images also convey powerful ideological messages that justify or challenge their inclusion or exclusion in various social settings. For women athletes, their bodies can be represented as determined competent competitors or reduced to erotic sexual objects or mannish muscle molls with ambiguous or lesbian sexuality.

Visual images of athletes have for decades been used to symbolically reflect the strength of American populism despite the real structures of inequality that block equal access to opportunities and prestige. For more than a century, extending from the late eighteenth century to World War II, women's bodies were constructed as naturally inferior to and dependent upon the strength of masculinity. Images of adult women emphasized their softness, their delicateness, their maternal qualities justifying that their "natural" domain was the home. Although women were restricted from activities in the public domain including athletics, visual images showing young girls clothed in dresses engaged in boys' activities conveyed a more populist ideological message.

Girls were selected for magazine illustrations from the nineteenth and early twentieth centuries playing America's game of baseball with boys in fields or as symbols of the love for the game by all of the people regardless of gender. Advertisements also incorporated this populist message. One for P and G soap on the cover of *Ladies' Home Journal* in September 1931 "shows a young girl from Portsmouth, Ohio completing a skirts high, hard slide into home plate," safe, of course, and smiling with sheer delight. Its caption reads: "What's right with the world when girls just *will* be boys?" Numerous magazine covers in the 1930s, extending to the early 1950s, featured girls playing baseball as artwork on their covers to represent this slice of populist Americana.[34] However, delighted as we may be to see pictures of "lone ponytails" unconscious of gender, happily competing with or against boys, the persistence of this image also suggests the persistent structured inequality behind the egalitarian facade. The underlying reality is that baseball is not a people's game. It is still a nowoman's land where only young prepubescent girls can transgress the gender boundary, temporarily.

Chapter Notes

The following abbreviations are used: ABGRC — A. Bartlett Giamatti Research Center at the Baseball Hall of Fame; LLMA — Little League Museum Archive.

Chapter 1

1. Barbara Gregorich, *Women at Play* (New York: Harcourt Brace & Co., 1993), 22.

2. Gregorich, *Women at Play*, 22–26; Gai Ingham Berlage, *Women in Baseball* (Westport, Ct.: Praeger, 1994), 46–53; "Alta Weiss All-Star."

3. Sara Corbett, "Baseball for Life," *The New York Times Sports Magazine* (3 June 2006): 52.

4. "Alta Weiss," *Sporting Life* (11 April 1908), ABGRC.

5. Corbett, "Baseball," 52.

6. Kimberle Crenshaw, "Mapping the Margins: Intersectionality, Identity Politics and Violence Against Women of Color," *Stanford Law Review* 43 (1991): 6, 1297.

7. Don Sabo, "Psychological Impacts of Athletic Participation on American Women: Facts and Fables," in *Women and Sports in the United States*, eds. Jean O'Reilly and Susan K. Cahn (Boston: Northeastern University Press, 2007), 61–75.

8. Eileen McDonagh and Laura Papano, *Playing with the Boys: Why Separate Is Not Equal in Sports* (Oxford: Oxford University Press, 2008); O'Reilly and Cahn, *Women and Sports in the United*

States; *Women's Studies Quarterly: Women and Sports* 33 (2005): 1, 2; Susan Birrell and Mary G. McDonald, eds. *Reading Sport* (Boston: Northeastern University Press, 2000); Colette Dowling, *The Frailty Myth* (New York: Random House, 2000); Michael Messner, *Taking the Field: Women, Men and Sports* (Minneapolis: University of Minnesota Press, 2002); Jim McKay, Michael Messner and Don Sabo, eds. *Masculinities, Gender and Sports* (London: Sage, 2000); Michael Messner and Donald F. Sabo, *Sex, Violence and Power in Sports* (Freedom, CA: The Crossing Press, 1994); Michael Messner, *Power at Play: Sports and the Problem of Masculinity* (Boston: Beacon Press, 1992); Pat Griffen, *Strong Women, Deep Closets* (Champaign, Ill: Human Kinetics, 1998); Lisa Disch and Mary Jo Kane, "When a Looker is Really a Bitch: Lisa Olsen, Sport and the Heterosexual Matrix," *Signs* 21 (1996): 2, 278–307; Susan K. Cahn, "From the 'Muscle Moll' to the 'Butch' Player: Mannishness, Lesbianism and Homophobia in U.S. Women's Sports," *Feminist Studies* 19 (1993): 2, 343–368.

9. Nick Trujillo, "Hegemonic Masculinity on the Mound," in *Reading Sport*, eds. Susan Birrell and Mary G. McDonald (Boston: Northeastern University Press, 2000), 15, 17; Michael A. Messner,

Taking the Field (Minneapolis: University of Minnesota Press, 2002), x.

10. Trujillo, "Hegemonic Masculinity," 15, 17; Cahn, "Muscle Moll," 344.

11. Michael Sokolove, "The Uneven Playing Field," *The New York Times Magazine*, 11 May, 2008.

12. Patricia Hill Collins, *Black Feminist Thought* (New York: Routledge, 1990), 68.

13. Sabo, "Psychological Impacts," 65–66.

14. Donald F. Sabo and Joe Panepinto, "Football Ritual and the Social Reproduction of Masculinity," in *Men and Masculinity*, ed. Theodore F. Cohen (Belmont, CA.: Wadsworth/Thomson Learning, 2000), 79.

15. Timothy Beneke, *Proving Manhood* (Berkley: University of California Press, 1997), 40.

16. Alan M. Klein. *Sugarball* (New Haven: Yale University Press, 1991), 72.

17. Brett G. Stroudt, "You're Either In or You're Out": School Violence, Peer Discipline, and the (Re)Production of Hegemonic Masculinity," *Men and Masculinities* 8 (2006): 3, 281.

18. Women's Sports Foundation, "Baseball and Softball: Should Girls and Women Have to Choose?" A Women's Sports Foundation Position Statement" (31 July 2007): 2.

19. Women's Sports Foundation, "Co-ed Participation — Issues Related to Girls and Boys Competing with and Against Each Other in Sports and Physical Activity Settings: The Foundation Position," 6.

20. Messner, *Taking the Field*, xvi; Natalie Adams, Alison Schmitke, and Amy Franklin, "Tomboys, Dykes, and Girly Girls: Interrogating the Subjectivities of Adolescent Female Athletes," *Women's Studies Quarterly, Women and Sports*, 33 (2005): 1,2, 17.

21. McDonagh and Pappano, *Playing with the Boys*, 29.

22. Women's Sports Foundation, "Baseball and Softball," 1.

23. Gary Alan Fine, *With the Boys* (Chicago: University of Chicago Press, 1987), 105–108.

24. Messner and Sabo, *Sex, Violence and Power in Sports*, 43–51.

25. Stoudt, "You're Either in or You're Out," 284.

26. For analysis of "Baseball Annies," see George Gmelch, *Inside Pitch* (Washington, D.C.: Smithsonian Institution Press, 2001), 162–172; Jean Hastings Ardell, *Breaking Into Baseball* (Carbondale: Southern Illinois University Press, 2005), 51–78.

27. Crenshaw, "Mapping the Margins," 6, 1297.

28. Messner, *Taking the Field*, 93.

29. Berlage, *Women in Baseball*; Gai Ingham Berlage, "Transition of Women's Baseball: An Overview," *Nine* 9 (2000): 1, 72–82; Gai Ingham Berlage, "Women, Baseball, and the American Dream," in *Baseball and the American Dream*, ed. Robert Elias (Armonk, N.Y.: M. E. Sharpe, 2001); Gregorich, *Women at Play*; Ardell, *Breaking Into Baseball*; John M. Korvach, *Women's Baseball* (Charleston, S.C.: Arcadia Publishing, 2005).

30. Colette Dowling, *The Frailty Myth* (New York: Random House, 2000); Britain A. Scott and Julie A. Derry, "Women in Their Bodies: Challenging Objectification Through Experiential Learning," *Women's Studies Quarterly: Women and Sports* 33 (2005): 1, 2, 188–209.

Chapter 2

1. Messner, *Power at Play*, 13–14.

2. Rodger Streitmatter, *Mightier than the Sword: How the News Media Have Shaped American History* (Boulder, CO.: Westview 1997), 41, 47.

3. Gai Ingham Berlage. "The Colorado Silver Bullets: Can Professional Women's Baseball Succeed," ABGRC, 6.

4. Berlage, *Women in Baseball*, 2–3.

5. Darryl Brock and Robert Elias, "To Elevate the Game: Women and Early Baseball," in *Baseball and the American Dream*, ed. Robert Elias (Armonk, N.Y.: M. E. Sharpe, 2001), 229.

6. Berlage, *Women in Baseball*, 9–24; Berlage, "Transition of Women's Baseball," 73; Kovach, *Women in Baseball*, 9–14.

7. Cahn, "Muscle Moll," 346.

8. Berlage, *Women in Baseball*, 11–12; Berlage, "Women, Baseball, American Dream," 237.

9. Berlage, *Women in Baseball*, 11.

10. Capt. Debra A. Shattuck, "Bats, Balls and Books: Baseball and Higher Education for Women at Three Eastern Women's Colleges, 1866–1891," *Journal of Sport History* 19 (1992): 101.

11. Shattuck, "Bats, Balls and Books," 2, 100, 108.

12. Shattuck, "Bats, Balls and Books," 92; Berlage, *Women in Baseball*, 6, 27; Berlage "Women, Baseball, American Dream," 236.

13. "Women Wield the Bat," *The Washington Post* (11 April 1890), ABGRC.

14. Berlage, *Women in Baseball*, 6; Ardell, *Breaking into Baseball*, 103.

15. Berlage, *Women in Baseball*, 30–31.

16. *Ibid.*, 29–30; Berlage, "Transition of Women's Baseball," 75–76.

17. Barbara Gregorich, "A Champion for All Seasons," *Pennsylvania Heritage*, Summer (1998), 6–7.

Chapter 3

1. "Girls Who Play Baseball," *The New York Times* (13 September 1893), ABGRC.

2. Cahn, "Muscle Molls," 348–349.

3. Berlage, *Women in Baseball*, 34.

4. *Ibid.*, 38.

5. Gregorich, *Women at Play*, 12.

6. *Cincinnati Enquirer* (24 August 1900), ABGRC.

7. Berlage, *Women in Baseball*, 35.

8. *Ibid.*; Berlage, "Transition of Women's Baseball," 76; Gregorich, *Women at Play*, 33.

9. "NY Bloomer Girls v. Judson Class A Red Coats of King Cotton League," n.d., ABGRC.

10. *New York Tribune* (20 March 1890), ABGRC.

11. *The Nashua Reporter* (8 August 1907), ABGRC.

12. *Cincinnati Enquirer* (6 October 1905), ABGRC.

13. Barrie Thorne, "Children and Gender: Constructions of Difference," in *Gender Through the Prism of Difference*, eds. Maxine Baca Zinn, Pierrette Hondagneu-Sotelo, Michael A. Messner (Boston: Allyn and Bacon, 2000), 33–37.

14. Debbie Jakala, *Times Herald* (17 April 1992), ABGRC; Amy Moritz, *Eagle Times* (15 August 2003); *Daily Messenger* (14 July 2003).

15. Kerry Williams, *Central Jersey Sports* (26 May 1994).

16. Monty Mosher, 12 July 1995, ABGRC; Berlage, *Women in Baseball*, 40.

17. Gregorich, *Women at Play*, 45–46.

18. *Ibid.*, 42–43, 48.

19. Sabo and Panepinto, "Football Ritual," 80–86.

20. Gregorich, *Women at Play*, 44; *The Staten Island Advance* (4 April 1931), ABGRC.

21. Berlage, *Women in Baseball*, 40.

22. *The Sun Tattler* (31 May 1961), ABGRC.

23. Gregorich, *Women at Play*, 6–11, 42–43, 48.

24. *Ibid.*, 44.

25. *Ibid.*; *The Staten Island Advance* (4 April 1931), ABGRC.

26. Gregorich, *Women at Play*, 42.

27. *Indianapolis Freeman* (1 April 1910), ABGRC.

28. Kovach, *Women's Baseball*, 21.

29. *AfroAmerican* (12 August 1921), ABGRC.

30. William E. Brandt, "Woman Whiffs Ruth and Gehrig," in *The Greatest Baseball Stories Ever Told*, ed. Jeff Silverman (Guilford, Ct.: The Lyons Press, 2001), 225–228.

31. David Jenkins, *Chattanooga News-Free Press* (11 April 1982), ABGRC; Berlage, *Women in Baseball*, 73–79; Ardell, *Breaking into Baseball*, 109.

32. Kovach, *Women's Baseball*, 57.

33. Messner, *Power at Play*, 164.

34. *Chattanooga News* (3 April 1931), ABGRC.

35. *Ibid.*, 4 February 1933.

36. Allen Morris, *Chattanooga News-Free Press* (7 September 1975), ABGRC.

37. Gregorich, *Women at Play*, 73–77; Berlage, *Women in Baseball*, 79–82;

Berlage, "Transition in Women's Baseball," 77.

38. Pat Griffin, "Changing the Game: Homophobia, Sexism, and Lesbians in Sport," in *Women and Sports in the United States*, O'Reilly and Cahn, 217–218.

39. Cahn, "Muscle Moll," 344.

Chapter 4

1. Berlage, "The Colorado Silver Bullets," 4, 7.

2. Patricia Vignola, "The Patriotic Pinch Hitter," *Nine* 12 (2004): 2, 102, 104.

3. Berlage, *Women in Baseball*, 153–154.

4. Merrie A. Fidler, *The Origins and History of the All-American Girls Professional Baseball League* (Jefferson, N.C.: McFarland & Company, 2006), 36.

5. *All-American Girls Professional Baseball League Scrapbook, Chicago Colleens versus Springfield Sallies*, 1950, ABGRC.

6. Barbara Liebrich, "Florida Nine Tries to Sign Woman Player," *All-American Girls Professional Baseball League Scrapbook, 1950* (3 August 1950), ABGRC.

7. Streitmatter, *Mightier than the Sword*, 137–152. Quotes on 137, 141, 142.

8. Cahn, "Muscle Molls," 344.

9. *Ibid.*, 344.

10. Griffen, "Changing the Game," 220–221.

11. Berlage, *Women in Baseball*, 134; Lois Browne, *Girls of Summer* (Toronto: Harper Collins, 1992), 39.

12. Quoted in Fidler, *The Origins and History*, 57.

13. *All-American Girls Professional Baseball League Scrapbook, Rockford Peaches, 1948*, ABGRC.

14. Fidler, *The Origins and History*, 16.

15. *All-American Girls Professional Baseball League Scrapbook, Chicago Colleens versus Springfield Sallies*, 1950, ABGRC.

16. Vignola, "The Patriotic Pinch Hitter," 104–105.

17. "All-American Girls Professional Baseball League Rules of Conduct, 1943–

1954," in *Women and Sports in the United States*, eds. Jean O'Reilly and Susan K. Cahn (Boston: Northeastern University Press, 2007), 59–60.

18. Addie Suehsdorf, "Sluggers in Skirts," *All-American Girls Professional Baseball League Yearbook, Chicago Colleens versus Springfield Sallies*, 1949, ABGRC; Sue Macy, *A Whole New Ballgame* (New York: Puffin Books, 1993), 66.

19. Ernestine Petras, interview by author, Haskell, New Jersey, 4 March 2008.

20. Fidler, *The Origins and History*, 166–172.

21. Jane Kruger, *All-American Girls Professional Baseball League Yearbook, Chicago Colleens versus Springfield Sallies*, 1949, ABGRC.

22. Ernestine Petras, interview by author, Haskell, New Jersey, 10 July 2007.

23. Browne, *Girls of Summer*, 60–63; Ardell, *Breaking into Baseball*, 116–117.

24. Griffen, "Changing the Game," 219.

25. Cahn, "Muscle Molls," 360.

26. Robert Sullivan, "Who Said Girls Couldn't Play Baseball," *Sunday News* (4 July 1948), ABGRC.

27. Cooperstown, *Kenosha Evening News* (21 June 1947), ABGRC.

28. Jennie Vimmerstedt, *Jamestown Post Journal* (29 August 1950), ABGRC; *All-American Girls Professional Baseball League Scrapbook, Chicago Colleens versus Springfield Sallies*, 1950, ABGRC.

29. Ernestine Petras, interview by author, Haskell, New Jersey, 4 March 2008.

30. *All-American Girls Professional Baseball League Scrapbook, Chicago Colleens versus Springfield Sallies*, 1950, ABGRC.

31. *The Washington Post* (15 April 1950), ABGRC; *All-American Girls Professional Baseball League Scrapbook, Chicago Colleens versus Springfield Sallies*, 1950, ABGRC.

32. Ernestine Petras, interview by author, Haskell, New Jersey, 10 July 2007.

33. *All-American Girls Professional Baseball League Scrapbook, Chicago Colleens versus Springfield Sallies*, 1950, ABGRC.

34. Hardy Rowland, "It Wasn't Men's

Baseball, But It Was the Best Imitation a Group of Girls Can Give," *Little Rock Gazette* (19 May 1946), ABGRC.

35. Ernestine Petras, interview by author, Haskell, New Jersey 10 July 2007.

36. Morris Markey, "Hey Ma You're Out," *All-American Girls Professional Baseball League Scrapbook, Chicago Colleens versus Springfield Sallies,* 1950, ABGRC.

37. Ken E. News, "Comets Have all the Hopes Aspirations of the Girls in the Stands," *Kenosha Evening News* (9 July 1948), ABGRC.

38. *All-American Girls Professional Baseball League, Yearbook, Chicago Colleens and Springfield Sallies,* 1949, ABGRC; Macy, *Whole New Ballgame,* 72–73.

39. Ernestine Petras, interview by author, Haskell, New Jersey, 10 July 2007.

40. Rowland, "It Wasn't Baseball," ABGRC.

41. Paul Horowitz, *Newark Evening News* (15 August 1949), ABGRC; *All-American Girls Professional Baseball League, Yearbook, Chicago Colleens and Springfield Sallies,* 1949, ABGRC.

42. Ernestine Petras, interview by author, Haskell, New Jersey, 10 July 2007.

43. Addie Suehsdorf, "Sluggers in Skirts," *All-American Girls Professional Baseball League, Yearbook, Chicago Colleens and Springfield Sallies,* 1949, ABGRC; Macy, *Whole New Ballgame,* 65; Ernestine Petras, interview by author, Haskell, New Jersey, 10 July 2007.

44. N. A. Turkheimer, *The Roanoke Times* (9 August 1949), ABGRC; *All-American Girls Professional Baseball League, Yearbook, Chicago Colleens and Springfield Sallies,* 1949, ABGRC.

45. Ernestine Petras, interview by author, Haskell, New Jersey, 4 March 2008.

46. Macy, *Whole New Ballgame,* 27.

47. Bill Fay, "Belles of the Ballgame," *All-American Girls Professional Baseball League, Yearbook, Chicago Colleens and Springfield Sallies,* 1949, ABGRC.

48. Ernestine Petras, interview by author, Haskell, New Jersey, July 10, 2007.

49. *Ibid.*

50. *Ibid.*; Browne, *Girls of Summer,* 81–82.

51. Macy, *Whole New Ballgame,* 27; Browne, *Girls of Summer,* 84.

52. Max Carey, letter to All American Girls Baseball League, 28 October 1949, ABGRC.

53. Browne, *Girls of Summer,* 78–79; Macy, *Whole New Ballgame,* 27–29.

54. Ernestine Petras, interview by author, Haskell, New Jersey, 4 March 2008.

55. *Ibid.,* 10 July 2007.

56. Fidler, *The Origins and History,* 161–162.

57. Ernestine Petras, interview by author, Haskell, New Jersey, 10 July 2007.

58. Fidler, *The Origins and History,* 87–88.

59. Colin Howell, "Canada," in *Baseball Without Borders,* ed. George Gmelch (Lincoln: University of Nebraska Press, 2006), 219.

60. Charles Strand, "Girls Baseball Moguls Smoke Pipe of Peace," *New York Post* (18 June 1948), ABGRC; Lou Hanelis letter to All-American Girls Professional Baseball League, 1948, *All-American Girls Baseball League Scrapbook,* 1949, ABGRC.

61. Markey, "Hey Ma You're Out."

62. Lynn Gray, *New York Post* (18 June 1948), ABGRC.

63. "Women and Cuban Baseball," http://www.cubaball.com/Images/History/Women/women.html.

64. Berlage, *Women in Baseball,* 147; Browne, *Girls of Summer,* 127–136.

65. Fidler, *The Origins and History,* 99–102.

66. Dan Cobian, "Women in Baseball: Latinas in the All-American Girls Professional Baseball League," *Chicana and Latina Studies,* Working Paper Series, 1–7.

67. Fidler, *The Origins and History,* 101–102.

68. *Ibid.,* 102–104; Gregorich, *Women at Play,* 153–157.

69. Ernestine Petras, interview by author, Haskell, New Jersey, 4 March 2008.

70. Cobian, "Latinas in the All-American Girls Professional Baseball League," 1–7.

71. Berlage, *Women in Baseball,* 177, 179.

72. Gregorich, *Women at Play,* 164.

73. Berlage, *Women in Baseball*, 177–178; Browne, *Girls of Summer*, 196.

74. Johnny Travers, "Gal Shortstop's Bid Given Short 'No' by O.B. Officials," *The Sporting News* (2 July 1952), ABGRC.

75. George M. Trautman, National Association of Professional Baseball Leagues, 24 June 1952, ABGRC.

76. Jules Traitman, "Girls Out as Pro Baseball Players," *Patriot News* (23 June 1952), ABGRC.

77. Jules Tygiel, "Black Ball," in *Total Baseball*, 8th edition, eds. John Thorn, Phil Birnbaum, Bill Deane, Rob Neyer, Alan Schwarz, Donald Dewey, Nicholas Acocella, Peter Wayner (Toronto: Sport Media Publishing, 2004), 669; Lawrence D. Hogan, *Shades of Glory: The Negro Leagues and the Story of African American Baseball* (Washington, D.C.: National Geographic, 2006), 343.

78. *The Sunday Patriot News* (23 June 2002), ABGRC.

79. Pat Harmon, "Cincinnati Almost Had First Girl in Organized Baseball," *Cincinnati Post* (24 June 1952), ABGRC.

80. S. A. Schreiner, "Do You Want Women in Baseball?" *Jr. Parade* (10 August 1952), ABGRC.

81. "Girl Player Stirs up Battle" (23 June 1952), ABGRC.

82. Tracy Everbach, "Breaking Baseball Barriers: The 1953–54 Negro League and Expansion of Women's Public Roles," *American Journalism* 22 (2005): 1, 22.

83. "Signing of Girl to Play Pro Ball Stirs Furore" (23 June 1952), ABGRC.

84. Editorial, "A Woman's Place is in the Grandstand," *The Sporting News* (23 June 1952), ABGRC.

85. Furman Bisher, "Girls of Summer: An All-Female Lineup for the Sun Sox?" (1 October 1984), ABGRC.

Chapter 5

1. Tygiel, "Black Ball," 668.

2. Kimberle Crenshaw, "Intersectionality and Identity Politics: Learning from Violence Against Women of Color," in *Feminist Theory*, eds. Wendy K. Kolmar and Frances Bartkowski (New York: McGraw Hill, 2005), 535.

3. Patricia Madoo Lenermann and Jill Niebrugge-Brantley, *The Women Founders* (Boston: McGraw Hill, 1998), 157.

4. Anna Julia Cooper, "The Status of Woman in America," from *A Voice of the South: By a Black Woman of the South*, in *Feminist Theory*, eds. Wendy K. Kolmar and Frances Bartkowski (New York: McGraw Hill, 2005), 104.

5. bell hooks, *Feminist Theory* (Cambridge, MA: South End Press, 2000), 16.

6. Crenshaw, "Intersectionality," 535.

7. Ardell, *Breaking into Baseball*, 113.

8. *Ibid.*, 110; Letter from Bob Davids Regarding Women in the Negro Leagues, 26 February 1996, ABGRC.

9. *Women in Baseball*, 129; Tygiel, "Black Ball," 665; Michelle Green, "Meeting Mamie," *Sports Fan Magazine*, 12, (2003): 46, ABGRC.

10. Everbach, "Breaking Baseball Barriers," 13, 21–25.

11. Berlage, *Women in Baseball*, 127–128; Ardell, *Breaking into Baseball*, 111–113.

12. Larry Lester, "Stone (Alberga), Marcenia Lyle 'Toni,'" in *Encyclopedia of Women and Baseball*, eds. Leslie A. Heaphy and Mel Anthony (Jefferson, N.C.: McFarland, 2006), 278.

13. Alan J. Pollock, *Barnstorming to Heaven: Syd Pollock and His Great Black Teams* (Tuscaloosa: The University of Alabama Press, 2006), 240–41.

14. "The Lady Played Second Base," ABGRC.

15. "Ball Player," *Ebony*, 1953.

16. Ardell, *Breaking into Baseball*, 110–111; "The Lady Played Second Base," ABGRC; Lester, "Stone," 279.

17. *Ibid.*

18. *Ibid.*

19. Pollock, *Barnstorming*, 242; Lester, "Stone," 279 .

20. "Feminine Stars," (17 February 1999): 3, ABGRC; Lester, "Stone," 279.

21. Ardell, *Breaking into Baseball*, 112; Pollock, *Barnstorming*, 243; Lester, "Stone," 279.

22. Everbach, "Breaking Baseball Barriers," 17.

23. Pollock, *Barnstorming*, 242.

24. Gregorich, *Women at Play*, 171; Pollock, *Barnstorming*, 242–243; Lester, "Stone," 279.

25. Gregorich, *Women at Play*, 175; Pollock, *Barnstorming*, 243.

26. "Ball Player," *Ebony*, 1953, 52.

27. *Ibid.*

28. Bill Kruissink, "First Woman in Pro Baseball Remembers," *Alameda Journal*, 2 April 1996.

29. "Gal on Second Base," 1953; Lester, "Stone," 279.

30. Everbach, "Breaking Baseball Barriers," 20–21.

31. "Lady Ball Player," *Ebony* (1953): 52, ABGRC.

32. Pollock, *Barnstorming*, 255.

33. *Ibid.*, 240.

34. "The Gal on Second Base," 1953, ABGRC.

35. Everbach, "Breaking Baseball Barriers," 20.

36. Ron Thomas, "Baseball Pioneer Looks Back," *San Francisco Chronicle*.

37. Pollock, *Barnstorming*, 244.

38. Everbach, "Breaking Baseball Barriers," 22–23.

39. Doug Grow, "League of Her Own: Tomboy Stone Dead at 76," *Minneapolis Star Tribune*, 5 November 1996.

40. Gregorich, *Women at Play*, 174.

41. Pollock, *Barnstorming*, 112.

42. "Lady Played Second Base"; Lester, "Stone," 279.

43. Pollock, *Barnstorming*, 244–245.

44. Susan Sword, "Toni Stone," *San Francisco Chronicle*, 6 November 1996.

45. Pollock, *Barnstorming*, 239–240; Lester, "Stone," 279.

46. Ron Thomas, "Baseball Pioneer Looks Back," *San Francisco Chronicle*, ABGRC.

47. "Ball Player," *Ebony* (1953): 52.

48. Pollock, *Barnstorming*, 239.

49. Hill-Collins, *Black Feminist Thought*, 107–108.

50. Everbach, "Breaking Baseball Barriers," 21.

51. Sword, "Toni Stone," ABGRC.

52. Pollock, *Barnstorming*, 248.

53. *Ibid.*

54. Everbach, "Breaking Baseball Barriers," 20.

55. *Ibid.*, 17.

56. Pollock, *Barnstorming*, p. 256.

57. "Stars," 3; Lester, "Stone," 279.

58. Pollock, *Barnstorming*, 258.

59. Everbach, "Breaking Baseball Barriers," 24.

60. Pollock, *Barnstorming*, 252.

61. Michelle Y. Green, *A Strong Right Arm* (New York: Puffin Books, 2002), 6.

62. Michelle Y. Green, "Meeting Mamie," *Sports Fan Magazine* 12 (2003): 6.

63. Green, *Strong Right Arm*, 23.

64. *Ibid.*, 22–23.

65. *Ibid.*, 7–8.

66. *Ibid.*

67. Green, "Meeting Mamie," 6.

68. Green, *Strong Right Arm*, 39.

69. Green, "Meeting Mamie," 6.

70. Green, *Strong Right Arm*, 43–44.

71. Merrie Fidler, "All American Girl Professional Baseball League," *Touching Bases Newsletter*, January 1905.

72. *Ibid.*; Dan Silverman, "No League of their Own," ABGRC.

73. Eugene L Meyer, "A League of Her Own: Baseball's Proud Peanut," *The News Tribune*, 5 April 1999; Lester, "Stone," 279.

74. Green, "Meeting Mamie," 47.

75. Donna Britt, "Peanut is Her Name, Baseball is Her Game," *The Detroit Free Press*, 16 September 1999.

76. Joseph White, "Peanut Struck Out Her Share of Guys," 11 May 1998.

77. "Stars," 3.

78. White, "Peanut Struck Out Her Share," ABGRC.

79. Meyer, "Baseball's Proud Peanut."

80. Green, "Meeting Mamie," 47.

81. Pollock, *Barnstorming*, 258.

82. Everbach, "Breaking Baseball Barriers," 19.

83. Hill-Collins, *Black Feminist Thought*, 113; Crenshaw "Intersectionality," 536.

Chapter 6

1. Karen Rosen, "A Female Team in Pro-Baseball," *Atlanta Constitution* (16 August 1984), ABGRC.

2. Gregorich, *Women at Play*, 79.

3. Rosen, "A Female Team."

4. DeLand, "Sun Sox Seek Berth in FSL, but There's One Hitch," *Florida Sun News*, (19 September 1984), ABGRC.

5. Larry McCarthy, "ERA Pitch: Stage Set for Women's Team to Join Class A Baseball League," *Reading Pennsylvania Times* (9 September 1984), ABGRC.

6. Bob Hope, quoted in Gregorich, *Women at Play*, 182.

7. Bisher, "Girls of Summer."

8. "Women Living Dreams in Baseball Tryouts," *Tifton Georgia Gazette*, (18 September 1984), ABGRC.

9. Ernest Reese, "Baseball a Men's Sport?" ABGRC.

10. "Women Living Dreams," ABGRC; "Sun Sox Tryouts End Predictably," 19 September, 1984.

11. Bisher, "Girls of Summer."

12. Dick Soonton, "Women in the Florida League? What a Snow Job," *Lakeland Florida Ledger* (20 September 1984), ABGRC.

13. Daniel T. Parker, *The Sports Wrangler* (20 September 1984), ABGRC.

14. Reese, "Baseball a Men's Sport?"

15. "Women Living Dreams"; Jeff Denberg, "Its Ladies Day at the Sun Sox Tryouts," *Atlanta Georgia Constitution* (18 September 1984).

16. Karen Rosen, "Florida State League Says No to Sun Sox," *Atlanta Georgia Journal* (27 September 1984), ABGRC.

17. Carol L. Whittington, "Gender Identities are Confusing," *Tampa Tribune* (7 December 1984), ABGRC.

18. Mitch Albom, "Women on Base? Decide on the Field." *Ft. Lauderdale Sun Sentinel* (26 September 1984), ABGRC.

19. Berlage, "The Colorado Bullets," 41.

20. Steve Zipay, "Niekro Set to Prove a Point," *Newsday* (16 December 1993), ABGRC; *USA Today*, 7–13 February 1996.

21. Berlage, "The Colorado Silver Bullets," 8.

22. Paul Nowell, "All-Women's Team Out of its League," *Times Union* (9 May 1994), ABGRC.

23. Ardell, *Breaking into Baseball*, 122.

24. Phil Niekro quoted in Pete Williams, "Silver Lining: Bullets Showed They Belong," *USA Today* (7–13 September 1994), ABGRC.

25. Maria Malloy, "Coor's Field of Stifled Dreams," *Business Week* (24 January 1994), ABGRC.

26. Susan Fornoff, "Playing Hardball," *The Sporting News* (30 May 1994), ABGRC.

27. Jay Greenberg, "Gals of Summer Take Their Cuts," *New York Post* (8 March 1994), ABGRC.

28. *USA Today* (9 May 1994), ABGRC.

29. Malloy, "Coor's Field of Stifled Dreams."

30. Carolyn White, "Silver Bullets Brace for Sunday's Opener," *USA Today* (6 May 1994), ABGRC.

31. Stuart Miller, "A Few More Pitches for Gender Equality," *Inside Sports* (June 1994), ABGRC.

32. Ray McNulty, "Wiley Finds Her Field of Dreams," *New York Post* (6 May 1994), ABGRC.

33. Dave Kindred, *The Colorado Silver Bullets: For the Love of the Game* (Atlanta: Longstreet Press, 1995), 88.

34. Ross Newhan, "Girls of Summer," *Times Union* (8 May 1994), ABGRC; Fornoff, "Playing Hardball."

35. Fornoff, "Playing Hardball."

36. Rachael Shuster, "Baseball Team Opens Doors, Minds," *USA Today* (21 February 1994), ABGRC; Mollory, "Coor's Field of Stifled Dreams."

37. Barbara Walder, "All-Women's Baseball Team is Both Silly and Boring" (8 April 1994), ABGRC.

38. Ray McNulty, "Old-Timer Says Team Won't Last," *New York Post* (9 May 1994), ABGRC; Claire Smith, "Swings and Misses Aren't Heart of the Matter in This Game," 9 May 1994.

39. Fornoff, "Playing Hardball."

40. Smith, "Swings and Misses."

41. Kindred, *Colorado Silver Bullets*, 40.

42. George Vesey, "A Sporting Gesture Touches 'Em All," *The New York Times* (30 April 2008).

43. Fine, *With the Boys*, 86.

44. "The New Americans," Kartemquin Films, 2002.

45. Kindred, *Colorado Silver Bullets,* 34.

46. Stephan R. Walk, "Moms, Sisters, and Ladies: Women Student Trainers in Men's Intercollegiate Sport," in *Masculinities, Gender Relations, and Sport,* eds., Jim McKay, Michael A. Messner and Don Sabo (London: Sage Publications, 2000), 31–46.

47. Susan Fornoff, "Hanes Does it Her Way," *The Sporting News* (30 May 1994), ABGRC.

48. "Historic Debut," *USA Today* (4 June 1996).

49. Berlage, "The Colorado Bullets," 41–42.

50. The phrase "lone ponytail" was first used by University of North Carolina soccer player Yael Averbusch, who played on boys' teams and wrote about her experiences at age twelve. See Yael Averbusch, "The Lone Ponytail," *Soccer Junior Magazine* (1999).

51. Brill, *Winning Women,* 63–65; Gregorich, *Women at Play,* 197–198; Alice Digilio, "Girl Sues to Play Ball," *The Washington Post* (17 March 1988), ABGRC.

52. Brill, *Winning Women,* 65; Gregorich, *Women at Play,* 198.

53. Brill, *Winning Women,* 68; Gregorich, *Women at Play,* 198.

54. *Jo Ann Carnes v. Tennessee Secondary School Athletic Association, Board of Education of Morgan County, John W. Galloway, Jake Gamble and Carl Edward Kreis,* 415 F. Supp. 569; 1976 U.S. Dist. LEXIS 15185 (1976).

55. *Nancy Maren Croteau and Raymond Nelson Croteau v. Rick Fair, Jack Lynch, Edward Kelly and The Prince William County School Board,* 686 F. Supp. 552; U.S. Dist. LEXIS 5799 (1988); Brill, *Winning Women,* 67; Gregorich, *Women at Play,* 199; Digilio, "Girl Sues to Play Ball"; Tony Kornheiser, "Julie Croteau's Play Deserves to be Judged On the Baseball Field, Not in the Court Room," *The Washington Post,* 19 March 1988; Caryle Murphy, "Team Backs Pr. William Coach in Sex Bias Case," *The Washington Post* (1988); Darlene Mehrer, "Girl Cut from H.S. Baseball Team Sues," *Basewoman* (June 1988).

56. Brill, *Winning Women,* 67.

57. Carolyn White, "Female Player 'Just One of the Team,'" *USA Today* (13 March 1989), ABGRC.

58. Stephen Steed, "Who's on First? A Girl in This Case," *USA Today* (5 May 1988), ABGRC.

59. Brill, *Winning Women,* 69,75.

60. *Ibid.,* 70–71; Gregorich, *Women at Play,* 200–01.

61. Mariah Burton Nelson, "Player: Sexism Cut Sort Career," *USA Today,* 6 June 1991, ABGRC.

62. Brill, *Winning Women,* 73–74.

63. *USA Today,* 1–7 May 1996, ABGRC.

64. Brad Parks, "Croteau's Love of Baseball Exceeds Pain of Past Slights," *The Washington Post,* ABGRC.

65. Brill, *Winning Women,* 76.

66. Jennifer Ring, "Why Shouldn't Girls Play Baseball? It's time for the U.S. to stop discouraging girls from the national pastime," *The Los Angeles Times* (27 July 2006), Girls Play Baseball, http://girlsplaybaseball.wordpress.com/2006/09/27/.

67. Gregorich, *Woman at Play,* 182.

68. Gai Ingham Berlage, "The Colorado Bullets," *Baseball Research Journal* 27 (1998): 40, ABGRC.

69. Mehrer, "Girl Cut from H.S. Baseball Team Sues," ABGRC.

Chapter 7

1. Brill, *Winning Women,* 74–76, 78–79; Gregorich, *Women at Play,* 203.

2. Brill, *Winning Women,* 79–80; Jean Hastings Ardell, "Ila Borders, Pitcher," *The National Pastime* 20 no. 19 (2000): 1–2.

3. Brill, *Winning Women,* 81.

4. *Ibid.,* 82.

5. *Ibid.;* Ardell, "Ila Borders," 1.

6. Ardell, "Ila Borders," 2.

7. Suzanne Laberge and Mathieu Albert, "Conceptions of Masculinity and Gender Transgressions in Sport Among Adolescent Boys," in *Masculinities, Gender Relations and Sport,* eds. Jim McKay, Michael A. Messner and Don Sabo (London: Sage Publications, 2000), 195–221.

8. Brill, *Winning Women*, 83; Ardell, "Ila Borders," 2–3.
9. Brill, *Winning Women*, 83.
10. Ardell, "Ila Borders," 3.
11. Brill, *Winning Women*, 84.
12. Ardell, "Ila Borders," 3.
13. Brill, *Winning Women*, 86; Ardell, "Ila Borders," 4.
14. Ardell, "Ila Borders," 4–5.
15. Brill, *Winning Women*, 87.
16. Ardell, *Breaking into Baseball*, 129.
17. Ardell, "Ila Borders," 5.
18. Ardell, *Breaking into Baseball*, 136.
19. Brill, *Winning Women*, 89.
20. Ardell, *Breaking into Baseball*, 131.
21. Ardell, "Ila Borders," 5–6.
22. *Ibid.*, 8.
23. Sharon Lennon, "What Is Mine," in *Listen Up: Voices from the Next Feminist Generation*, ed. Barbara Findlen (Seattle: Seal Press, 1995), 120–131.
24. Lee Anne Bell, "Something's Wrong Here and Its Not Me: Challenging the Dilemmas That Block Girls' Success," in *Women: Images and Realities*, eds. Amy Kesselman, Lily D. McNair and Nancy Schniedewind (McGraw Hill: Boston, 2003), 83–88.
25. Ardell, "Ila Borders," 5.
26. Everbach, "Breaking Baseball Barriers," 29.
27. Ardell, "Ila Borders," 6.

Chapter 8

1. Fidler, *The Origins and History*, 15.
2. *Ibid.*, 16
3. *Ibid.*, 16, 20.
4. *Ibid.*, 18, 20.
5. *Ibid.*, 23.
6. Berlage, *Women in Baseball*, 96–97.
7. Lance and Robin Van Auken, *Play Ball: The Story of Little League Baseball* (University Park, PA: The Pennsylvania State University Press, 2001), 12–13.
8. Fidler, *The Origins and History*, 25; Ardell, *Breaking into Baseball*, 82–83.
9. Berlage, *Women in Baseball*, 91.
10. *Ibid.*
11. *Ibid.*
12. Gregorich, *Women at Play*, 61–62
13. Berlage, *Women in Baseball*, 93.

14. *Ibid.*, 93–94.
15. Berlage, *Women in Baseball*, 94.
16. *Ibid.*, 95.
17. *Ibid.*; Gregorich, *Women at Play*, 60–65.

Chapter 9

1. Van Auken, *Play Ball*, 143.
2. Carl E. Stotz, *A Promise Kept* (Jersey Shore, PA: Zebrowski Historical Services Publishing Company, 1992), 16.
3. Van Auken, *Play Ball*, 145, 151.
4. *Ibid.*, 164.
5. *Ibid.*, 116–117; Fine, *With the Boys*, 7, 27.
6. File on Girls, 1950–1968, LLMA.
7. Exhibit "Celebrating the 30th Anniversary of Girls in Little League," 2004, LLMA.
8. Ardell, *Breaking Into Baseball*, 83–84; Berlage, *Women in Baseball*, 97.
9. McDonagh and Pappano, *Playing with the Boys*, 206.
10. File on Girls Litigations, 1974, "She Was in a League of Her Own in '63," *New York Times* (31 March 1974), LLMA.
11. File on Girls, 1950–1968, LLMA.
12. Van Auken, *Play Ball*, 147.
13. Carolyn Ann King by Gerald King, *Ypsilanti Community American Little League, and the City of Ypsilanti v. Little League Baseball, S.B. Stanton*, 505 F.2d 264; 1974 U.S. App. LEXIS 6288 (1974).
14. *Ibid.*; LLMA, Press Clippings Relating to Girls in Baseball, *Long Island Press*, 24 May 1973.
15. Carolyn Ann King by Gerald King, *Ypsilanti Community American Little League, and the City of Ypsilanti v. Little League Baseball, S.B. Stanton*, 505 F.2d 264; 1974 U.S. App. LEXIS 6288 (1974).
16. *Ibid.*
17. Maria Pepe, interview by author, Jersey City, New Jersey, 19 March 2007.
18. James Farina, interview by author, Hoboken, New Jersey, 11 June 2007.
19. Philip Read, "It Took a Hoboken Girl to Strike Out Little League's Ban," *The Star Ledger* (6 May 2005), LLMA; Ruth Padawer, "She Came to Play: Women Athletes Can Thank Trailblazer,

Her Coach," *The Record* (23 November 2003) LLMA; Maria Pepe, interview by author, Jersey City, New Jersey, 19 March 2007.

20. James Farina, interview by author, Hoboken, New Jersey, 11 June 2007.

21. *Ibid.*; Daniel Hays, "Maria Jolts Little League," *The Evening News* (9 May 1972) LLMA.

22. James Farina, interview by author, Hoboken, New Jersey, 11 June 2007.

23. "Alumni Profile: Maria Pepe," *FDU Magazine*, Fall/Winter, 1998.

24. Padawer, "She Came to Play"; Read, "It Took a Hoboken Girl"; Maria Pepe, interview by author, Jersey City, New Jersey, 19 March 2007.

25. McDonagh and Pappano, *Playing with the Boys*, 208.

26. Maria Pepe, interview by author, Jersey City, New Jersey, 19 March 2007.

27. "Maria Pepe Sees Fruits of Playing in 1971," Associated Press Sports Center (8 July 2005).

28. Daniel Hays, "Maria's Mother Cool to N.O.W. Suit, But Proud of Little League Daughter," *The Evening News* (25 May 1972), LLMA; Read, "It Took a Hoboken Girl"; Padawer, "She Came to Play"; Maria Pepe, interview by author, Jersey City, New Jersey, 19 March 2007; James Farina, interview by author, Hoboken, New Jersey, 11 June 2007.

29. "Alumni Profile: Maria Pepe."

30. Maria Pepe, interview by author, Jersey City, New Jersey, 19 March 2007.

31. File Girls' Litigation, 1974, LLMA.

32. *Ibid.*

33. File Civil Rights, 1971, 1972–1974; letter written 20 June 1973, LLMA.

34. File: Press Clippings Relating to Girls in Baseball, LLMA.

35. Dr. Thomas Johnson, "An Analysis of Sex Differences as They Affect Little League Baseball," LLMA.

36. "Boys and Girls Together," *The New York Times* (5 January 1974), LLMA.

37. *National Organization for Women, Essex County Chapter, Division on Civil Rights v. Little League Baseball, Inc.*, 127 N.J. Super. 522; 318 A.2d 33; 1974 N.J. Super. LEXIS 756; 66 A.L.R.3d 1247 (1974).

38. McDonagh and Pappano, *Playing with the Boys*, 209.

39. *National Organization for Women, Essex County Chapter, Division on Civil Rights v Little League Baseball, Inc.*, 127 N.J. Super. 522; 318 A.2d 33; 1974 N.J. Super. LEXIS 756; 66 A.L.R.3d 1247 (1974).

40. *Ibid.*

41. *Ibid.*

42. *Ibid.*

43. *Ibid.*

44. File Girls Litigation, 1974, letter from R.B. Alexander to Peter J. McGovern, 2 April 1974, LLMA.

45. Frank Deford, "Now Georgy-Porgy Runs Away," *Sports Illustrated* (22 April 1974).

46. Berlage, *Women in Baseball*, 101.

47. Deford, "Now Georgy-Porgy."

48. *Ibid.*

49. *Ibid.*

50. *Ibid.*

51. *Allison "Pookie" Fortin and Robert Fortin v Darlington Little League, Inc.*, 376 F. Supp. 473; 1974 U.S. Dist. LEXIS 8530 (1974).

52. *Allison "Pookie" Fortin, et.al., v Darlington Little League, Inc. etc. et.al.*, 514 F.2d 344; 1975 U.S. App. LEXIS 15392 (1975).

53. *Ibid.*

54. *Ibid.*

55. *Ibid.*

56. Press Clippings Relating to Girls in Baseball, Edward Wood, "A Game for All or Just the Boys," *The Providence Sunday Journal* (28 May 1974), LLMA.

57. *Ibid.*

58. Press Clippings Relating to Girls in Baseball, Homer Metz, *Providence Rhode Island Journal* (28 April 1974), LLMA.

59. Press Clippings Relating to Girls in Baseball, Jack Kofoed, "Girls and Little League — Do Courts, Nature Disagree," *Miami Herald* (2 April 1974), LLMA.

60. File Girl's Litigation, 1974, Bob Allison, *Gazette Sports*, Phoenix, Ariz. (1 April 1974), LLMA.

61. File Girl's Litigation, 1974, *Sun Gazette*, Williamsport, Penn. (5 August 1974), LLMA.

62. Press Clippings Relating to Girls in

Baseball, George James, "Defending the Credo," *The Record* (11 March 1974), LLMA.

63. File Civil Rights, 1971, 72–74, Richard J. Seltzer, "Hazardous Game for Girls?" Rockville, Maryland (9 June 1973), LLMA.

64. Press Clippings Relating to Girls in Baseball, *Daily News* (15 June 1974), LLMA.

65. File Civil Rights, 1971–1974, Bill Gleason, ""Woman in Majors? Its Just a Matter of Time," *Philadelphia Inquirer* (18 June 1973), LLMA.

66. File Press Clippings Relating to Girls in Baseball, LLMA.

67. Lennon, "What is Mine," 123–124.

68. Maria Pepe Exhibit, LLMA.

69. Maria Pepe Exhibit; File Civil Rights, 1971–1974, LLMA.

70. Fine, *With the Boys*, 51, 154.

71. *Ibid.*, 102–114; 155–157.

72. Stoudt, "You're Either In or You're Out," 273–287.

73. Pawtucket Slaterettes, Press releases, http://www.slaterettes.com.

74. File Girls Planning Discussion 1973, Letter by Creighton J. Hale, 9 November 1973, LLMA.

75. "Boys and Girls Together," *The New York Times* (5 January 1974), LLMA.

76. Press Clippings Relating to Girls in Baseball, Wood, "A Game for All," LLMA.

77. Ardell, *Breaking into Baseball*, 82; McDonagh and Pappano, *Playing with the Boys*, 10.

78. "Maria Pepe Sees Fruits of Playing in 1971."

79. Berlage, *Women in Baseball*, 103.

80. John Kovach, "Where's the Pony-tail?," Presentation at the Popular and American Culture Conference, Boston, Mass., April, 2007.

81. Van Auken, *Play Ball*, 202.

82. Kovach, "Where's the Ponytail."

83. *Little League Baseball World Series Media Guide*, 2004, LLMA.

84. Wandoo Makurdi, "Irina Kovach: In a League of Her Own," Women's Sports Foundation, http://www.womenssports foundation.org/cgi-bin/iowa/athletes/article.html?record=274.

85. "Maria Pepe Sees Fruits of Playing in 1971."

86. Berlage, "Transition of Women's Baseball," 79.

87. Van Auken, *Play Ball*, 202.

Chapter 10

1. George Vesey, "Softball Is Losing a Chance to Celebrate," *The New York Times*, Sports, (28 February 2008).

2. Women's Sports Foundation, "Baseball and Softball: Should Girls and Women Have to Choose: A Women's Sports Foundation Position Paper" (31 June 2007): 2.

3. Michael Gasparino, "Playing Hardball: Women's Baseball Seeking Respect," New York NOW/New York Sports On Line-Baseball, http://www.nysol.com/baseball_women.html.

4. Vanessa Selbst, telephone conversation with author, 21 February 2008.

5. Averbusch, "The Lone Ponytail."

6. Marcia Chambers, "Barred from Men's-Only Event, Woman Sues Public Gold Club," *The New York Times* (19 February 2008).

7. Bill Pennington, "Title IX Trickles Down to Girls of Generation Z," *The New York Times* (29 June 2004).

8. *Ibid.*

9. Women's Sports Foundation, "Co-ed Participation — Issues Related to Girls and Boys Competing With and Against Each Other in Sports and Physical Activity Settings: The Foundation Position," 1–2.

10. *New York State Division on Human Rights, on Complaint of Bernice Gera v New York-Pennsylvania Professional Baseball League, et.al.,* 36 A.D.2dd 364; 320 N.Y.S.2nd 788; 1971 N.Y. App Div. LEXIS 4177; 3 Fair Empl. Prac. Cas. (BNA) 483 (1971).

11. Michael Lewis, "Absolutely, Power Corrupts," *New York Times Magazine* (24 April 2005): 46–51.

12. *Ibid.*

13. Sara Corbett, "Baseball for Life," *The New York Times Sports Magazine* (June 2006).

14. *Ibid.*

15. Allan Simpson, "2005 Baseball for the Ages," *Baseball America* (October-December 2005).

16. Corbett, "Baseball for Life,"; Simpson, "2005 Baseball for the Ages."

17. Dave Zinn, "How Baseball Strip-Mines the Dominican Republic" (28 October 2005), CommonDreams.org.

18. Pawtucket Slaterettes Press Releases, http://www.slaterettes.com.

19. Chicago Pioneers, http://www.chicagopioneers.com/about.htm.

20. Carolina Miners, http://www.carolinaminers.com/about.htm.

21. Jim Glennie, "The Recent Development of Women's International Baseball Competitions," American Women's Baseball Federation, 2 April 2006.

22. Jennifer Ring, "Why Shouldn't Girls Play Baseball?" *The Los Angeles Times* (27 August 2006); Girls Play Baseball, http://girlsplaybaseball.wordpresss.com.

23. Dan Zak, "The Girls of Summer," *The Washington Post* (27 May 2007); Michael Weinreb, "Playing for Fun and Little Else, On Football's Edge," *The New York Times* (18 July 2006).

24. Messner and Sabo, *Sex, Violence and Power in Sports*, 172.

25. Andrea Kahn, "35 Years of Title IX," *The New York Times Sports Magazine* (19 August 2007); McDonagh and Pappano, *Playing with the Boys*, 254–256.

26. Thomas J. Kueck and Ben Beagle, "Shy Smile. Mean Fastball," *The New York Times* (19 May 2005).

27. Karen Crouse, "Also Seeing Life Through a Face Mask," *The New York Times* (29 October 2006). For additional information relating to legal cases involving girls playing on boys' football teams, see McDonagh and Pappano, *Playing with the Boys*, 125–134.

28. *Ibid.*

29. Stephan R. Walk, "Moms, Sisters, and Ladies: Women Student Trainers in Men's Intercollegiate Sport," in *Masculinities, Gender Relations, and Sport*, eds. Jim McKay, Michael A. Messner and Don Sabo (Thousand Oaks, CA: Sage, 2000), 35–38.

30. Tamar Lewin, "In Twist for High School Wrestlers, Girl Flips Boy," *The New York Times* (17 February 2007). For additional information relating to legal cases involving girls on boys' wrestling teams, see McDonagh and Pappano, *Playing with the Boys*, 134–137.

31. Crenshaw, "Intersectionality," 533.

32. Crenshaw, "Mapping the Margins," 1297.

33. Murray Chass, "Should a Clubhouse Be a Chapel?" *The New York Times* (2 February 2008): D1, D3.

34. John M. Kovach, *Women's Baseball* (Charleston, S.C.: Arcadia Publishing, 2005).

Bibliography

Documents and Records

A. Bartlett Giamatti Research Center (ABGRC)

All American Girls Professional Baseball League Scrapbook. 1948. Rockford Peaches.
All American Girls Professional Baseball League Scrapbook. 1949. Chicago Colleens versus Springfield Sallies.
All American Girls Professional Baseball League Scrapbook. 1950. Chicago Colleens versus Springfield Sallies.
Author unknown. 1954. "Feminine Stars." *Indianapolis Clowns Program.* File: Women in the Negro Leagues.
Berlage, Gai Ingham, date unknown. "The Colorado Silver Bullets: Can Professional Women's Baseball Succeed?" unpublished manuscript.
Carey, Max. Letter to All American Girls Professional Baseball League, 28 November 1949. File: Max Carey.
Davids, Bob. Letter regarding women in the Negro Leagues, 26 February 1996. File: Women in the Negro Leagues.
Hanelis, Lou. Letter to All American Girls Professional Baseball League, National Girls Baseball League, Atlantic Coast Girls' Baseball League, 1948. All American Girls Professional Baseball League 1949 scrapbook.
Trautman, George M. Official statement: National Association of Professional Baseball Leagues, 24 June 1952. File: Eleanor Engel.
Martin, Jamie. 2004. "Negro Leagues Gave Female Baseball Legend Her Start." Mamie 'Peanut' Johnson speaks at Library of Congress. U.S. Department of State, International Information Programs, 1 October.

Little League Museum Archive (LLMA)

Alexander, R. B. District Administrator, Letter to Peter J. McGovern, Chairman, Little League Baseball, 2 April 1974. File: Girl's Litigations, 1974.
Exhibit Celebrating the 30th Anniversary of Girls in Little League.
File: Girls, 1950–1968.
File: Civil Rights, 1971–1974.
File: Girls Planning Discussion, 1973.
File: Girls' Litigation, 1974.
File: Press Clippings Relating to Girls in Baseball.
File: Dr. Thomas Johnson.

Hale, Creighton J. Letter to President of Little League Baseball, 9 November 1973. File: Girls Planning Discussion, 1973.
Johnson, Dr. Thomas. 1974. "An Analysis of Sex Differences as They Affect Little League Baseball." File: Dr. Thomas Johnson.
Young, Norma. Letter to Robert H. Stirrat, Director of Public Relations, 1968, and Stirrat's reply, 5 June 1968. File: Girls, 1950–1968.

LEGAL DOCUMENTS

Allison "Pookie" Fortin and Robert Fortin, Plaintiffs, v. Darlington Little League, Inc. (American Division), et al., Defendants. Civ. A. No. 74-76, United States District Court for the District of Rhode Island. 376 F. Supp. 473: 1974 U.S. Dist. LEXIS 8530, 15 May 1974.
Allison "Pookie" Fortin, et al., Plaintiffs, Appellants, v. Darlington Little League, Inc., et al., Defendants, Appellees. No. 74-1216, United States Court of Appeals for the First Circuit. 514 F.2d 344; 1775 U.S. App. LEXIS 15392, 31 March 1975.
Carolyn Ann King, by Gerald E. King, her next friend, Ypsilanti Community American Little League, and the City of Ypsilanti, Plaintiffs-Appellants, v. Little League Baseball, Inc., a Federal Corporation, S.B. Stanton, Agent for Little League Baseball, Inc., Defendants-Appellees. No. 73-1940, United States Court of Appeals for the Sixth Circuit. 505 F.2d 264; 1974 U.A. App. LEXIS 6288, 30 October 1974.
Jo Ann Carnes v. Tennessee Secondary School Athletic Association, Board of Education of Morgan County, John W. Galloway, Jake Gambie and Carl Edward Kreis. Civ. No. 3-76-137, United States District Court for the Eastern District of Tennessee, Northern Division. 415 F. Supp. 569; 1976 U.S. Dist. LEXIS 15185, 10 May 1976.
Nancy Maren Croteau and Raymond Nelson Croteau, as parents and next of friends of Julie Croteau, Plaintiffs, v. Rick Fair, in his individual capacity and in his official capacity as teacher and head varsity baseball coach of Osbourn Park Senior High School, and Jack Lynch, in his individual capacity and in his official capacity as Principal of Osbourn Park Senior High School, and Edward Kelly, Superintendent of Prince William County Schools, and the Prince William County School Board, Defendants. Civil Action No. 88-0294-A, United States District Court For the Eastern District of Virginia, Alexandria Division. 686 F. Supp. 552; 1988 U.S. Dist. LEXIS 5799, 28 March 1988.
National Organization for Women, Essex County Chapter, Judith S. Weiss, President; Gilbert H. Francis, Director, Division on Civil Rights, Complainants-Respondents, v. Little League Baseball, Inc., Respondent-Appellant. Superior Court of New Jersey, Appellate Division, 127 N.J. Super.522; 318 A.2d 33; 1974 N.J. Super. LEXIS 756; 66 A.L.R.3d 1247, 29 March 1974.
New York State Division of Human Rights, on Complaint of Bernice Gera, Respondent, v. New York-Pennsylvania Professional Baseball League et al., Petitioners, Supreme Court of New York, Appellate Division, Fourth Department. 36 A.D.2d 364; 320 N.Y.S.2d 788; 1971 N.Y. App. Div. LEXIS 4177; 3 Fair Empl. Prac. Cas. (BNA) 483; 3 Empl. Prac. Dec. (CCH) P8208, 27 April 1971.

Interviews

Farina, James. Hoboken, New Jersey, 11 June 2007.
Pepe, Maria. Jersey City, New Jersey, 19 March 2007.

Petras, Ernestine. Haskell, New Jersey, 10 July 2007, 4 March 2008.
Selbst, Vanessa. Telephone interview. 21 February 2008.

Books and Book Chapters

"All American Girls Professional Baseball League Rules of Conduct." In *Women and Sports in the United States*, edited by Jean O'Reilly and Susan K. Cahn. Boston: Northeastern University Press, 2007.

Ardell, Jean Hastings. *Breaking into Baseball*. Carbondale: University of Southern Illinois Press, 2005.

Bell, Lee Anne. "Something's Wrong Here and It's Not Me: Challenging the Dilemmas That Block Girls' Success." In *Women: Images and Realities*, edited by Amy Kesselman, Lily D. McNair and Nancy Schneidewind. Boston: McGraw Hill, 2003.

Beneke, Timothy. *Proving Manhood*. Berkeley: University of California Press, 1997.

Berlage, Gai Ingham. "Socio-cultural History of the Origin of Women's Baseball at the Eastern Women's Colleges During the Victorian Period." In *Cooperstown Symposium on Baseball and the American Culture*, edited by Alvin L. Hall. Oneonta: SUNY College at Oneonta, 1989.

_____. *Women in Baseball*. Westport, CT: Praeger, 1994.

_____. "Women, Baseball, and the American Dream." In *Baseball and the American Dream*, edited by Robert Elias. Armonk, NY: M. E. Sharpe, 2001.

Birrell, Susan, and Mary G. McDonald. *Reading Sport: Critical Essays on Power and Representation*. Boston: Northeastern University Press, 2000.

Brandt, William E. "Woman Whiffs Ruth and Gehrig." In *The Greatest Baseball Stories Ever Told*, edited by Jeff Silverman. Guilford, CT: The Lyons Press, 2001.

Brill, Marlene Targ. *Winning Women in Baseball & Softball*. Hauppauge: Barron's, 2000.

Brock, Darryl, and Robert Elias. "To Elevate the Game: Women and Early Baseball." In *Baseball and the American Dream*, edited by Robert Elias. Armonk, NY: M.E. Sharpe, 2001.

Brown, Lois. *Girls of Summer*. Toronto: Harper Collins, 1992.

Collins, Patricia Hill. *Black Feminist Thought*. New York: Routledge, 1990.

Cooper, Anna Julia. "The Status of Woman in America." In *A Voice of the South: By a Black Woman of the South*. In *Feminist Theory*, edited by Wendy K. Kolmar and Frances Bartkowski. New York: McGraw Hill, 1892.

Crenshaw, Kimberle. "Intersectionality and Identity Politics: Learning from Violence Against Women of Color." In *Feminist Theory*, edited by Wendy K. Kolmar and Frances Bartkowski. New York: McGraw Hill, 1997.

Daniels, Dayna Beth. "The Forgotten Discipline: Sport Studies and Physical Education." In *Transforming the Disciplines: A Women's Studies Primer*, edited by Elizabeth L. McNabb, Mary Jane Cherry, Susan Popham and Rene Perri Prys. New York: The Haworth Press, 2001.

Dowling, Colette. *The Frailty Myth*. New York: Random House, 2000.

Fidler, Merrie A. *The Origins and History of the All-American Girls Professional Baseball League*. Jefferson, N.C.: McFarland, 2006.

Fine, Gary Alan. *With the Boys*. Chicago: University of Chicago Press, 1987.

Gmelch, George, and J. J. Weiner. *In the Ballpark: The Working Lives of Baseball People*. Washington, D.C.: Smithsonian Books, 1999.

_____. *Inside Pitch: Life in Professional Baseball*. Washington, D.C.: Smithsonian Books, 2001.

_____, ed. *Baseball Without Borders*. Lincoln: University of Nebraska Press, 2007.
Green, Michelle Y. *A Strong Right Arm*. New York: Puffin Books, 2002.
Gregorich, Barbara. *Women at Play*. New York: Harcourt Brace, 1993.
Griffen, Pat. *Strong Women, Deep Closets*. Champaign, IL: Human Kenetics, 1998.
_____. "Changing the Game: Homophobia, Sexism and Lesbians in Sport." In *Women and Sport in the United States*, edited by Jean O'Reilly and Susan K. Cahn. Boston: Northeastern University Press, 2007.
Hogan, Lawrence D. *Shades of Glory: The Negro Leagues and the Story of African American Baseball*. Washington, D.C.: National Geographic, 2006.
Hooks, Bell. *Feminist Theory*. Cambridge, MA: South End Press, 2000.
Howell, Colin. "Canada." In *Baseball Without Borders*, edited by George Gmelch. Lincoln: University of Nebraska Press, 2006.
Kindred, David. *The Colorado Silver Bullets: For Love of the Game*. Atlanta: Longstreet Press, 1995.
Klein, Alan M. *Sugarball*. New Haven: Yale University Press, 1991.
Kovach, John M. *Women's Baseball*. Charleston: Arcadia Publishing, 2005.
Laberge, Suzanne, and Mathieu Albert. "Conceptions of Masculinity and Gender Transgressions in Sport Among Adolescent Boys." In *Masculinities, Gender Relations and Sport*, edited by Jim McKay, Michael A. Messner and Don Sabo. London: Sage, 2000.
Lenermann, Patricia Madoo, and Jill Niebrugge-Brantley. *The Women Founders*. Boston: McGraw Hill, 1998.
Lennon, Sharon. "What Is Mine." In *Listen Up: Voices from the Next Feminist Generation*, edited by Barbara Findlen. Seattle: Sea Press, 1995.
Lester, Larry. "Stone (Alberga), Marcenia Lyle 'Toni.'" In *Encyclopedia of Women and Baseball*, edited by Leslie A. Heaphy and Mel Anthony May. Jefferson, NC: McFarland, 2006.
Macy, Sue. *A Whole New Ballgame*. New York: Puffin Books, 1993.
McDonagh, Eileen, and Laura Papano. *Playing with the Boys*. New York: Oxford University Press, 2008.
McKay, Jim, Michael A. Messner, and Don Sabo. *Masculinities, Gender Relations, and Sport*. Thousand Oaks, CA: Sage, 2000.
Messner, Michael A. *Taking the Field: Women, Men and Sports*. Minneapolis: University of Minnesota Press, 2002.
_____. *Power at Play: Sports and the Problem of Masculinity*. Boston: Beacon Press, 1992.
Messner, Michael A., and Donald F. Sabo. *Sex, Violence and Power in Sports*. Freedom, CA.: The Crossing Press, 1994.
O'Reilly, Jean, and Susan K. Cahn, eds. *Women and Sports in the U.S.* Boston: Northeastern University Press, 2007.
Pollock, Alan. J. *Barnstorming to Heaven*. Tuscaloosa: The University of Alabama Press, 2006.
Roschelle, Anne R. "Dream or Nightmare?: Baseball and the Gender Order." In *Baseball and the American Dream*, edited by Robert Elias. Armonk, NY: M. E. Sharpe, 2001.
Sabo, Don. "Psychological Impacts of Athletic Participation on American Women: Facts and Fables." In *Women and Sports in the United States*, edited by Jean O'Reilly and Susan K. Cahn. Boston: Northeastern University Press, 2007.
Sabo, Donald F., and Joe Panepinto. "Football Ritual and the Social Reproduction of Masculinity." In *Men and Masculinity*, edited by Theodore F. Cohen. Belmont, CA: Wadsworth, 2001.

Stotz, Carl E. *A Promise Kept.* Jersey Shore, PA: Zebrowski Historical Services Publishing Co., 1992.
Streitmatter, Rodger. *Mightier than the Sword.* Boulder, CO.: Westview Press, 1977.
Thorne, Barrie. "Children and Gender Constructions of Difference." In *Gender Through the Prism of Difference*, edited by Maxine Baca Zinn, Pierrette Hondagneu-Sotelo and Michael A. Messner. Boston: Allyn and Bacon, 2000.
Trujillo, Nick. "Hegemonic Masculinity on the Mound." In *Reading Sport*, edited by Susan Birrell and Mary G. McDonald. Boston: Northeastern University Press, 2000.
Tygiel, Jules. "Black Ball." In *Total Baseball*, 8th edition, edited by John Thorn, Phil Birnbaum, Bill Deane, Rob Neyer, Alan Schwarz, Donald Dewey, Nicholas Acocella, and Peter Wayner. Ontario, CA: Sports Media Publishing, 2004.
Van Auken, Lance, and Robin Van Auken. *Play Ball: The Story of Little League Baseball.* University Park: Pennsylvania State University Press, 2001.
Walk, Stephan R. "Moms, Sisters and Ladies: Women Student Trainers in Men's Intercollegiate Sport." In *Masculinities, Gender Relations and Sport*, edited by Jim McKay, Michael A. Messner, and Don Sabo. London: Sage, 2000.
Youngen, Lois J. "A League of Our Own." In *Baseball and the American Dream*, edited by Robert Elias. Armonk, NY: M. E. Sharpe, 2001.

Periodical Articles

Adams, Natalie, Alison Schmitke and Amy Franklin. "Tomboys, Dykes and Girly Girls: Interrogating the Subjectivities of Adolescent Female Athletes." *Women's Studies Quarterly: Women and Sports* 33.1–2 (2005): 1–34.
"Alta Weiss." 1908. *Sporting Life.* 11 April. ABGRC File: Alta Weiss.
"Alta Weiss-All Star." ABGRC File: Alta Weiss. (Author, date unknown.)
"Alumni Profile: Maria Pepe." 1998. *FDU Magazine*, Fall-Winter.
Ardell, Jean Hastings. "Ila Borders, Pitcher." *The National Pastime* 20.19 (1 January 200): 1–6.
Averbusch, Yael. 1999. "The Lone Ponytail." *Soccer Jr. Magazine.*
Berlage, Gai Ingham. "The Colorado Bullets." *Baseball Research Journal* 27 (1998): 40–42.
_____. "Transition of Women's Baseball: An Overview." *Nine* 9.1 (Fall 2000): 72–82.
Cahn, Susan K. 1993. "From the 'Muscle Moll' to the 'Butch' Player: Mannishness, Lesbianism and Homophobia in U.S. Women's Sports." *Feminist Studies* 19.2 (1993): 343–368.
Cobian, Dan. n.d. "Women in Baseball: Latinas in the All-American Girls Professional Baseball League." *Chicana and Latina Studies*, Working Paper Series.
Corbett, Sarah. 2006. "Baseball for Life." *The New York Times Sports Magazine* (3 June 2006): 52.
Crenshaw, Kimberle. "Mapping the Margins: Intersectionality, Identity Politics, and Violence Against Women of Color." *Stanford Law Review* 43.6 (1991): 124–199.
Deford, Frank. 1974. "Now Georgy-Porgy Runs Away." *Sports Illustrated*, 22 April.
Disch, Lisa, and Mary Jo Kane. 1996. "When a Looker Is Really a Bitch: Lisa Olson, Sport and the Heterosexual Matrix." *Signs: Journal of Women in Culture and Society* 21.2 (1996): 278–307.
Everbach, Tracy. 2005. "Breaking Baseball Barriers: The 1953–54 Negro League and Expansion of Women's Public Roles." *American Journalism* 22.1 (Winter 2005): 13–34.

Fidler, Merrie A. 2005. *AAGPBL Touching Bases Newsletter,* January.
Green, Michelle Y. 2003. "Meeting Mamie." *Sports Fan Magazine,* issue 12, pp. 46–47.
Gregorich, Barbara. 1993. "Blues, Bloomers and Bobbies." *Pennsylvania Heritage* 19.3 (Summer 1993): 32–37.
_____. "A Champion for All Seasons." *Pennsylvania Heritage* 24 (Summer 1994): 4–9.
_____. "You Can't Play in Skirts." *Timeline* (July/August 1994): 38–43.
"Historic Debut." *USA Today,* 4 June 1996. ABGRC File: Colorado Silver Bullets. (Author unknown.)
Kahn, Andrea. 2007. "35 Years of Title IX." *The New York Times Sports Magazine,* 19 August.
Kelley, Brent. 1999. "'Peanut' Johnson: The First Woman to Win a Pro Ballgame." *Sports Collectors Digest,* 22 October.
Lacy, Sam. 1953. "First Woman in Pro Ball." *Afro Magazine.*
"The Lady Played Second Base." ABGRC File: Women in the Negro Leagues. (Author, date unknown.)
Lewis, Michael. 2005. "Absolutely, Power Corrupts." *The New York Times Magazine,* 24 April.
Malloy, Maria. 1994. "Coor's Field of Stifled Dreams." *Business Week,* 24 January.
Mehrer, Darlene. 1988. "Girl Cut from H.S. Baseball Team Sues." *Basewoman,* June.
Miller, Stuart. 1994. "A Few More Pitches for Gender Equality." *Inside Sports,* June.
Nelson, Mariah Burton. 1991. "Player: Sexism Cut Short Career." *USA Today,* 6 June.
Sagert, Kelly Boyer. 1998. "Girl Wonder: Born to Pitch." *Over the Back Fence,* Fall, pp. 16–19.
Schreiner, S. A. 1952. "Do You Want Women in Baseball?" *Junior Parade,* 10 August.
Scott, Britain A., and Julie A. Derry. "Women in Their Bodies: Challenging Objectification Through Experiential Learning." *Women's Studies Quarterly: Women and Sports* 33.1–2 (2005): 188–209.
Shattuck, Capt. Debra A. "Bats, Balls and Books: Baseball and Higher Education for Women at Three Eastern Women's Colleges, 1866–1981." *Journal of Sport History* 19.2 (Summer 1992): 91–109.
Shuster, Rachael. 1994. "Baseball Team Opens Doors, Minds." *USA Today,* 21 February.
Simpson, Allan. 2005. "Baseball for the Ages." *Baseball America,* October–December.
Smith, Gene. "The Girls of Summer." *American Heritage* (July/August 1994): 110–111.
Stoudt, Brett G. 2006. "'You're Either In or You're Out': School Violence, Peer Discipline, and the (Re)Production of Hegemonic Masculinity." *Men and Masculinities* 8.3 (January 2006): 273–287.
Travers, Johnny. 1952. "Gal Shortstop's Bid Given Short 'No' by O.B. Officials." *The Sporting News,* 2 July.
USA Today, 7–13 February 1996. ABGRC File: Colorado Silver Bullets. (Author unknown.)
Vignola, Patricia. "The Patriotic Pinch Hitter: The AAGBL and How the American Woman Earned a Permanent Spot on the Roster." *Nine* 12.2 (Spring 2004): 102–113.
White, Carolyn. 1989. "Female Player 'Just One of the Team.'" *USA Today,* 13 March.
Williams, Kerry. 1994. "Hardball Was a Job for Girls." *Central Jersey Sports,* 26 May.
Williams, Pete. 1994. "Silver Lining: Bullets Showed They Belong." *USA Today,* 7–13 September.

Newspaper Articles — Writer Unknown

1890. "Women Wield the Bat." *The Washington Post*, 4 October. ABGRC File: Women in Baseball, 19th century.

1890. *New York Tribune*, 20 March. ABGRC File: Bloomer Girls.

1893. "Girls Who Play Baseball." *The New York Times*, 3 September. ABGRC File: Women in Baseball, 19th century.

1900. *Cincinnati Enquirer*, 24 August. ABGRC File: Bloomer Girls.

1905. *Cincinnati Enquirer*, 6 October. ABGRC File: Bloomer Girls.

1910. "Black Broncho Baseball." *Indianapolis Freeman*, 1 April. ABGRC File: Bloomer Girls.

1921. "Black Sox Bloomers Lose to Excelseor Girls of Sparrows Point 17–14." *AfroAmerican*, 12 August. ABGRC File: Bloomer Girls.

1931. *The Staten Island Advance*, 4 April. ABGRC File: Bloomer Girls.

1931. *Chattanooga News*, 3 April. ABGRC File: Jackie Mitchell.

1933. *The Lookout Chattanooga*, 4 February. ABGRC File: Jackie Mitchell.

1950. *The Washington Post*, 15 April. ABGRC, All American Girls Professional Baseball League, 1950 Scrapbook.

1952. "Girl Player Stirs Up Battle." 23 June. ABGRC File: Eleanor Engle.

1952. "Signing of Girl to Play Pro Ball Stirs Furore." 23 June. ABGRC File: Eleanor Engle.

1952. "A Woman's Place Is in the Grandstand." *The Sporting News*, 2 July. ABGRC File: Eleanor Engle.

1953. "Lady Ball Player." *Ebony*. ABGRC File: Women in the Negro Leagues.

1953. "The Gal on Second Base." ABGRC File: Women in the Negro League.

1961. *Sun Tattler*, 31 May. ABGRC File: Bloomer Girls.

1974. *Williamsport Sun Gazette*, 5 August. LLMA File: Girls Press.

1984. "Women Living Dreams in Baseball Tryouts." *Tifton Georgia Gazette*, 18 September. ABGRC File: Florida Sun Sox.

2002. *The Sunday Patriot News*. 23 June. ABGRC File: Eleanor Engel.

2003. *Daily Messenger*, 14 July. ABGRC File: Bloomer Girls.

Newspaper Articles — Bylined

Albom, Mitch. 1984. "Women on Base? Decide on Field." *Ft. Lauderdale Sun Sentinel*, 26 September.

Allison, Bob. 1974. *Gazette Sports*, Phoenix, Ariz., 1 April.

Bisher, Furman. 1984. "Girls of Summer: An All Female Lineup for the Sun Sox?" 1 October. ABGRC File: Florida Sun Sox.

Britt, Donna. 1999. "Peanut Is Her Name, Baseball Is Her Game." *The Detroit Free Press*, 16 September.

Chambers, Marcia. 2008. "Barred from Men's-Only Event, Woman Sues Public Gold Club." *The New York Times*, 19 February.

Chass, Murray. 2008. "Should a Clubhouse Be a Chapel." *The New York Times*, 2 February.

Crouse, Karen. 2006. "Also Seeing Life Through a Face Mask." *The New York Times*, 29 October.

Denberg, Jeff. 1984. "It's Ladies Day at the Sun Sox Tryouts." *Atlanta Georgia Constitution*, 18 September.

_____. 1984. "Sun Sox Tryouts End Predictably." *Atlanta Georgia Journal*, 19 September.

Digilio, Alice. 1988. "Girl Sues to Play Baseball." *The Washington Post*, 17 March.

Fay, Bill. 1949. "Belles of the Ballgame." ABGRC, All American Girls Professional Baseball League, 1949 Scrapbook.

Fornoff, Susan. 1994. "Playing Hardball." *The Sporting News*, 30 May.

Gleason, Bill. 1973. "Woman in the Majors? It's Just a Matter of Time." *Philadelphia Inquirer*, 18 June.

Gray, Lynn. 1948. *New York Post*, 18 June.

Greenberg, Jay. 1994. "Gals of Summer Take Their Cuts." *New York Post*, 8 March.

Grow, Doug. 1996. "League of Her Own: Tomboy Stone Dead at 76." *Minneapolis Star Tribune*, 5 November.

Harmon, Pat. 1952. "Cincinnati Almost Had the First Girl in Organized Baseball." *Cincinnati Post*, 24 June.

Hawley, David. 1996. "Toni Stone, a Baseball 'Tomboy' Among Men Dies." *Saint Paul Pioneer*, 5 December.

Hays, Daniel. 1972. "Maria Jolts Little League." *The Evening News*, 9 May.

_____. 1972. "Maria's Mother Cool to N.O.W. Suit, but Proud of Little League Daughter." *The Evening News*, 25 May.

Horowitz, Paul. 1949. *Newark Evening News*, 15 August. ABGRC, All American Girls Professional Baseball League, 1949 Scrapbook.

Jakala, Debbie. 1992. "Nun's First Calling Was Pitching Strikes." *Times Herald*, 17 April.

James, George. 1974. "Defending the Credo." *The Record*, 11 March.

Jenkins, David. 1982. *Chattanooga News-Free Press*, 11 April.

Johnson, Dr. Thomas. 1974. "Boys and Girls Together." *The New York Times*, 5 January.

Kofoed, Jack. 1974. "Girls and Little League — Do Courts, Nature Disagree." *Miami Herald*, 2 April.

Kornheiser, Tony. 1988. "Julie Croteau's Play Deserves to Be Judged on the Baseball Field, Not in the Courtroom." *The Washington Post*, 19 March.

Kruger, Jane. 1949. ABGRC, All American Girls Professional Baseball League, 1949 Yearbook.

Kruissink, Bill. 1996. "First Woman in Pro Baseball Remembers." *Alameda Journal*, 2 April.

Kueck, Thomas J., and Ben Beagle. 2005. "Shy Smile, Mean Fastball." *The New York Times*, 19 May.

Lewin, Tamar. 2007. "In Twist for High School Wrestlers, Girl Flips Boy." *The New York Times*, 17 February.

Liebrich, Barbara. 1950. "Florida Nine Tries to Sign Woman Player." 3 August, ABGRC, All American Girls Professional Baseball League, 1950 Scrapbook.

Markey, Morris. 1950. "Hey Ma You're Out." ABGRC, All American Girls Professional Baseball League, 1950 Scrapbook.

McCarthy, Larry. 1984. "ERA Pitch: Stage Set for Women's Team to Join Class A Baseball League." *Reading Pennsylvania Times*, 9 September.

McNulty, Ray. 1994. "Wiley Finds Her Field of Dreams." *New York Post*, 6 May.

_____. 1994. "Old-Timer Says Team Won't Last." *New York Post*, 9 May.

Mersh, Mike. 1984. "Fact: Women Can't Compete With Men." *Bradenton Florida Herald*, 30 September.

Meyer, Eugene L. 1999. "A League of Her Own: Baseball's Proud Peanut." *The News Tribune*, 5 April.

Morris, Alan. 1975. "Jackie Struck Out Babe Ruth and Lou Gehrig." *Chattanooga News-Free Press*, 7 September.

Mosher, Monty. 1995. "Former Bloomer Girl Hit, Pitched with the Best." 12 July.

Moritz, Amy. 2003. *Eagle Times*, 15 August.

Murphy, Caryle. 1988. "Team Backs Pr. William Coach in Sex Bias Case." *The Washington Post.*

Newhan, Ross. 1994, "Girls of Summer." *Times Union*, 8 May.

News, Ken E. 1948. "Comets Have All the Hopes, Aspirations of the Girls in the Stands." *Kenosha Evening News*, 9 July.

Nowell, Paul. 1994. "All Women's Team Out of Its League." *Times Union*, 9 May.

Padawer, Ruth. 2003. "She Came to Play: Women Athletes Can Thank Trailblazer, Her Coach." *The Record*, 23 November.

Parks, Brad. "Croteau's Love of Baseball Exceeds Pain of Past Slights." *The Washington Post.* ABGRC File: Julie Croteau.

Pennington, Bill. 2004. "Title IX Trickles Down to Girls of Generation Z." *The New York Times*, 29 June.

Reese, Ernest. 1984. "Baseball a Men's Sport?" ABGRC File: Florida Sun Sox.

Reid, Philip. 2005. "It Took a Hoboken Girl to Strike Out Little League's Ban." *The Star Ledger*, 6 May.

Ring, Jennifer. 2006. "Why Shouldn't Girls Play Baseball? It's Time for the U.S. to Stop Discouraging Girls from the National Past Time." *The Los Angeles Times*, 27 July.

Rosen Karen. 1984. "Florida State League Says No to Sun Sox." *Atlanta Georgia Journal*, 27 September.

Seltzer, Richard J. 1973. "Hazardous Game for Girls?" Rockville, Maryland, 9 June.

Shemanske, Susan. 1997. *The Journal Times*, 19 July.

Silverman, Dan. n.d. "No League of Their Own." ABGRC File: Women in the Negro Leagues.

Smith, Claire. 1994. "Swings and Misses Aren't Heart of the Matter in This Game." ABGRC File: Colorado Silver Bullets.

Soonton, Dick. 1984. "Women in the Florida League? What a Snow Job." *Lakeland Florida Ledger*, 20 September.

Strand, Charles. 1948. "Girls Baseball Moguls Smoke Pipe of Peace." *New York Post*, 18 June.

Suehsdorf, Addie. 1949. "Sluggers in Skirts." ABGRC, All American Girls Professional Baseball League, 1949 Yearbook.

Sword, Susan. 1996. "Toni Stone." *San Francisco Chronicle*, 6 November.

Thomas, Ron. n.d. "Baseball Pioneer Looks Back." *San Francisco Chronicle.*

Traitman, Jules. 1952. "Girls Out as Pro Baseball Players." *Patriot News*, 23 June.

Turkheimer, N. A. 1949. *The Roanoke Times*, 9 August, ABGRC, All American Girls Professional Baseball League, 1949 Scrapbook.

Vesey, George. 2008. "Softball is Losing a Chance to Celebrate." *The New York Times*, 28 February.

Vecsey, George. 2008. "A Sporting Gesture Touches 'Em All." *The New York Times*, 30 April.

Vimmerstedt, Jennie. 1950. "Colleen's Ace Pitcher Hopes to Teach Physical Ed." *Jamestown Post Journal*, 29 August.

Voorhees, Deborah. 1999. "Three Women Got Their Chance to Play." *The Dallas Morning News*, 17 February.

Walder Barbara, 1994. "All-Women's Baseball Team Is Both Silly and Boring." 8 April, ABGRC File: Colorado Silver Bullets.

Weinreb, Michael. 2006. "Playing for Fun and Little Else, on Football's Edge." *The New York Times*, 18 July.

White, Joseph. 1998. "'Peanut' Struck Out Her Share of Guys." *The Associated Press*, 9 May.
Whittington, Carol L. 1984. "Gender Identities Are Confusing." *Tampa Tribune*, 7 December.
Zak, Dan. 2007. "The Girls of Summer." *The Washington Post*, 27 May.
Zipay, Steve. 1993. "Niekro Set to Prove a Point." *Newsday*, 16 December.

Internet and Miscellaneous Sources

Associated Press. 2005. "Maria Pepe Sees Fruits of Playing in 1971." *Sports Center*, 8 July.
Carolina Miners. http://www.carolinaminers.com/about.htm.
Chicago Pioneers. http://www.chicagopioneers.com/about/htm.
Gasparino, Michael. n.d. "Playing Hardball: Women's Baseball Seeking Respect." NY NOW/NY Sports on Line-Baseball. http://www.nysol.com/baseball_women.html.
Glennie, Jim. 2006. "The Recent Developments of Women's International Baseball Competitions." American Women's Baseball Federation, 2 April.
Kovach, John. 2007. "Where's the Ponytail?" Presentation at the Popular and American Culture Conference, Boston, Mass., April.
Makurdi, Wandoo. n.d. "Irina Kovach: In a League of Her Own." Women's Sports Foundation. http://www.womenssportsfoundation.org/cgi- bin/iowa/athletes/article.html?/record=274.
Pawtucket Slaterettes. http://www.slaterettes.com.
"Women and Cuban Baseball." http://www.cubaball.com/Images?History/Women/women.html/.
Women's Sports Foundation. 2007. "Baseball and Softball: Should Girls and Women Have to Choose?" A Women's Sports Foundation Position Statement. 31 July.
Women's Sports Foundation. n.d. "Co-ed Participation — Issues Related to Girls and Boys Competing With and Against Each Other in Sports and Physical Activity Settings: The Foundation Position."
Zinn, Dave. "How Baseball Strip-Mines the Dominican Republic." 28 October 2005. CommonDreams.org.

Index